Women and Economics

*A Study of the Economic Relation
Between Men and Women as a
Factor in Social Evolution*

Charlotte Perkins Gilman

With a New Introduction
by Michael Kimmel and Amy Aronson

UNIVERSITY OF CALIFORNIA PRESS
Berkeley · Los Angeles · London

University of California Press
Berkeley and Los Angeles, California

University of California Press, Ltd.
London, England

First University of California Press Paperback, 1998

Introduction © 1998 by
Michael Kimmel and Amy Aronson

Library of Congress Cataloging-in-Publication Data

Gilman, Charlotte Perkins, 1860–1935.
    Women and economics : a study of the economic relation
between men and women as a factor in social evolution /
Charlotte Perkins Gilman ; with a new introduction by
Michael Kimmel and Amy Aronson.
    p. cm.
    Originally published: Boston : Small, Maynard & Co., 1898.
Includes index.
    ISBN 0-520-20998-2 (pbk. : alk. paper)
    1. Women—Economic conditions. I. Title.
HQ1381.G66 1998
305.42—dc21
                             97-52172
                             CIP

Printed in the United States of America

9 8 7 6 5 4 3 2 1

The paper used in this publication is both acid-free and totally
chlorine-free (TCF). It meets the minimum requirements of
American Standard for Information Sciences—Permanence of
Paper for Printed Library Materials, ANSI Z39.48-1984. ⊗

CONTENTS

INTRODUCTION
TO THE 1998 EDITION

Michael Kimmel and Amy Aronson

EXACTLY a century ago, in 1898, Charlotte Perkins Gilman's first nonfiction book, *Women and Economics*, was published to universal acclaim. The book's publication catapulted its 38-year-old author into intellectual celebrity. Almost overnight she became "the leading intellectual in the women's movement."[1] Her ideas were widely circulated and discussed; she was in great demand on the lecture circuit, and her intellectual circle included some of the most prominent thinkers of the age.

Yet by the mid-1960s, she was nearly forgotten, and *Women and Economics* long out of print. Thirty years ago, the eminent historian Carl Degler reintroduced Gilman's most distinguished work to a new generation of readers. Degler attributed Gilman's fall from popular view in part to the postsuffrage doldrums in which the American women's movement had found itself since the mid-1920s. But he, then perched in Poughkeepsie at Vassar College, sensed the emergent tenor of the times in the years immediately following the publication of Betty Friedan's *The Feminine Mystique* in 1963—a renewed restlessness among American women about the yawning gap between the lives they wanted to live and the lives to which they had been consigned. Degler grasped the need of these increasingly politicized feminist intellectuals for foremothers, mentors who had been there before, wrestled with the same issues. By editing *Women and Economics*, Degler returned Charlotte Perkins Gilman to history.

Of course, he did not do it alone. After *Women and Economics* was reissued, Gilman's most famous works of fiction were also rediscovered and republished. Perhaps her most famous short story, "The Yellow Wallpaper," which chronicled the descent into madness of a woman when she was prevented from experiencing a vital public life, was anthologized in 1973 by Elaine Hedges; in 1980 by Gilman's biographer, Ann Lane; in 1989 by Lynne Sharon Schwartz; and in 1992 by Barbara Solomon. The most renowned of Gilman's utopian novels, *Herland*, which had only been serialized in her monthly magazine, the *Forerunner*, in 1915, was republished in 1979, and has remained a feminist classic, a touchstone work in which readers are invited to imagine the way society could develop if only there were no men in it.

Despite this recent interest, however, *Women and Economics*, Gilman's signal book, has once again gone out of print. We are reviving it now for its fresh and continuing insight to a generation of feminists and social thinkers poised—as they were when the book was written—on the cusp of a new century.

Degler's edition of *Women and Economics* spoke to what a second wave of feminist women wanted—indeed, needed—to read in the 1960s through the early 1990s. Second Wave feminism took its impetus, in part, from Friedan's indictment of the cult of domesticity. In her eyes, women had become virtual prisoners of their own homes, unable to work, unable really to have much of a public life at all. These sentiments echoed Gilman's insistence that women's economic independence was the single most important element in their emancipation.

By the 1980s, though, women had come to achieve that public presence and even a modicum of that economic independence Gilman advocated. The walls that had so long kept women out of the public sphere had begun to crumble—as decisively, if not as rapidly or completely, as the deliberate dismantling of the Berlin Wall. Women had entered the professions, the work world, the military (and its academies); women were in the House and the Senate, the statehouse and the courthouse.

Many American women began to realize that the exodus from their homes to the workplace accomplished only half a revolution, both socially and personally. Many yearned also for the pleasures of motherhood, for family and domestic life. Suddenly, "having it all" became the motto of a new wave of American women. Could women have it all? Could they have the involving, exciting, important careers

to which they now believed they had become entitled, while at the same time having the warm, loving support of family life? Or would they, like Gilman and the women of her generation, have to
sacrifice one for the other?

Of course, Gilman understood that men face no
such painful choice. To a large extent, men already
do "have it all"—the careers and the nurturing families to come home to—and the reason those who do
have it all *do* is precisely the reason that women do
not. Listen to how contemporary, how prescient, are
Gilman's words from an essay in 1906:[2]

> We have so arranged life that a man may have
> a home and family, love, companionship, domes-
> ticity, and fatherhood, yet remain an active citi-
> zen of age and country. We have so arranged
> life, on the other hand, that a woman must
> "choose"; must either live alone, unloved, unac-
> companied, uncared for, homeless, childless,
> with her work in the world for sole consolation;
> or give up all world-service for the joys of love,
> motherhood, and domestic service.

Gilman had figured out what contemporary women
have also begun to understand—half a revolution
was no revolution at all; if women were simply going to trade their kitchen aprons for power suits,
they would remain unfulfilled in partial, gender-

limited lives. In that sense, as well, Gilman understood that men were going to have to be a necessary element in the liberation of women.

Her analysis stressed the connection between work and home, between the public and private sectors. She understood that women's maternal nurturing had been overdeveloped, at the cost of the underdevelopment of their abilities for rational and critical thinking and civic participation. By contrast, she argued, men's capacities for success in the public sphere had been overdeveloped, and at the expense of their abilities to care and nurture.

Gilman also understood that for the social transformation promised by feminism to succeed, both women *and* men would have to change, that shifts in one sphere would redound to the other. And she believed throughout her life and writing that women's entry into the public arena and the reforms of the family she proposed would be a win-win situation—for both women and men. The public sphere would no longer be deprived of women's particular abilities, and men would also be able to enlarge the possibilities to experience and express the emotional sustenance of family life.

Gilman joined many of her reform-minded contemporaries in making what are today called "social constructionist" arguments, suggesting that the personality forms we observe have their roots not in some intrinsic, biological predisposition, but are fashioned from the circumstances of people's lives, from the materials and ideas we find around us. She argued that it was not women's "nature" to be passive, weak, helpless, and dependent, any more than it was man's "nature" to be domineering, aggressive, arrogant, and oppressive. "It is not that women are really smaller-minded, weaker-minded, more timid and vacillating," she wrote in *The Home* (1903), "but that whosoever, man or woman, lives always in a small dark place, is always guarded, protected, directed and restrained, will become inevitably narrowed and weakened by it. The woman is narrowed by the home and the man is narrowed by the woman."[3]

Fourteen years later, the writer and bohemian radical Floyd Dell echoed these sentiments in an essay entitled "Feminism for Men." From a man's point of view, the strict separation of spheres was both unnecessary and severely limited. It made the home, as he put it, "a little dull." He wrote:

When you have got a woman in a box, and you pay rent on the box, her relationship to you insensibly changes character. It loses the fine excitement of democracy. It ceases to be companionship, for companionship is only possible in a democracy. It is no longer a sharing of life together—it is a breaking of life apart. Half a life —cooking, clothes, and children; half a life—

business, politics, and baseball. It doesn't make much difference which is the poorer half. Any half, when it comes to life, is very near to none at all.

Feminism, Dell concluded, was "going to make it possible for the first time for men to be free."[4]

But in other ways, Gilman completely departed from her contemporaries. For one thing, she disavowed the term "feminism," preferring in its place a vaguer, yet more inclusive term, "humanism." Further, the domestic reforms she advocated—cooperative kitchens, the professionalization of housework and child care—carried her beyond the agendas even of most women reformers of her day. Where she was graphic and concrete about the reforms of the home, many other thinkers remained nostalgic or romantic.

On the other hand, where these other writers were graphic and concrete, Gilman was often elliptical, evasive, and downright negative. Especially about sex. Dell and other bohemian radicals at the turn of the century preached "free love," and sexual liberation born of a peculiar reading of Freudian psychology. Gilman repudiated Freud, and came pretty close—repeatedly, in various works and several genres—to denouncing sexual pleasure altogether.

Still, Gilman predicted that changes were in the offing at the turn of the twentieth century, and embraced the many advances she saw as imminent in the future. Who would have predicted it would take the entire century to begin to free women from the home, and that the transformation of men's lives would be only a glimmer of possibility by the century's end?

So now, poised as we are at the edge of a new millennium, fired once again by the possibilities of transformation that would allow women and men to live full, rich, nourishing lives—both as productive workers and as caring and loving partners and parents—we can again rediscover *Women and Economics*, and find that both Gilman's analysis of the relations between women and men, and her hopes for their transformation, may yet, again, speak to us.

With the republication of her autobiography in 1975, a major biography published in 1990, and the republication of many of her books, the story of Gilman's life is fairly well known. She was born Charlotte Anna Perkins on July 3, 1860, in Hartford, Connecticut, to one of the nineteenth century's most prominent families. Her father, Frederick Beecher Perkins, was the grandson of Lyman Beecher and nephew of Henry Ward Beecher and Harriet Beecher Stowe. Frederick's sister, Emily (who became Charlotte's favorite aunt), was married to Edward Everett Hale. Charlotte's mother, Mary Ann Fitch Westcott, was a descendant of Roger Williams.

Despite their prominence, however, Charlotte's father was a ne'er-do-well and a dilettante. He attended Yale but never graduated, studied law but never practiced, and abandoned the family soon after Charlotte's birth, returning only for occasional visits before the couple formally divorced in 1873. (Charlotte had one older brother, Thomas. Two other siblings died in their first year.) That fall, Charlotte moved into a female-dominated household in Providence, consisting of her mother, grandmother, and great-grandmother, and she began to attend young ladies' school.

Never particularly feminine—she was physically strong and vigorous, and was passionate about sports—Charlotte first thought to be an artist, and entered the newly opened Rhode Island School of Design in 1878. Family problems intervened, and she left school without graduating; her early training, however, provided her with the basis to earn a living as a commercial artist.

Early in 1882, she met Charles Walter Stetson, a promising young artist in Providence. Their courtship was difficult and turbulent. Charlotte had resolved to remain single and devote herself to her career. As she wrote in her autobiography:[5]

On the one hand I knew it was normal and right in general, and held that a woman should be able to have marriage and motherhood, and do her work in the world also. On the other, I felt strongly that for me it was not right, that the nature of the life before me forbade it, that I ought to forgo the more intimate personal happiness for complete devotion to my work.

Nevertheless, soon she capitulated to Walter's earnest courtship. "I knew of course that the time would come when I must choose between two lives," she wrote in her autobiography, "but never did I dream that it would come so soon, and that the struggle would be so terrible."[6] Charlotte talked herself out of her misgivings, and willed herself to accept Walter's proposal. They were married in May 1884.

The marriage was ill fated from the start. Despite Walter's efforts—he was attentive and dutiful, and even, she says, helped with the housework—Charlotte felt torn between marital obligations and the lure of her career. The tension only redoubled when her daughter, Katherine, was born in March 1885. At first, Charlotte was overjoyed by motherhood, but she gradually sank into what she described as a "growing melancholia," a "constant dragging weariness miles below zero."[7]

Her emotional distress became increasingly acute. "Here was a charming home," she wrote, "loving and devoted husband; an exquisite baby, healthy intelligent and good; a highly competent mother to run things; a wholly satisfactory servant—and I lay all day on the lounge and cried."[8] Even her essays from these years describe marriage as a life-or-death struggle for women, tearing them between two irreconcilable passions—motherhood and career.[9]

By 1887, Charlotte's depression had become so serious and debilitating that she sought the advice of Dr. S. Weir Mitchell, the Philadelphia physician who had gained national fame for his treatment of a somewhat trendy, elite condition called "neurasthenia." Mitchell saw neurasthenia—a nervous disorder marked by both anxiety and depression—as a consequence of the overcivilized modern life, "that of the business man exhausted from too much work, and the society woman exhausted from too much play," as Charlotte described it.[10] In both cases, neurasthenia was marked by gender nonconformity. For men, that meant passivity and lassitude, derived from the sedentary effects of the modern workplace; for women, by contrast, neurasthenia was marked by depression over the balance between work and family, and the inability to function as properly feminine.

Mitchell's remedies returned to traditional gender norms and a strict separation of spheres. "I no more want women to be preachers, lawyers, or platform orators than I want men to be seamstresses, or nurses of children," Mitchell had told the graduating class at Radcliffe College in 1890. Men were

urged to experience the tonic freshness of the out-
doors by spending, perhaps, a few weeks at "dude
ranches," which had been newly developed for precisely that purpose. And women were counseled to
seek plenty of exposure to their babies and bed rest.

As Charlotte recalled, Mitchell told her: "Live as
domestic a life as possible. Have your child with
you all the time. Lie down an hour after each meal.
Have but two hours intellectual life a day. And never
touch a pen, brush, or pencil as long as you live."
She tried. She "went home, followed those direc-
tions rigidly for months, and came perilously close
to losing my mind."[11]

Instead, she got out of bed, took her daughter,
and left her husband, traveling first to Pasadena and
then to Oakland, California, to live with her best
friend, Grace Channing. Her diary entry read:
"Thirty years old. Made a wrong marriage—lots of
people do. Am heavily damaged but not dead."

In California, Charlotte threw herself into work,
becoming a follower of Edward Bellamy's Nationalist Movement. The publication of her first major
poem, the satiric "Similar Cases" in the *Nationalist*,
the movement's magazine, made her an instant
celebrity. (William Dean Howells, also a Nationalist,
said it was the best satire since James Russell Low-
ell's 1848 verse collection, *The Biglow Papers*.) Her
literary career had begun.

And what a prodigious career it was! Between

1888, when she left Walter Stetson, to her death in 1935, Gilman published eight novels, 171 short stories, 473 poems, and 1,472 nonfiction pieces—nine of them books.[12] In her *Forerunner* magazine alone, she wrote critical articles, editorials, essays, poetry, reviews, short fiction, and two serialized books a year; the full seven-year run of the magazine equaled some twenty-eight full-length books.[13] Yet prolific as she was, Gilman's writing turned on a few dominant themes: the transformations of marriage, the family, and the home. And even these returned insistently to her central argument, "the economic independence and specialization of women as essential to the improvement of marriage, motherhood, domestic industry, and racial improvement."[14] The liberation of women—and of children and of men, for that matter—required getting women out of the house, both practically and ideologically. It was work that was "the normal life of every human being; work, which is joy and growth and service, without which one is a pauper and a parasite."

Charlotte certainly followed her own advice. She became a celebrated author and widely popular lecturer, traveling across the country and, soon enough, abroad as well, advocating woman suffrage and social reform. "The Yellow Wallpaper," her barely fictionalized account of her own struggles with neurasthenia and its "cures," was published in *New England Magazine* in January 1892; the next year, she published her first book, *In This Our World,* a book of poems that was well received by critics.[15]

In 1898, Charlotte published *Women and Economics,* her breakthrough work of nonfiction, and probably her single greatest book. Subtitled *A Study of the Economic Relation Between Men and Women as a Factor in Social Evolution,* the book was an immediate success, widely read and discussed both in the United States and abroad. The book, which the *Nation* called "the most significant utterance on the subject of women since Mill's *The Subjection of Women,*" established Charlotte as the leading intellectual in the American women's movement.

In this work, Gilman drew from several different sources to produce a groundbreaking and original synthesis. From Marx and others, she took the idea that the central arena of human life is the realm of production, and that the workplace is the site of both oppression and liberation. What's more, she also agreed that the differences among people are to be found not in nature, in biological differences, but rather in the ways they are raised.[16] But unlike Marx, who had limited his discussion to economic classes, Gilman applied the idea to gender. Women and men are far more alike than they are different, she argued, but they are socialized to be dramatically different, and at a cost to both. From Darwin she took the idea of progress and evolution. We have changed, she observed, and thus we can change and we must change. A theory of evolution underlies all Gilman's work, from her critique of the home as an anachronistic throwback to her vision of a future of economic independence and professional housework and child care. From Thorstein Veblen she took the blistering critique of woman as ornament, as a medium of exchange between men. And from the sociologist Lester Ward she took the idea that women, not men, were the originators of evolution, the origin of the species. Ward was, Gilman wrote, "quite the greatest man I have ever known," and his "gynecocentric" theory she thought "the greatest single contribution to the world's thought since Evolution."[17]

Gilman may have drawn upon the ideas of these thinkers, but she did not become part of the movements inspired by them. Though she relied upon Darwin's theory of evolution, she did not become a social Darwinist. Though she drew upon Marx and socialism, she did not become a socialist.[18] In fact, while Gilman wrote and edited for numerous organizational publications—she edited the suffrage column for the *People*, the Providence Knights of Labor weekly, and was a contributing editor for the *American Fabian* and *Woman's Journal*, for example—she was often marginal to the prevailing orthodoxies of her age. As she wrote:[19]

Among the various unnecessary burdens of my life is that I have been discredited by conserva-

tive persons as a Socialist, while to the orthodox
Socialists themselves I was quite outside the
ranks. Similarly the anti-suffrage masses had
me blackly marked "Suffragist," while the suf-
fragists thought me a doubtful if not dangerous
ally on account of my theory of the need of economic independence to women.

Explicitly rejecting the term "feminist," she was especially uncomfortable with the sexual liberationist
ethic that was emerging as an important strand of
feminist thought. This discomfort also led her to be
fully dismissive of Freud.

Women and Economics ushered in a period of prolific writing that scarcely diminished until her
death. Gilman began writing articles regularly for
some of the most popular magazines of her day, including the *Saturday Evening Post, Century, Scribner's,
Appleton's,* the *Independent,* and the *Woman's Home
Companion.* Six major works of nonfiction secured
her reputation as one of the most important public
intellectuals of her time. These included *Concerning
Children* (1900), *The Home* (1903), *Human Work*
(1904), *Women and Social Service* (1907), *The Man-
Made World* (1911), and *His Religion and Hers*
(1923). In all venues, Gilman's writing largely re-
volved around the central issues that, as she wrote
in 1916, dominated her life: "the economic independence of women, the expert care of children in ad-

dition to that of their mothers and the professionalizing of 'domestic industry.'"[20]

Charlotte's personal life was stable if unorthodox. She lived in Oakland with her daughter, Kate, her mother, and Adeline Knapp, a reporter for the San Francisco *Call*, in a relationship that most biographers agree was lesbian. Grace, her closest friend, lived nearby, with Walter, whom she married in 1894, when his divorce from Charlotte became final. (They remained friends all their lives, and Kate lived periodically with Grace and her father.)

In 1900, Charlotte remarried, this time to her first cousin, George Houghton Gilman, who was seven years her junior. Houghton (called "Ho") was also the great-grandson of Lyman Beecher and nephew of Daniel Coit Gilman, the first president of Johns Hopkins University. Charlotte moved to New York, where Ho maintained his law practice, and the couple lived there for more than two decades in a place she described as "that unnatural city where every one is an exile."[21]

Those two decades were productive and happy ones for Gilman. Her books continued to receive significant attention. Many of her proposals were radical—even for our age, let alone hers. She was among the first to see the need for innovations in child rearing and in housework to ease the burdens of working women. While middle-class reformers began professionalizing their own pursuits as well

as envisioning the positive outcomes of specialized
expertise in others, Gilman was perhaps the first
(and certainly the most influential) reformer to pro-
pose the professionalization of housework and child
care, freeing women to pursue their goals in the
workplace, and assigning to trained professionals
the tasks that she argued were so haphazardly and
unevenly done by mothers and wives. Housework
was really work, and therefore ought to be "done
by the hour by specially trained persons, with the
service of cooked meals to the home," she wrote.[22]
She designed cooperative kitchens in urban apartment buildings, which, she argued, would facilitate
women's balancing of work and family and also
provide some social support and contact for wives
who were homebound.

Other reforms today seem obvious and relatively
tame, like nursery schools and child care facilities—
great, airy nurseries where small children could be
taught social skills and new ideas by women trained
as professionals to do it.

In 1909, Gilman launched her 32-page monthly
magazine, the *Forerunner*, in part because, as she
wrote, no one else would publish all her work. Her
aims, as she put them in the magazine's inaugural
issue, were "to stimulate thought; to arouse hope,
courage and impatience; to offer practical suggestions and solutions, to voice the strong assurance
of better living, here, now, in our own hands to

make."[23] Available by subscription only, the *Fore-runner* reached a circulation varying between five thousand and seven thousand, and sold for ten cents an issue or a dollar a year, about the same price as commercial monthlies at the time (although some ran up to a hundred pages, including advertising).[24] Like any magazine, the *Forerunner* contained virtually every genre of writing, from essays to poetry to sermons, satires to serialized novels. But unlike any other magazine of its magnitude before or since, every word of it, including the small amount of advertising copy that she would allow, was written by Gilman herself. And, like many magazines then and now, the *Forerunner* was not easy to keep afloat financially; despite Gilman's celebrity, it earned only about half of its production costs through subscription fees, and Houghton regularly lent Charlotte money to keep it going.[25] Still, with all these pressures competing for her time and attention during the *Forerunner*'s seven years and two months in print, she practiced virtually every mode and genre of expression, and produced six complete books of nonfiction and five works of fiction for its pages.

These years, the years before World War I, witnessed Charlotte's greatest public celebrity. In 1913, she addressed the International Suffrage Convention in Budapest, and also lectured in England, Germany, and Scandinavia. A series of lectures delivered in New York and London in 1914 received extensive coverage in the *New York Times* and elsewhere. Her six-lecture series "The Larger Feminism" enthralled an audience that averaged over two hundred per lecture, and another series, "Our Male Civilization," also produced significant notice.

Following the United States' entry into the Great War, however, Charlotte broke ranks with many of her former allies in the peace movement (Charlotte had helped to organize and promote the Women's Peace Parade in 1914), largely out of antipathy to the Germans. Several of her closest friendships were ruptured by her support of the American entry into the war.

After the war, and especially after the gaining of suffrage by women in 1920, Gilman's popularity began to wane; her embrace by critics was chillier, and she had increasing difficulty finding publishers for her work, especially her fiction from the now-defunct *Forerunner*.

In 1923, she published *His Religion and Hers*, an idiosyncratic work that contrasts the male conception of life (as postponement and preparation for the afterlife) with the female (as paradise in the present time and place). Echoing earlier works, she distinguishes women's practicality from the mundane narrowing of horizons imposed by their current state.

In January 1932, Charlotte was diagnosed with

breast cancer. Though she sought treatment, the death of her husband in May 1934 and the gradual spread of the cancer led her to decide to take her own life:[26]

Human life consists in mutual service. No grief, pain, misfortune or "broken heart" is excuse for cutting off one's life while any power of service remains. But when all usefulness is over, when one is assured of unavoidable and imminent death, it is the simplest of human rights to choose a quick and easy death in place of a slow and horrible one.

On August 17, 1935, after saying goodbye to friends and family, Charlotte Perkins Gilman lay down in her bed and covered her face with a cloth soaked in chloroform. In the end, she wrote in a note, she "preferred chloroform to cancer."[27]

Even in death she remained an outsider, a non-conformist who lived as an individual, accountable to herself and to her vision. (No one would have had to convince her of the morality of Dr. Kevorkian's ministrations.) Her autobiography, *The Living of Charlotte Perkins Gilman*, published later that year, takes the reader up to the moment when she dies (her suicide note was appended), and has left a valuable source for understanding Gilman's temperament and career. "The one predominant duty is to find one's work and do it," she writes in the book's last lines, "and I have striven mightily at that. The religion, the philosophy, set up so early, have seen me through."[28]

Women and Economics was the first—and the most significant—work that Gilman produced. It is the touchstone text for virtually all her ideas, "the sum of her life-work" according to Zona Gale in the foreword to Gilman's autobiography.[29] Her later works of nonfiction elaborate themes first raised in its pages. Here she touches on all the themes that dominated her work, including male-female relationships, child care, housework, domestic relationships, and male domination of the economy, politics, religion, and social life. Those topics that she did not discuss first in *Women and Economics* were left untreated in her nonfiction; it was only in her fiction that she took up the question of violence against women and the envisioning of a society without male domination.

Written over a six-week period of intensive and steady writing despite the fact that Gilman was traveling and lecturing at the time, *Women and Economics* was immediately seized by her feminist friends and colleagues as a breakthrough work when it was published in May 1898. Jane Addams called it a "masterpiece," and Florence Kelley wrote that it was "the first real, substantial contribution made by a woman to the science of economics."[30]

And it received immediate critical acclaim. Writing in the *Woman's Journal* Henry Brown Blackwell called it "brilliant, suggestive, instructive, and inspiring." In the *Dial*, Arthur Woodford hailed Gilman's "profound social philosophy," which, coupling "a wealth of illustration" with "enough wit and sarcasm to make the book very entertaining reading," made her book "almost startling in the vividness of its truth." The *Nation* also praised its originality—the "new point of view, with a new largeness of outlook . . . a new imaginativeness in interpretation, and finally, a temper which, being good, is perhaps newest of all." And Annie Muzzey, writing in the *Arena*, welcomed Gilman's "declaration of freedom to reject the false and meretricious, and to exalt the real and abiding union of man and woman."[31]

Both the *Nation* and the *London Daily Chronicle* compared the book favorably to John Stuart Mill's *The Subjection of Women*. The former called it "the most significant utterance on the subject since Mill's," while the latter noted that since Mill "there has been no book dealing with the whole position of women to approach it in originality of conception and brilliancy of exposition."[32]

Other reviewers were somewhat less effusive, but acknowledged the originality of Gilman's argument or the fluidity of her prose. The reviewer for the *New York Times Saturday Review of Books* noted

Gilman's "adroit" argument about women's lack of training for the mundane tasks of motherhood; the housewife finds herself "an amateur cook, and amateur cleaner, an amateur needlewoman, and, as Mrs. Stetson uniquely puts it, an amateur mother." The *Literary World*, a Boston magazine, praised Gilman above other feminist writers of the time for not dwelling on suffrage, and also hailed her "pleasant wit," so that one might read her book "without the annoyance which so often nettles a reader who has heard much of the 'woman question.'" A reviewer for the *Chicago Tribune* insisted that the book "lacks beauty; it is too clever . . . it stirs no deep reverberations of the soul . . . but you can quote it, and remember its points."[33]

Academic reviewers saw the work as "the cleverest, fairest and most forcible presentation" of the rights of women, despite the lack of academic scholarship. Even conservative reviewers offered the book a sort of grudging respect. "While the ideals of this author may not appeal to us," wrote the reviewer in the *Independent*, "we must admit that there is some force in her criticisms, and some reason in her suggestions."[34]

It was no less welcome abroad, where it was translated into seven languages, including Dutch, Russian, Hungarian, and Japanese. Perhaps the most effusive review came from the *Westminster Gazette* in London:

This book unites in a remarkable degree the charm of a brilliantly written essay with the inevitable logic of a proposition of Euclid. It deals, of course, with the woman question, but in a manner so striking, from a standpoint so novel, with a wit so trenchant yet void of offence, that no apology is needed for its publication in England after making something of a sensation in the United States. Nothing that we have read for many a long day can approach it in clearness of perception, in power of arrangement, and in lucidity of expression.

No wonder that in its time it was "considered by feminists of the whole world as the outstanding book on Feminism," according to the *New York City Review of Literature.*[35]

Gilman's clever style and compelling arguments are evident in the book's opening pages. She challenges the Victorian assumptions that the observed differences between women and men are somehow reflective of biological differences. Yet it is also true, she notes, that women *are* inferior to men. Such inferiority is socially produced by the fact that we are the only animal species in which females are economically dependent upon males.

Stylistically, Gilman is playful; she anticipated possible objections to her arguments and answers them before they can ossify into critique. One might protest, she writes, that as wives, women earn a share of the "family wage" paid to the husband. But women only consume and do not produce, she answers. Critics will say that she is a "partner" in the marriage, which justifies this division of labor into male producer and woman consumer. But this misunderstands the nature of the marital partnership, which extends only in relation to children and to love. A male composer does not have his wife finish his compositions when he dies. A man's work is not destroyed when his wife dies.

If she is not a true partner, Gilman asks, how does a woman earn her living? Through domestic labor, through housework, some might say. True enough. The work of the wife at home allows the husband to produce more outside it. But so does the work of a horse. In fact, she argues, women are not really rewarded for their work in the home. Making the first of a series of class-based sarcastic observations she notes that the "women who do the most work get the least money, and the women who have the most money do the least work."[36]

Perhaps, then, it is as mothers that women are rewarded. Not true again, says Gilman. If that were true, economic status would be connected to how many children one had; in fact those women with the fewest children seem to have the highest status, while those with the most children seem to have the lowest status.

In the end, Gilman concedes, it must be for their domestic labor that women are rewarded. It is for the cleaning, the washing, the cooking, the mending, that women "earn" their keep. In fact, she argues, women "work longer and harder than most men, and not solely in maternal duties." What an ironic situation, Gilman claims. "In spite of her supposed segregation to maternal duties, the human female, the world over, works at extra-maternal duties for hours enough to provide her with an independent living, and then is denied independence on the ground that motherhood prevents her from working!"[37]

Men make their living by work; women make their living by marriage. Their status is determined not by the work they do, but by the work of their husbands. (One cannot imagine a male doctor identifying himself as "a housewife's husband.")

The consequences are dire, but different, for women and men. Women's economic dependence exaggerates the differences between the sexes. Men overemphasize their masculine traits—rationality, competitiveness, aggressiveness, restlessness—at the expense of their human qualities. Women exaggerate their feminine traits—passivity, physical ability to attract men—over their human qualities. As a result, she says, women are "over-sexed"—by which she means they overdevelop their specifically feminine traits at the expense of their human traits.

Gilman illustrates this difference with a hilarious and now justly famous distinction between a wild cow and a milk cow:

> The wild cow is a female. She has healthy calves, and milk enough for them; and that is all the femininity she needs. Otherwise than that she is bovine rather than feminine. She is a light, strong, swift, sinewy creature, able to run, jump, and fight, if necessary. We, for economic uses, have artificially developed the cow's capacity for producing milk. She has become a walking milk-machine, bred and tended to that express end, her value measured in quarts. The secretion of milk is a maternal function—a sex-function. The cow is over-sexed.

If she were to be released, Gilman suggests, she would revert to her bovine temperament and use her energies for the general good of all cows, "not all running to milk."[38]

The result of this overdevelopment of feminine qualities at the expense of human qualities is that men are more "human" than women. "Man is the human creature," she writes. "Woman has been checked, starved, aborted in human growth; and the swelling forces of race development have been driven back in each generation to work in her through sex functions alone."[39] Put the two together, and gender inequalities are exaggerated rather than muted.

Far ahead of her time, Gilman makes the argument that women's economic dependence and the overemphasis on physical attractiveness to ensure her economic survival are a form of low-level prostitution. "From the odalisque with the most bracelets to the debutante with the most bouquets," she continues, "woman's economic profit comes through the power of sex-attraction." Yet when we observe the extreme illustration of exactly this—in "the open market of vice," or prostitution—"we are sick with horror." On the other hand, when "we see the same economic relation made permanent, established by law, sanctioned and sanctified by religion, covered with flowers and incense and all accumulated sentiment, we think it innocent, lovely, and right." What hypocrisy! she sneers. Although in both cases "the female gets her food from the male by virtue of her sex-relationship to him," the "transient trade" we abhor; the "bargain for life" we celebrate."[40]

Having lifted the gauzy veil of romantic obscurantism from what is essentially an economic relationship, Gilman extends her economic metaphors to all aspects of gender relations. "He is the market, the demand. She is the supply." Her attractiveness is a form of currency in this marketplace; it is what she has to sell. But unlike other marketers, she cannot appear to be too eager to sell, lest that cheapen the product and reduce demand; "she must not even look as if she wanted it!" She writes with bitter irony of the "cruel and absurd injustice of blaming the girl for not getting what she is allowed no effort to obtain" and with compassion for the unmarried woman, who "must sit passive as the seasons go by, and her 'chances' lessen with each year." She seems to wince at the "strain on a highly sensitive nervous organism to have so much hang on one thing, to see the possibility of attaining it grow less and less yearly, and to be forbidden to take any step toward securing it!"[41]

The arrangement does little good for women or for men. Marriage is corrupted into a mercenary relationship. By marrying, the woman becomes her husband's "house-servant, or at least the housekeeper." It distorts their courtship as well as their married life. "She gets her living by getting a husband. He gets his wife by getting a living."[42]

What's more, such a system also impoverishes motherhood, which, in turn, does children little good. "The mother as a social servant instead of a home servant will not lack in true mother duty. She will love her child as well, perhaps better, when she is not in hourly contact with it, when she goes from its life to her own life, and back from her own life to its life, with ever new delight and power."[43] And "the child also," Gilman continues, "will feel this beneficent effect."[44] In the end, she argues,[45]

> The economically independent mother, widened and freed, strengthened and developed, by her social service, will do better service as a mother than it has been possible for her before. No one thing could do more to advance the interests of humanity than the wiser care and wider love of organized human motherhood around babies. This nobler mother, bearing nobler children, and rearing them in nobler ways, would go far toward making possible the world which we want to see.

The cause is simple; so too its solution. "The economic independence of woman will change all these conditions as naturally and inevitably as her dependence has introduced them."[46]

Every facet of women's lives can change. Marriage, for example. Gilman suggests that "a pure and lasting monogamous sex-union can exist without bribe of purchase, without the manacles of economic dependence, and that men and women so united in sex-relation will still be free to combine with others in economic relation."[47]

And motherhood—parenthood—can be reformed. A mother who is economically independent can be "a world servant instead of a house-servant; a mother knowing the world and living in it—can be to her children far more than has ever been possible before. Motherhood in the world will make that world a different place for her child."[48]

But how do we get from here to there, from women's economic dependency to such a pure and healthy marriage and family life? Perhaps Gilman's most important contribution is her ability to offer sweeping but specific reforms that would actualize her vision. In a nutshell, Gilman's solution was the professionalization of domestic work, and the freeing of women from being forced to do it because of their dependency. In this, she joined many socialist reformers of the era in seeking to resolve the economic contradiction between the social circumstances of production (goods and services are created in concert with others) and private, individual ownership. Production is social; ownership is private. Socialists believed that socializing the means of production would automatically resolve the tensions between classes.

But Gilman extended that argument to the relations between women and men, relations that were no less "political" than those between classes, because women's economic dependency upon men reproduced the relationship between workers and owners. In domestic life, she argued, production remained social, public, but consumption and caregiving were private, individual. We make things together, but consume them separately. The professionalization of housework and child care and the liberation of women to create new identities in the world of work could together create a new era for women and children, and a far more profound relationship between women and men.

Professionalization meant several things. First, it meant that child-care arrangements would have to change. "If it can be shown that our babies would be better off if part of their time was passed in other care than their mothers', then such other care would be right; and it would be the duty of motherhood to provide it."[49] Day care, provided by well-trained and professional day-care workers, would be far superior, Gilman believed, to the haphazard, erratic, and unpredictable care given to children by their mothers, no matter how well intended.

Housework also should be left to the experts. Cooking, for example, disfigures male-female relationships. "Is it not time that the way to a man's heart through his stomach should be relinquished for some higher avenue?" Gilman asks. "The stomach should be left to its natural uses, not made a thoroughfare for stranger passions and purposes; and the heart should be approached through higher channels." The current system leaves us poorly

nourished, both physically and spiritually—so Gilman proposes the professionalization of cooking,
putting it in "the hands of trained experts." That
way, a woman could "stand beside man as the comrade of his soul, not the servant of his body."[50]

Apartment houses could be built without
kitchens, since "a family unit which is only bound
together with a table cloth is of questionable value,"
and the building itself could construct a large, collective, buildingwide kitchen in the basement, where
women could prepare the occasional meal coopera-
tively, thus satisfying their need for socializing as
well as domestic work, nurturing themselves while
they nurture their families.

The result of these changes, Gilman argues,
would be neither the reduction of motherhood nor
the estrangement of wifely affections. In fact, it
would mean a larger motherhood, with women free
to love and care for their children, which is, after
all, what they do best, and leaving all the other
work to others, who are trained to do it. And it
would mean a larger domestic partnership for the
married couple, with women freed to pursue the
very interests and public lives that will make them
more interesting, more desirable, and more affectionate to their spouses.

Gilman was sanguine about the possibilities of
change, in part because it all seemed so simple.
"The economic independence of woman will change

all these conditions as naturally and inevitably as her dependence has introduced them." And so, she concludes, when "the mother of the race is free, we shall have a better world."[51]

———————

It all seemed so simple, and indeed the changes were upon us. All that remained was to spell out exactly the dynamics of the transition in which we were already engaged. Virtually all Gilman's subsequent writing was an elaboration of the themes first raised in *Women and Economics*. Her first two subsequent books focused on motherhood from two angles she had already suggested—child care and housework. These were the common points of objection to women's rights and economic independence, the areas where women were thought to be so desperately needed at home. *Concerning Children* (1900) and *The Home* (1903) take up where *Women and Economics* left off, specifying the ways in which such notions were economically, emotionally, and morally suspect.

First, the children. We raise our children all wrong, Gilman flatly argues. Although there is nothing more important than the raising of children—"on its right treatment rests the progress of the world," she argues[52]—we ask people who have no training, but who mean well, mothers, to do it, and when they can't we ask servants or nurses to pitch in, though neither of these has any partic-

ular training in the proper care of children either.
  But who can train the baby any better than the
mother? Gilman asks herself rhetorically:

> If the mother can, by all means let her. But can
> she? We do not hear mothers protesting that
> they can teach their grown-up sons and daugh-
> ters better than college professors, nor their
> middle aged children better than their school
> teachers. Why, then, are they so certain that
> they can teach their babies better than trained
> baby-teachers? They are willing to consult a
> doctor if the baby is ill, and gladly submit to his
> dictation.... There is no wound to maternal
> pride in this case.

Such a sentiment is not only bad motherhood; it
flies against all available economic evidence, which
tells us that specialization is both natural and beneficial:[53]

> It is a pretty sentiment that the mother's love in
> some mysterious way makes all she does for the
> child superior to what another can do. But ap-
> ply the test of fact. Can she, with all her love,
> make as good a shoe as the shoemaker, as good
> a hair-brush, tooth-brush, tumbler, tea cup, pie-
> plate, spoon, fork, or knife, as the professional
> manufacturers of these things? Does mother-

love teach her to be a good barber? Can she cut her darling's hair so as to make him happy? Can she make a good chair or table or book or window? How silly it is to imagine that this "personality" inserted between the sheets makes the bed more conducive to healthy sleep than any other clean, well-aired, well-made bed!

And it's not good for the children, either, to grow up isolated and individually, which makes us "unnecessarily selfish," because "each child is so the focus of family attention all the time." Organized child care, performed by trained professionals, would free mothers and fathers alike, and would produce a generation of happier, healthier children. "A number of little ones together for part of every day, having their advantages in common, learning from infancy to say 'we' instead of 'I,' would grow up far better able to fill their places as helpful and happy members of society."[54]

Throughout the book, Gilman pauses to champion specific reforms besides child care. She counsels against corporal punishment, and in favor of parents' explaining to their children the reasons for their commands or requests. Despite her general uneasiness with the subject, Gilman also advises frank and honest discussion about sex and reproduction.

In *The Home* (1903), she turns her attention once more to motherhood, this time in relation to the house itself, and not as much its younger inhabitants. In a book that Gilman herself called "the most heretical—and the most amusing—of anything I've done,"[55] she argues that the home as presently organized is an evolutionary throwback, derived from an earlier time, a living anachronism that is no longer necessary.

More than half a century before Betty Friedan coined the term "the feminine mystique," Gilman was already tearing down the walls of women's "arbitrary imprisonment." And, like Friedan, Gilman argued that such "exclusive confinement" in the home made the woman less a person, that a "mental myopia" comes over her as she focuses only on the proximate, to the exclusion of the visionary.[56] This makes the woman far less attractive to her husband than misty ideology might suggest. "We are taught that man most loves and admires the domestic type of woman," she writes. "This is one of the roaring jokes of history. The breakers of hearts, the queens of romance, the goddesses of a thousand devotees, have not been cooks." In fact, she argues, if a man loves his wife, "it is in spite of the home— not because of it."[57]

Not only does the current organization of the home make little emotional sense, it makes virtually no economic sense. The individual woman is expected to be a master of a "swarming heap of rudimentary trades." But why? We don't expect each

xliv

person to make his or her own shoes, do we? Then why would we expect everyone to cook their own meals? Think of it this way, she writes in an article a year later:[58]

> We take half the people of the world and set them to wait upon the other half, thus limiting the output of their labor exactly as it would that of a lumber camp if half the men were assigned to wait upon the other half instead of chopping wood; or of an army if half the soldiers were "keeping tent" instead of fighting; or of a ship's crew if half the sailors were cooks.

She calculates that the traditional nuclear family—with working husband and a full-time domesticated wife—is three times more costly than what is necessary to meet the same needs. What waste! And who can afford it?

If women worked outside the home, she calculates, the husband would be "relieved of two-thirds of his expenses; provided with double supplies; properly fed and more comfortable at home than he even dreamed of being, and associated with a strong, free, stimulating companion all through life, will be able to work to far better purpose in the social service, and with far greater power, pride, and enjoyment."[59]

In this book, Gilman also raises a new issue, one to which she will return in later works, especially her fiction: violence against women. Though she was not the first to explore the question of domestic violence or marital rape, her emphasis that the origins of such abuses were to be found not in demented, perverse, or evil individuals, or in "demon rum," but in the structure of the arrangements between women and men, and especially in women's economic dependence on men, were astonishingly new, and would resound across the twentieth century as women became increasingly aware of the severity and the extent of such violence.

Here, she barely raises the issue. Women, current ideology holds, "must be guarded in the only place of safety, the home." But, she asks, "guarded from what? From men. From the womanless men who may be prowling about while all women stay at home. The home is safe because women are there. Out of doors is unsafe because women are not there. If women were there, everywhere, in the world which belongs to them as much as to men, then everywhere would be safe."[60]

In her 1904 book *Human Work*, Gilman expanded on her dominant and specifically economic focus on women's plight to make broader and grander arguments about the centrality of work in human life. While she called the work "the greatest book I have ever done, and the poorest," the book echoes contemporaneous themes about dignity of work articulated by, for example, Fabian socialists and William

Morris and the Arts and Crafts Movement in Britain, and Edward Bellamy and Thorstein Veblen in the United States. Work, she argued, was the generator of life—hers is both a Marxian labor theory of value and a psychological labor theory of values—and economic independence is the prerequisite for genuine emotional and psychological autonomy for all adults, women as well as men.[61]

A good deal of Gilman's subsequent work, both nonfiction and fiction, had been first published in the *Forerunner*. In *The Man-Made World* (1911), serialized in the magazine in 1910, Gilman continues to develop the distinctly sociological perspective on social development also at play in *Women and Economics*. She argues that our world has been built by a sleight of hand, the substitution of the "male" for the human and the simultaneous devaluation of all that is female. Whereas her earlier works sought to elevate women to the realms of the human, in this work she also tries to bring men down to earth, restore them to their masculine specificity as opposed to pretending that they are synonymous with humanity. Gilman is going to turn the tables. If, as she writes, "men have written copiously about women, treating them always as females, with an offensiveness and falsity patent to modern minds," then she will treat "men as males in contradistinction to their qualities as human beings," but without reproducing "the abusiveness and contempt that has been shown to women as females." In a sense, Gilman seeks to make masculinity visible.[62]

Its invisibility has negative consequences for both women and men. By their remaining feminine and specific, women's growth has been stunted; they live in a state of perpetual "arrested development," since they "cannot develop humanly, as he has, through social contact, social service, true social life." And for him, his personality is disfigured, his capacity for love and compassion muted, his family a "despotism."

Much of the book is taken up with observing the effects of "the unbridled dominance of one sex" in every arena she can think of—from child rearing (she discusses children's games, toys, and dolls) to education, to ethics and religion. Currently, she observes—presciently, given today's discussions about the academic "canon"—we discuss "women's literature" and its difference from "literature." Do we have a parallel of "masculine literature"? Gilman asks. Of course not, because "men are people! Women, being 'the sex' have their limited feminine interests, their feminine point of view, which must be provided for. Men, however, are not restricted— to them belongs the world's literature!"[63]

This critique of the false equation *man = world; women = her sex* resounds across other works that came later. For example, in *Herland*, Gilman gives full force to her rage at the difference:[64]

When we say *men, man, manly, manhood*, and all the other masculine derivatives, we have in the background of our minds a huge vague crowded picture of the world and all its activities. To grow up and "be a man," to "act like a man,"—the meaning and connotation is wide indeed. That vast background is full of marching columns of men, of changing lines of men, of long processions of men; of men steering their ships into new seas, exploring unknown mountains, breaking horses, herding cattle, ploughing and sowing and reaping, toiling at the forge and furnace, digging in the mine, building roads and bridges and high cathedrals, managing great businesses, teaching in all the colleges, preaching in all the churches; of men everywhere doing everything—"the world."

And when we say *women*, we think *female*—the sex.

Finally, in *His Religion and Hers* (1923), she explores how androcentric religion has distorted the spiritual impulse. Anticipating many contemporary spiritual feminist writers, Gilman argues that a feminist religion would be very different from the current masculinist one—a "birth-based" religion as opposed to a "death-based" religion, organized through the "immediate altruism" of the mother and child rather than the "posthumous egotism" of masculine immortality, and focused on the question "What must be done for the child who is born?" rather then "What happens to me after I die?"—the signal trademark of all masculine religions.[65]

In her nonfiction work, Gilman invariably describes women made weak, helpless, and feeble by economic dependence. But in her fiction, she was able to envision a stronger, bolder, more assertive femininity. For example, *What Diantha Did* (1910) describes the transformation of household economy and early childhood socialization by an independently minded woman. Gilman's *Forerunner* fiction consistently offers heroines who exemplify the need for full, independent identities, even after matrimony. In her many short stories about marriage, when mates or potential mates will not "love them and encourage [women] to be creative, contributing members of society... the message from Gilman is clear: don't marry."[66] And *Unpunished*, a long-unpublished murder mystery (circa 1929), utilizes the popular detective genre to explore the contrast between despotic and egalitarian marriage. That work centers around the murder of Mr. Vaughn, "the utmost manifestation of a dissolute patriarchy," a tyrannical patriarch, who has committed fraud, blackmail, and marital rape, and kept women and children virtual hostages. Solving the mystery are a husband-and-wife detective team, Jim and Bess Hunt, who share housework, and divide labor according to their respective abilities, not their respective genders. They respect each other's work; their complementary skills enable them to solve a mystery neither could have solved alone.[67]

This theme of strong, independent women is most fully realized, of course, in *Herland*, perhaps Gilman's most justly famous work of fiction. The book, now a feminist classic, is a utopian novel in which Gilman invites us to imagine the possibilities of women's unfettered development if they were completely free of any dependence on men, even for biological reproduction.

Herland is one of three feminist utopias originally published in the *Forerunner*, a group that includes as well *Moving the Mountain* (1911) and *Herland*'s sequel, *With Her in Ourland* (1916).[68] The women of Herland are strong, healthy, vibrant, and athletic, energized by "a sunny breeze of freedom." Here child care is collectively organized and professionalized (since all women in Herland have a desire for motherhood, but not all women are well suited for it); there is no poverty, no crime, no violence. There is no sentimentalized home to imprison, no marketplace competition to divide, no God to fear and obey—since they live in a virtual heaven on earth, the women of Herland have no need to believe in some abstraction called heaven.[69]

Less obvious, but no less central to Gilman's project, is her description of the three men who inadvertently stumble into Herland. These men capture three very different responses of American men to feminist reforms at the turn of the century.[70] Terry Nicholson is wealthy and arrogant, an unreconstructed patriarch, a "gay Lothario" who eventually commits marital rape and is exiled from the feminist paradise. Jeff Margrave accepts the women's ways a bit too readily and far too uncritically for Gilman's tastes; his "exalted gallantry" marks him as "something of a traitor." (To be sure, Gilman tells us, Margrave had something of "a following" among some of the women, but it was always the "more sentimental" and "less practical" ones who liked him.) Vandyck Jennings, the narrator, is a sociologist—rational, thoughtful, and careful. His conversion to the ways of Herland is considered and cautious, based on a judicious weighing of empirical evidence; he neither resists, nor does he become a sycophantic acolyte.[71]

It is Jennings who finds the women of Herland almost "inconveniently reasonable," especially compared to the women to whom he had become accustomed. Having now observed women's unfettered development, Jennings realizes that his (and our) definition of femininity is "not feminine at all, but mere reflected masculinity—developed to please us because they had to please us." In fact, Jennings muses, men don't really like women very much at all:[72]

> We talk fine things about women, but in our hearts we know that they are very limited beings—most of them. We honor them for their functional power, even while we dishonor them by our use of it; we honor them for their carefully enforced virtue, even when we show by our own conduct how little we think of that virtue; we value them, sincerely, for the perverted maternal activities which make our wives the most comfortable of servants, bound to us for life with the wages wholly at our own decision, their whole business, outside of the temporary duties of such motherhood as they may achieve, to meet our needs in every way. Oh, we value them, all right, "in their place."

It was from her place, that pedestal of reverence and contempt, from which Gilman sought to dislodge woman, to make her at once more human, active, and alive.

———

One other theme jumps out at the contemporary reader of *Herland*—Gilman's antipathy for and discomfort with sexuality. With one foot planted firmly in nineteenth-century Victorian morality, Gilman could not easily step into twentieth-century sexual liberation. In the novel, sexuality causes problems for all three of the newlywed couples and sets in motion the events that lead to their expulsion from paradise.

After their wedding, and without guile or affect, Jennings's wife, Ellador, asks him:[73]

"You mean—that with you—love between man and woman expresses itself in that way—without regard to motherhood? To parentage, I mean," she added carefully.

"Yes, surely. It is love we think of—the deep sweet love between two. Of course we want children, and children come—but that is not what we think about."

"But—but—it seems so against nature!" she said. "None of the creatures we know do that."

Personally, Gilman seems to have been a relative stranger to the pleasures of sexual passion. Whether this is because she was deeply, secretly, lesbian, as her biographers suggest (with her attraction to women emerging only once in her life), or because of the psychological consequences of her bout with postpartum depression and neurasthenia, or because, like some other feminists of her day, Gilman believed that "sexual freedom led to another form of female subordination,"[74] one cannot be certain.

But it is clear that she held a lifelong distaste for sexual desire and activity.

And wherever it came from, Gilman seems to have been even theoretically antipathetic to the *idea* of sexual liberation for women. In various of her *Forerunner* stories, sex is a male force and seduction a man's game; she often wrote in part to reveal "the cruel disproportion between his 'fun' and that lifelong injury and shame inflicted on a foolish, ignorant girl."[75] Even marital sexuality seems to have been misguided, damaging, or somewhat distasteful to her. None of the married couples in *Herland* manages actually to have sex, and in *Unpunished* what might appear to some as marital sex is exposed as rape and abuse. What Gilman did not see, as Rosalind Rosenberg writes, was that the sexual revolution of the first decades of the century "gave women something that was essential to their eventual liberation: a broader conception of their own physical needs and a greater confidence in their ability to control their physical destiny."[76]

In part this political antipathy may have come from her resolutely economic emphasis. It was through economic independence that women would become free; sexual expression might prove a distraction from the pursuit of their economic liberation. It may have simply been that sexual freedom is such an individual solution to what Gilman saw as a social problem. Feminism required social transformation, and sexual freedom was a way to express personal freedom that would, or at least could, leave existing social arrangements in place. Or it may be that Gilman felt that any sexual pleasure to be taken under existing circumstances would invariably be based upon motives and criteria derived from women's economic dependency, and could therefore not be a true expression of her real sexuality.

Regardless of her motives, or its permutations, sexuality as a mode of personal expression or as an aspect of liberation played little role in Gilman's vision of the future. Here she parted company with many of the radicals, socialists, and feminists with whom she shared so much. While many of them turned to Freud as a personal corollary to the collective social transformation offered by socialism, Gilman remained disgusted by his ideas, put off by "our absurd Sexolatry" derived from his "illogical assertions," and she declared his influence "evil" in a lecture entitled "The Fallacy of Freud."[77]

Gilman's sexual Victorianism was coupled with several other themes that may be problematic for modern readers. These themes hover at the edge of *Women and Economics* and emerge more fully in other works. In this book, she stresses the intersection of class and gender, but pays little attention to race. In fact, it is an inescapable conclusion that when Gilman referred to "the race," meaning humanity as a whole, she envisioned the white race (though it seems a bit of a strain to claim that she meant it to be understood as a racialized concept).[78] In various works, she specifies other races, especially blacks, as inferior, occupying a lower rung on a grand human evolutionary ladder, echoing the very social Darwinist sentiments that she despised when applied to gender. Especially in her private letters and diaries, but scattered throughout her writings in the *Forerunner* and elsewhere, Gilman invoked racist ideas, moved too easily to racist examples, and drew upon racist themes. One senses, as her biographer Ann Lane writes, that Gilman felt that "all of these strange people with their odd customs and language and look were not quite as good as her people."[79]

On the other hand, she occasionally discredits explicitly racist themes. In *Herland*, for example, Gilman puts racist sentiments only in Terry's mouth, so that the unreconstructed misogynist is also unmasked as a racist, down to the songs he hums. And the fact that "we have cheated the Indian, oppressed the African, robbed the Mexican," Gilman wrote in the *Forerunner*, "is ground for shame." And, as Lane also points out, at the 1903 convention of the National American Woman's Suffrage Association, Gilman's was the sole dissenting voice raised in opposition to a literacy requirement for the vote, frequently a racist ploy to continue the disenfranchisement of blacks.[80]

Gilman's ambivalent racism was frequently complemented by an often virulent nativism: she believed that healthy, native-born American stock would be gradually displaced (though she did not fear dilution through intermarriage) by "lesser" peoples streaming in from other countries—particularly from Germany, Russia, Poland, and southern Europe—at the turn of the century. Though she believed that some peoples were superior to others, she dissented from the eugenics movement that urged restricted breeding of these "lower races" because she felt that differences among races were social in origin, not biological.

Her major nativist nemesis remained the Jews. Gilman's anti-Semitism was pronounced and consistent throughout her life. Claiming that New York City, where she had never enjoyed living, had become one-third Jewish by 1920, she declared herself pleased to leave, to "escape forever this hideous city —and its Jews. The nervewearing noise—the dirt— the ugliness, the steaming masses in the subway." Her anti-Semitism again surfaced when she considered the Russian Revolution. Bolshevism, she said, was a "Russian-Jewish nightmare."[81]

In his 1966 introduction, Carl Degler assessed the value of *Women and Economics* both within the context of the emerging Second Wave of the women's movement, and within Gilman's work as a whole.

He suggested that Gilman's strength was in her social analysis, her sociology, and that she "showed little talent for imaginative writing" (although he does suggest that "The Yellow Wallpaper" was passable).[82] Such an assessment is, perhaps, a bit harsh, given the enduring popularity not only of that single short story, but also of *Herland*, which continues to find an audience of readers eager to believe that things would be altogether different (and better) if women ruled the world, or, even more simply, if they lived in a world without men.

Yet much of Gilman's other fiction suffers from a narrative style that can be both plodding and unstable by turns, even in a very short story, and from an incessant, often intrusive didacticism. The recent publication of two more of her novels, the detective story *Unpunished* and *Herland*'s sequel, *With Her in Ourland*, provides ample evidence that Gilman's strengths lay elsewhere.[83] These are useful novels more for their contribution to the biographical portrait of their author than for their deft narrative, complex characterization, or even propelling plot lines.

In her own time, Gilman had been a major thinker and writer, a leading public intellectual. In the 1960s, she had jibed with Second Wave readers who brought to *Women and Economics* the concerns of a generation of women who felt themselves, as Gilman had, trapped in the home, who yearned, as

Gilman did, to have a larger, public life, a life of meaningful work, of economic independence.

Today, women have earned those rights. Women have entered the workplace, the professions, the military, in unprecedented numbers. Women maintain the right to pursue their ambitions without harassment or discrimination, to insist on lives free of the threat of rape or violence, the right to enjoy sexual liberty and, however precariously, the right to choose.

To be sure, they still face significant obstacles to their complete entry into the public sphere, still face harassment and a multitude of minor and major discriminations, still fear rape and violence, still fear that their right to choose may be further eroded or compromised by those to whom women's autonomy is a threat. But there is also no question that women today feel themselves entitled to as full a public life and as full a sense of independence and integrity as men feel.

But their entry into the public arena has not brought women the liberation that Gilman, or Betty Friedan, predicted. Today's readers bring new and different concerns to Gilman's text—concerns born of the frustration that economic autonomy has not yet been won, and that the economic freedoms thus far gained have not translated into commensurate progress toward women's equality. An earlier generation believed that women needed to be freed *from* the home; today's women want to move easily and freely *between* home and work, comfortably balancing economic and family life.

Gilman understood that woman's freedom would require more than simply throwing open the doors of the homes that imprisoned her; it would require the transformation of the workplace and also the transformation of the home. The workplace was not a gender-neutral site, into which women, once liberated from the home, would simply integrate themselves. The workplace was, and continues to be, a male domain; it is no wonder that it also bears the marks of that now-visible identity. The workplace is a gendered arena, and women's success in that arena continues to be largely based on their ability to negotiate its masculine precepts and values.

In order for women to integrate into the workplace while maintaining a sense of themselves in their own terms, the workplace will have to change. It will need to become attuned to a more inclusive constellation of approaches, and become more "family-friendly," developing those mechanisms that enable workers to balance work and family successfully. And Gilman understood much of this. She advocated parental leave, for example, long before the Family and Medical Leave Act was a twinkle in any legislator's eye. "A year's vacation should be taken with each baby," she wrote in an essay in 1923.[84]

And she understood also that in order for women to be able to achieve economic independence, home and family life would have to be transformed, and that both structural and emotional changes were necessary. Her proposals for professionalized child care and organized and well-funded nurseries are finally becoming realities across the nation, while her more sweeping architectural innovations, like cooperative kitchens in urban apartments, remain on the experimental fringe of the American way of life.

And Gilman also understood that the home was not the safe "haven in a heartless world" that romantic sentimentalists had sold to women as the justification for the separation of spheres in the first place. Today's readers know that the home is the site of terror and violence against women as well, that more rapes and murders of women occur in the home than in any other place, that the men most likely to commit rape are either those to whom the women are married or those they are dating, and that nearly one-third of all women are, at some point, hit by their husbands. As early as the 1870s, Gilman protested men's violence and how it was used to keep women in their place. Once, when she had refused a male escort's offer to see her safely home, he remarked to her, somewhat bewildered, "But any man would be glad to protect a woman. Man is a woman's natural protector!" "Against what?" she asked. In her novels, like *Herland* and *Unpunished*, and in several of her essays and books, Gilman protested against the violence and the threat of violence that hold women back—both collectively and individually.

This leads to a last issue that contemporary readers bring to her work today. For women to be free of violence, for women to be free to pursue their economic autonomy in the public sphere and also to have the rich family lives they say they want, *men* are going to have to change as well. Men will have to cease seeing themselves as the unexamined norm, and begin to enlarge the meanings of masculinity to include those emotions and behaviors—nurturing, love, emotional intimacy, care—that have defined domestic life. To be sure, women's emancipation has been women's project, but if women are going to "have it all," men are going to have to share the work. Few feminist writers in the mid-1960s, let alone in 1898, understood the relationship between women's freedom and the changes for men; fewer still would have advocated them. But Gilman believed, as the famous labor song put it, "the rising of the women is the rising of the race."[85] And she well understood the portent of the feminist movement for men.

At the beginning of the century, Charlotte Perkins Gilman proclaimed the twentieth century as "the woman's century"—the century of her eman-

cipation from the home and from economic dependence on men. A century of struggle and activism
has produced only part of that emancipation, and it
remains for the next generation of readers, in the
next century, to grasp feminism's emancipatory
promise. Now is another moment, as Gilman pronounced then, the "chance for the mother of the
world to rise to her full place, her transcendent
power to remake humanity, to rebuild the suffering
world—and the world waits while she powders her
nose."[86]

NOTES

1. Carl Degler, "Introduction," in Charlotte Perkins Gilman,
   Women and Economics (New York: Harper and Row, 1966),
   p. xiii.
2. Charlotte Perkins Gilman, "Passing of Matrimony," in *Harper's Bazaar*, June 1906, p. 496.
3. Charlotte Perkins Gilman, *The Home: Its Work and Influence* (New York: Charlton Company, 1903), p. 129.
4. Floyd Dell, "Feminism for Men," in *The Masses*, volume 5,
   number 20 (July 1917); reprinted in Michael Kimmel and
   Thomas Mosmiller, eds., *Against the Tide: Profeminist Men
   in the United States, 1776–1990, a Documentary History*
   (Boston: Beacon Press, 1992), pp. 364, 361. Of course, to
   Gilman it *did* matter which half was the poorer half—at
   least men had the thrill of public participation—and if
   forced to choose between those halves, she would not have
   hesitated.

5. Charlotte Perkins Gilman, *The Living of Charlotte Perkins Gilman* (New York: Harper and Row, 1975), p. 83.

6. Ibid., p. 84.

7. Ibid., pp. 90, 91.

8. Ibid., p. 89. The "black helplessness" with its "deadness of heart, its aching emptiness of mind," which she felt, might have been what is now called postpartum depression. See, for example, Verta Taylor, *Rock-a-By Baby* (New York: Routledge, 1996).

9. See, for example, "On Advertising for Marriage," in *Alpha*, volume 2, and "The Answer," in *Woman's Journal*, volume 17, number 40 (October 2, 1886).

10. *The Living* (above, n. 5), p. 95.

11. Ibid., p. 96.

12. Gary Scharnhorst, *Charlotte Perkins Gilman: A Bibliography* (Metuchen, N.J.: Scarecrow Press, 1985).

13. Charlotte Perkins Gilman, *Herland: A Lost Feminist Utopian Novel*, ed. Ann J. Lane (New York: Pantheon, 1979), p. vi.

14. *The Living* (above, n. 5), p. 186.

15. Though "The Yellow Wallpaper" is now considered her finest work of fiction, she searched for two years to find a publisher. The story had been turned down by Howells when he was editor of the *Atlantic* in 1892, though he later included it in his collection *Great Modern Stories* in 1920.

16. As in Marx's famous epigram that "men make their own history," echoed in his most famous articulation of this social constructionist position, in the preface to his 1859 *Contribution to the Critique of Political Economy*, where he writes that "it is not the consciousness of men that determines their being, but, on the contrary, their being which determines their consciousness."

17. *The Living* (above, n. 5), p. 187.

18. In fact, she was antipathetic to much of the socialist planning of her era. A visit to the socialist community at Rus-

kin, Tennessee, for example, made her think it was simply "another of those sublimely planned, devoutly joined, and invariably deserted Socialist colonies. Only ignorance of the real nature of social relations can account for these high-minded idiocies." See ibid., p. 252.

19. Ibid., p. 198.

20. *Forerunner*, volume 7 (November 1916), p. 287.

21. *The Living* (above, n. 5), p. 316. The couple lived mostly on the Upper West Side. Of their last apartment, on Riverside Drive between 94th and 95th St., she wrote that "if the flat had had suitable closets, and if the other inhabitants had not encouraged New York's little traveling pets, it would have been about perfect" (p. 296). Since the editors of this volume live quite nearby, we can attest that little has changed since Charlotte's days.

22. Ibid., p 26.

23. *Forerunner*, volume 1 (December 1909), p. 33.

24. Larry Ceplair cites Gilman's own estimation of circulation in *Charlotte Perkins Gilman: A Nonfiction Reader* (New York: Columbia University Press, 1991), p. 188. See also Charlotte Perkins Gilman, "A Summary of Purpose," *Forerunner*, volume 7 (November 1916), p. 287.

25. Ceplair, *Charlotte Perkins Gilman* (above, n. 24), p. 190. See also, Gilman, *The Living* (above, n. 5), p. 305.

26. *The Living*, p. 333.

27. Ibid., p. 334.

28. Ibid.

29. Zona Gale, "Foreword" to *The Living* (above, n. 5), p. xxxi.

30. Both Addams and Kelley are cited in Mary A. Hill, *Charlotte Perkins Gilman: The Making of a Radical Feminist, 1860–1896* (Philadelphia: Temple University Press, 1980), p. 295.

31. Henry Brown Blackwell, review of *Women and Economics*, in *Woman's Journal*, June 25, 1898, p. 204; Arthur Wood-

ford, *Dial*, February 1, 1899, p. 85; *Nation*, June 8, 1899, p. 433.

32. *Nation*, June 8, 1899; *London Daily Chronicle*, June 26, 1899.

33. *New York Times Saturday Review of Books*, November 5, 1898, p. 738; *Literary World*, December 24, 1898, p. 451; *Chicago Tribune*, May 24, 1914.

34. Mabel Hurd, review in *Political Science Quarterly*, volume 14 (December 1899), p. 712; *Independent*, January 26, 1899, p. 283.

35. *Westminster Gazette*, August 29, 1899; *New York City Review of Literature*, August 19, 1933.

36. Below, pp. 14–15.

37. Below, pp. 20–21.

38. Below, pp. 43–44.

39. Below, p. 75.

40. Below, pp. 63–64.

41. Below, pp. 86, 88–89, 87.

42. Below, p. 219.

43. Below, p. 290.

44. Ibid.

45. Below, pp. 293–94.

46. Below, p. 312.

47. Below, p. 115.

48. Below, p. 269.

49. Below, p. 212.

50. Below, pp. 236, 237.

51. Below, pp. 312, 340.

52. Charlotte Perkins Gilman, *Concerning Children* (Boston: Small, Maynard, and Co., 1900), p. 42.

53. Ibid., p. 91.

54. Ibid., p. 46.

55. *The Living* (above, n. 5), p. 286.

56. Charlotte Perkins Gilman, *The Home* (New York: McClure, Phillips, and Co., 1903), pp. 22, 23, 216.

57. Ibid., pp. 280, 281.

58. Charlotte Perkins Gilman, "Domestic Economy," in the *Independent*, June 16, 1904, p. 1161.

59. *The Home* (above, n. 56), pp. 320, 322.

60. Ibid., p. 254.

61. Charlotte Perkins Gilman, *Human Work* (New York: Mc-Clure, Phillips, and Co., 1904). Gilman's assessment of the book is in *The Living* (above, n. 5), p. 275.

62. Charlotte Perkins Gilman, *The Man-Made World* (New York: Charlton Company, 1911), p. 8. This project coincides with that of one of the editors of this volume. Kimmel argues that one of the mechanisms by which male domination is perpetuated is that masculinity is equated with humanity—we use the generic male pronoun, for example—and thus the specificity of masculinity remains invisible. See, for example, Michael Kimmel, "Invisible Masculinity," in *Society*, September 1993, pp. 28–35; and the introduction to *Manhood in America: A Cultural History* (New York: Free Press, 1996).

63. *The Man-Made World* (above, n. 62), p. 91.

64. Gilman, *Herland* (above, n. 13), p. 137.

65. Charlotte Perkins Gilman, *His Religion and Hers* (New York: Century and Company, 1923), p. 50.

66. Aleta Cane, "The Heroine of Her Own Story: Appropriation and Subversion of Mass Media Marriage Plots in Three Short Stories from the *Forerunner*," unpublished paper delivered at the Second International Charlotte Perkins Gilman Conference, June 26–28, 1997, Skidmore College, Saratoga Springs, New York, p. 8.

67. Charlotte Perkins Gilman, *Unpunished*, edited and with an afterword by Catherine J. Golden and Denise D. Knight (New York: Feminist Press, 1997), p. 218.

68. See Carol Farley Kessler, *Charlotte Perkins Gilman: Her Progress Toward Utopia, with Selected Writings* (Syracuse:

Syracuse University Press, 1995), p. 36. See also Lane's account of the genre of the utopia in *Herland* (above, n. 13), pp. xii, xix–xxiii.

69. *Herland* (above, n. 13), pp. 99, 82.

70. See Michael Kimmel, "Men's Responses to Feminism at the Turn of the Century," *Gender & Society*, volume 1, number 2 (1987), pp. 261–83.

71. *Herland* (above, n. 13), pp. 124, 89, 51.

72. Ibid., p. 141.

73. Ibid., p. 138.

74. Lane, *Herland* (above, n. 13), p. xvi.

75. Charlotte Perkins Gilman, "His Mother," *Forerunner*, July 1914, pp. 169–73. Reprinted in Denise D. Knight, ed., *"The Yellow Wall-Paper" and Selected Stories of Charlotte Perkins Gilman* (Cranbury, N.J.: Associated University Presses, 1994), p. 74.

76. Rosalind Rosenberg, *Beyond Separate Spheres: Intellectual Roots of Modern Feminism* (New Haven: Yale University Press, 1982), p. 206.

77. See Ann J. Lane, *To "Herland" and Beyond: The Life and Work of Charlotte Perkins Gilman* (New York: Pantheon, 1990), pp. 332, 352. Lane attributes Gilman's antipathy to a simpler motive—her distrust that male doctors were using psychological insights to oppress women further. While doubtless true, this argument downplays Gilman's opposition to sexual liberation as the source of her antipathy to Freud's ideas.

78. For an excessively politically correct reading of Gilman's racism, see Gail Bederman, *Manliness and Civilization* (Chicago: University of Chicago Press, 1994).

79. See Lane, *To "Herland"* (above, n. 77), p. 256.

80. He sings, "The things that I learned from the yellow and black / They 'ave helped me a 'eap with the white": *Herland* (above, n. 13), p. 131. Note also his mock working-

class accent in the song, as Gilman is attributing such sentiments to the aristocratic, misogynist Nicholson mouthing a working-class, imperialist racism. None but the most determinedly myopic and ideologically blindered reader could possibly mistake her recitation as anything but critical. See also Lane, *To "Herland"* (above, n. 77), p. 256.

81. Ibid., p. 337; Gilman, *The Living* (above, n. 5), p. 320.

82. Degler, "Introduction" (above, n. 1), p. xviii.

83. See Gilman, *Unpunished* (above, n. 67); and Charlotte Perkins Gilman, *With Her in Ourland* (New York: Praeger, 1997).

84. Charlotte Perkins Gilman, "The New Generation of Women," *Current History*, August 18, 1923, p. 734.

85. Dell, "Feminism for Men," in Kimmel and Mosmiller, eds., *Against the Tide* (above, n. 4), p. 361.

86. *The Living* (above, n. 5), p. 331.

PROEM

In dark and early ages, through the primal forests
    faring,
Ere the soul came shining into prehistoric night,
Twofold man was equal; they were comrades dear and
    daring,
Living wild and free together in unreasoning delight.

Ere the soul was born and consciousness came slowly,
Ere the soul was born, to man and woman, too,
Ere he found the Tree of Knowledge, that awful tree
    and holy,
Ere he knew he felt, and knew he knew.

Then said he to Pain, "I am wise now, and I know you!
No more will I suffer while power and wisdom last!"
Then said he to Pleasure, "I am strong, and I will
    show you
That the will of man can seize you,—aye, and hold
    you fast!"

Food he ate for pleasure, and wine he drank for glad-
    ness.
And woman? Ah, the woman! the crown of all delight!
His now,—he knew it! He was strong to madness
In that early dawning after prehistoric night.

His,—his forver! That glory sweet and tender!

*Ah, but he would love her! And she should love but
    him!*
*He would work and struggle for her, he would shelter
    and defend her,—*
*She should never leave him, never, till their eyes in
    death were dim.*

*Close, close he bound her, that she should leave him
    never;*
Weak still he kept her, lest she be strong to flee;
And the fainting flame of passion he kept alive forever
With all the arts and forces of earth and sky and sea.

And, ah, the long journey! The slow and awful ages
*They have labored up together, blind and crippled, all
    astray!*
*Through what a mighty volume, with a million shame-
    ful pages,*
*From the freedom of the forests to the prisons of
    to-day!*

*Food he ate for pleasure, and it slew him with dis-
    eases!*
*Wine he drank for gladness, and it led the way to
    crime!*
*And woman? He will hold her,—he will have her
    when he pleases,—*
*And he never once hath seen her since the pre-historic
    time!*

*Gone the friend and comrade of the day when life was
    younger,*
She who rests and comforts, she who helps and saves.
Still he seeks her vainly, with a never-dying hunger;
Alone beneath his tyrants, alone above his slaves!

*Toiler, bent and weary with the load of thine own
    making!*
*Thou who art sad and lonely, though lonely all in
    vain!*
*Who hast sought to conquer Pleasure and have her
    for the taking,*
*And found that Pleasure only was another name for
    Pain—*

Nature hath reclaimed thee, forgiving dispossession!
God hath not forgotten, though man doth still forget!
*The woman-soul is rising, in despite of thy trans-
    gression—*
Loose her now, and trust her! She will love thee yet!

*Love thee? She will love thee as only freedom
    knoweth!*
*Love thee? She will love thee while Love itself doth
    live!*
Fear not the heart of woman! No bitterness it showeth!
The ages of her sorrow have but taught her to forgive!

PREFACE

This book is written to offer a simple and natural explanation of one of the most common and most perplexing problems of human life,—a problem which presents itself to almost every individual for practical solution, and which demands the most serious attention of the moralist, the physician, and the sociologist—

To show how some of the worst evils under which we suffer, evils long supposed to be inherent and ineradicable in our natures, are but the result of certain arbitrary conditions of our own adoption, and how, by removing those conditions, we may remove the evils resultant—

To point out how far we have already gone in the path of improvement, and how irresistibly the social forces of to-day are compelling us further, even without our knowledge and against our violent opposition,—an advance which may be greatly quickened by our recognition and assistance—

To reach in especial the thinking women of to-day, and urge upon them a new sense, not only of their social responsibility as individuals, but of their measureless racial importance as makers of men.

It is hoped also that the theory advanced will prove sufficiently suggestive to give rise to such further study and discussion as shall prove its error or establish its truth.

I.

SINCE we have learned to study the development of human life as we study the evolution of species throughout the animal kingdom, some peculiar phenomena which have puzzled the philosopher and moralist for so long, begin to show themselves in a new light. We begin to see that, so far from being inscrutable problems, requiring another life to explain, these sorrows and perplexities of our lives are but the natural results of natural causes, and that, as soon as we ascertain the causes, we can do much to remove them.

In spite of the power of the individual will to struggle against conditions, to resist them for a while, and sometimes to overcome them, it remains true that the human creature is affected by his environment, as is every other living thing. The power of the individual will to resist natural law is well proven by the life and death of the ascetic. In any one of those suicidal martyrs may be seen the will, misdirected by the ill-informed intelligence, forcing the body to defy every natural impulse,— even to the door of death, and through it.

But, while these exceptions show what the human will can do, the general course of life shows the inexorable effect of conditions upon humanity. Of these conditions we share with other living things the environment of the material universe. We are affected by climate and locality, by physical, chemical, electrical forces, as are all animals and plants. With the animals, we farther share the effect of our own activity, the reactionary force of exercise. What we do, as well as what is done to us, makes us what we are. But, beyond these forces, we come under the effect of a third set of conditions peculiar to our human status; namely, social conditions. In the organic interchanges which constitute social life, we are affected by each other to a degree beyond what is found even among the most gregarious of animals. This third factor, the social environment, is of enormous force as a modifier of human life. Throughout all these environing conditions, those which affect us through our economic necessities are most marked in their influence.

Without touching yet upon the influence of the social factors, treating the human being merely as an individual animal, we see that he is modified most by his economic conditions, as is every other animal. Differ as they may in color and size, in strength and speed, in minor adaptation to minor conditions, all animals that live on grass have distinctive traits in common, and all animals that eat flesh have distinc-

tive traits in common,— so distinctive and so
common that it is by teeth, by nutritive appa-
ratus in general, that they are classified, rather
than by means of defence or locomotion. The
food supply of the animal is the largest passive
factor in his development; the processes by
which he obtains his food supply, the largest
active factor in his development. It is these
activities, the incessant repetition of the exertions by which he is fed, which most modify
his structure and develope his functions. The
sheep, the cow, the deer, differ in their adaptation to the weather, their locomotive ability,
their means of defence; but they agree in main
characteristics, because of their common method
of nutrition.

The human animal is no exception to this rule.
Climate affects him, weather affects him, enemies affect him; but most of all he is affected,
like every other living creature, by what he does
for his living. Under all the influence of his
later and wider life, all the reactive effect of
social institutions, the individual is still inexorably modified by his means of livelihood: "the
hand of the dyer is subdued to what he works
in." As one clear, world-known instance of the
effect of economic conditions upon the human
creature, note the marked race-modification of
the Hebrew people under the enforced restric-

tions of the last two thousand years. Here is a people rising to national prominence, first as a pastoral, and then as an agricultural nation; only partially commercial through race affinity with the Phœnicians, the pioneer traders of the world. Under the social power of a united Christendom — united at least in this most unchristian deed — the Jew was forced to get his livelihood by commercial methods solely. Many effects can be traced in him to the fierce pressure of the social conditions to which he was subjected : the intense family devotion of a people who had no country, no king, no room for joy and pride except the family; the reduced size and tremendous vitality and endurance of the pitilessly selected survivors of the Ghetto; the repeated bursts of erratic genius from the human spirit so inhumanly restrained. But more patent still is the effect of the economic conditions,— the artificial development of a race of traders and dealers in money, from the lowest pawnbroker to the house of Rothschild; a special kind of people, bred of the economic environment in which they were compelled to live.

One rough but familiar instance of the same effect, from the same cause, we can all see in the marked distinction between the pastoral, the agricultural, and the manufacturing classes in any nation, though their other conditions be the same.

4

On the clear line of argument that functions and organs are developed by use, that what we use most is developed most, and that the daily processes of supplying economic needs are the processes that we most use, it follows that, when we find special economic conditions affecting any special class of people, we may look for special results, and find them.

In view of these facts, attention is now called to a certain marked and peculiar economic condition affecting the human race, and unparalleled in the organic world. We are the only animal species in which the female depends on the male for food, the only animal species in which the sex-relation is also an economic relation. With us an entire sex lives in a relation of economic dependence upon the other sex, and the economic relation is combined with the sex-relation. The economic status of the human female is relative to the sex-relation.

It is commonly assumed that this condition also obtains among other animals, but such is not the case. There are many birds among which, during the nesting season, the male helps the female feed the young, and partially feeds her; and, with certain of the higher carnivora, the male helps the female feed the young, and partially feeds her. In no case does she depend on him absolutely, even during this sea-

5

son, save in that of the hornbill, where the female,
sitting on her nest in a hollow tree, is walled in
with clay by the male, so that only her beak
projects ; and then he feeds her while the eggs
are developing. But even the female hornbill
does not expect to be fed at any other time.
The female bee and ant are economically dependent, but not on the male. The workers are
females, too, specialized to economic functions
solely. And with the carnivora, if the young
are to lose one parent, it might far better be the
father : the mother is quite competent to take
care of them herself. With many species, as in
the case of the common cat, she not only feeds
herself and her young, but has to defend the
young against the male as well. In no case is
the female throughout her life supported by the
male.

In the human species the condition is permanent and general, though there are exceptions,
and though the present century is witnessing
the beginnings of a great change in this respect.
We have not been accustomed to face this fact
beyond our loose generalization that it was
"natural," and that other animals did so, too.

To many this view will not seem clear at
first ; and the case of working peasant women
or females of savage tribes, and the general
household industry of women, will be instanced

6

against it. Some careful and honest discrimination is needed to make plain to ourselves the
essential facts of the relation, even in these
cases. The horse, in his free natural condition,
is economically independent. He gets his living by his own exertions, irrespective of any
other creature. The horse, in his present condition of slavery, is economically dependent.
He gets his living at the hands of his master;
and his exertions, though strenuous, bear no
direct relation to his living. In fact, the horses
who are the best fed and cared for and the
horses who are the hardest worked are quite
different animals. The horse works, it is true;
but what he gets to eat depends on the power
and will of his master. His living comes through
another. He is economically dependent. So
with the hard-worked savage or peasant women.
Their labor is the property of another: they
work under another will; and what they receive
depends not on their labor, but on the power
and will of another. They are economically
dependent. This is true of the human female
both individually and collectively.

In studying the economic position of the sexes
collectively, the difference is most marked. As
a social animal, the economic status of man rests
on the combined and exchanged services of vast
numbers of progressively specialized individuals.

The economic progress of the race, its mainte‑
nance at any period, its continued advance,
involve the collective activities of all the trades,
crafts, arts, manufactures, inventions, discoveries,
and all the civil and military institutions that go
to maintain them. The economic status of any
race at any time, with its involved effect on all
the constituent individuals, depends on their
world-wide labors and their free exchange.
Economic progress, however, is almost exclusively
masculine. Such economic processes as women
have been allowed to exercise are of the earliest
and most primitive kind. Were men to perform
no economic services save such as are still per‑
formed by women, our racial status in econom‑
ics would be reduced to most painful limitations.

To take from any community its male workers
would paralyze it economically to a far greater
degree than to remove its female workers. The
labor now performed by the women could be
performed by the men, requiring only the setting
back of many advanced workers into earlier
forms of industry ; but the labor now performed
by the men could not be performed by the
women without generations of effort and adapta‑
tion. Men can cook, clean, and sew as well as
women ; but the making and managing of the
great engines of modern industry, the threading
of earth and sea in our vast systems of transpor‑

tation, the handling of our elaborate machinery of trade, commerce, government,— these things could not be done so well by women in their present degree of economic development.

This is not owing to lack of the essential human faculties necessary to such achievements, nor to any inherent disability of sex, but to the present condition of woman, forbidding the development of this degree of economic ability. The male human being is thousands of years in advance of the female in economic status. Speaking collectively, men produce and distribute wealth; and women receive it at their hands. As men hunt, fish, keep cattle, or raise corn, so do women eat game, fish, beef, or corn. As men go down to the sea in ships, and bring coffee and spices and silks and gems from far away, so do women partake of the coffee and spices and silks and gems the men bring.

The economic status of the human race in any nation, at any time, is governed mainly by the activities of the male: the female obtains her share in the racial advance only through him.

Studied individually, the facts are even more plainly visible, more open and familiar. From the day laborer to the millionnaire, the wife's worn dress or flashing jewels, her low roof or her lordly one, her weary feet or her rich equipage,— these speak of the economic ability of the husband. The comfort, the luxury, the necessities of life itself, which the woman receives, are obtained by the husband, and given her by him. And, when the woman, left alone with no man to "support" her, tries to meet her own economic necessities, the difficulties which confront her prove conclusively what the general economic status of the woman is. None can deny these patent facts,— that the economic status of women generally depends upon that of men generally, and that the economic status of women individually depends upon that of men individually, those men to whom they are related. But we are instantly confronted by the commonly received opinion that, although it must be admitted that men make and distribute the wealth of the world, yet women earn their share of it as wives. This assumes either that the husband is in the position of employer and the wife as employee, or that marriage is a "partnership," and the wife an equal factor with the husband in producing wealth.

Economic independence is a relative condition at best. In the broadest sense, all living things are economically dependent upon others,— the animals upon the vegetables, and man upon both. In a narrower sense, all social life is economically interdependent, man producing collectively what he could by no possibility produce separately. But, in the closest interpretation, individual economic independence among human beings means that the individual pays for what he gets, works for what he gets, gives to the other an equivalent for what the other gives him. I depend on the shoemaker for shoes, and the tailor for coats; but, if I give the shoemaker and the tailor enough of my own labor as a house-builder to pay for the shoes and coats they give me, I retain my personal independence. I have not taken of their product, and given nothing of mine. As long as what I get is obtained by what I give, I am economically independent.

Women consume economic goods. What economic product do they give in exchange for what they consume? The claim that marriage is a partnership, in which the two persons married produce wealth which neither of them, separately, could produce, will not bear examination. A man happy and comfortable can produce more than one unhappy and uncomfortable, but this is as true of a father or son as of a husband. To take from a man any of the conditions which make him happy and strong is to cripple his industry, generally speaking. But those relatives who make him happy are not therefore his business partners, and entitled to share his income.

11

Grateful return for happiness conferred is
not the method of exchange in a partnership.
The comfort a man takes with his wife is not in
the nature of a business partnership, nor are her
frugality and industry. A housekeeper, in her
place, might be as frugal, as industrious, but
would not therefore be a partner. Man and
wife are partners truly in their mutual obligation to their children,— their common love,
duty, and service. But a manufacturer who
marries, or a doctor, or a lawyer, does not
take a partner in his business, when he takes a
partner in parenthood, unless his wife is also a
manufacturer, a doctor, or a lawyer. In his
business, she cannot even advise wisely without
training and experience. To love her husband,
the composer, does not enable her to compose;
and the loss of a man's wife, though it may
break his heart, does not cripple his business,
unless his mind is affected by grief. She is in
no sense a business partner, unless she contributes capital or experience or labor, as a
man would in like relation. Most men would
hesitate very seriously before entering a business partnership with any woman, wife or not.

If the wife is not, then, truly a business partner, in what way does she earn from her husband the food, clothing, and shelter she receives
at his hands? By house service, it will be

instantly replied. This is the general misty idea upon the subject,— that women earn all they get, and more, by house service. Here we come to a very practical and definite economic ground. Although not producers of wealth, women serve in the final processes of preparation and distribution. Their labor in the household has a genuine economic value.

For a certain percentage of persons to serve other persons, in order that the ones so served may produce more, is a contribution not to be overlooked. The labor of women in the house, certainly, enables men to produce more wealth than they otherwise could; and in this way women are economic factors in society. But so are horses. The labor of horses enables men to produce more wealth than they otherwise could. The horse is an economic factor in society. But the horse is not economically independent, nor is the woman. If a man plus a valet can perform more useful service than he could minus a valet, then the valet is performing useful service. But, if the valet is the property of the man, is obliged to perform this service, and is not paid for it, he is not economically independent.

The labor which the wife performs in the household is given as part of her functional duty, not as employment. The wife of the poor man, who works hard in a small house, doing all the work for the family, or the wife of the rich man, who wisely and gracefully manages a large house and administers its functions, each is entitled to fair pay for services rendered.

To take this ground and hold it honestly, wives, as earners through domestic service, are entitled to the wages of cooks, housemaids, nursemaids, seamstresses, or housekeepers, and to no more. This would of course reduce the spending money of the wives of the rich, and put it out of the power of the poor man to "support" a wife at all, unless, indeed, the poor man faced the situation fully, paid his wife her wages as house servant, and then she and he combined their funds in the support of their children. He would be keeping a servant : she would be helping keep the family. But nowhere on earth would there be "a rich woman" by these means. Even the highest class of private housekeeper, useful as her services are, does not accumulate a fortune. She does not buy diamonds and sables and keep a carriage. Things like these are not earned by house service.

But the salient fact in this discussion is that, whatever the economic value of the domestic industry of women is, they do not get it. The women who do the most work get the least

money, and the women who have the most
money do the least work. Their labor is
neither given nor taken as a factor in economic
exchange. It is held to be their duty as women
to do this work; and their economic status
bears no relation to their domestic labors, unless an inverse one. Moreover, if they were
thus fairly paid,— given what they earned, and
no more,— all women working in this way would
be reduced to the economic status of the house
servant. Few women — or men either — care
to face this condition. The ground that women
earn their living by domestic labor is instantly
forsaken, and we are told that they obtain
their livelihood as mothers. This is a peculiar
position. We speak of it commonly enough,
and often with deep feeling, but without due
analysis.

In treating of an economic exchange, asking
what return in goods or labor women make
for the goods and labor given them,— either to
the race collectively or to their husbands individually,— what payment women make for their
clothes and shoes and furniture and food and
shelter, we are told that the duties and services
of the mother entitle her to support.

If this is so, if motherhood is an exchangeable
commodity given by women in payment for
clothes and food, then we must of course find

some relation between the quantity or quality of the motherhood and the quantity and quality of the pay. This being true, then the women who are not mothers have no economic status at all; and the economic status of those who are must be shown to be relative to their motherhood. This is obviously absurd. The childless wife has as much money as the mother of many,— more; for the children of the latter consume what would otherwise be hers; and the inefficient mother is no less provided for than the efficient one. Visibly, and upon the face of it, women are not maintained in economic prosperity proportioned to their motherhood. Motherhood bears no relation to their economic status. Among primitive races, it is true,— in the patriarchal period, for instance,—there was some truth in this position. Women being of no value whatever save as bearers of children, their favor and indulgence did bear direct relation to maternity; and they had reason to exult on more grounds than one when they could boast a son. To-day, however, the maintenance of the woman is not conditioned upon this. A man is not allowed to discard his wife because she is barren. The claim of motherhood as a factor in economic exchange is false to-day. But suppose it were true. Are we willing to hold this ground, even in theory? Are we willing to consider motherhood as a business, a form of commercial exchange? Are the cares and duties of the mother, her travail and her love, commodities to be exchanged for bread?

It is revolting so to consider them; and, if we dare face our own thoughts, and force them to their logical conclusion, we shall see that nothing could be more repugnant to human feeling, or more socially and individually injurious, than to make motherhood a trade. Driven off these alleged grounds of women's economic independence; shown that women, as a class, neither produce nor distribute wealth; that women, as individuals, labor mainly as house servants, are not paid as such, and would not be satisfied with such an economic status if they were so paid; that wives are not business partners or co-producers of wealth with their husbands, unless they actually practise the same profession; that they are not salaried as mothers, and that it would be unspeakably degrading if they were, — what remains to those who deny that women are supported by men? This (and a most amusing position it is),— that the function of maternity unfits a woman for economic production, and, therefore, it is right that she should be supported by her husband.

The ground is taken that the human female is not economically independent, that she is fed by the male of her species. In denial of this, it is first alleged that she is economically independent,— that she does support herself by her own industry in the house. It being shown that there is no relation between the economic status of woman and the labor she performs in the home, it is then alleged that not as house servant, but as mother, does woman earn her living. It being shown that the economic status of woman bears no relation to her motherhood, either in quantity or quality, it is then alleged that motherhood renders a woman unfit for economic production, and that, therefore, it is right that she be supported by her husband. Before going farther, let us seize upon this admission,— that she *is* supported by her husband.

Without going into either the ethics or the necessities of the case, we have reached so much common ground: the female of genus homo is supported by the male. Whereas, in other species of animals, male and female alike graze and browse, hunt and kill, climb, swim, dig, run, and fly for their livings, in our species the female does not seek her own living in the specific activities of our race, but is fed by the male.

Now as to the alleged necessity. Because of her maternal duties, the human female is said to be unable to get her own living. As the maternal duties of other females do not unfit them

18

for getting their own living and also the livings of their young, it would seem that the human maternal duties require the segregation of the entire energies of the mother to the service of the child during her entire adult life, or so large a proportion of them that not enough remains to devote to the individual interests of the mother.

Such a condition, did it exist, would of course excuse and justify the pitiful dependence of the human female, and her support by the male. As the queen bee, modified entirely to maternity, is supported, not by the male, to be sure, but by her co-workers, the "old maids," the barren working bees, who labor so patiently and lovingly in their branch of the maternal duties of the hive, so would the human female, modified entirely to maternity, become unfit for any other exertion, and a helpless dependant.

Is this the condition of human motherhood? Does the human mother, by her motherhood, thereby lose control of brain and body, lose power and skill and desire for any other work? Do we see before us the human race, with all its females segregated entirely to the uses of motherhood, consecrated, set apart, specially developed, spending every power of their nature on the service of their children?

We do not. We see the human mother

worked far harder than a mare, laboring her life long in the service, not of her children only, but of men ; husbands, brothers, fathers, whatever male relatives she has ; for mother and sister also ; for the church a little, if she is allowed ; for society, if she is able ; for charity and education and reform,— working in many ways that are not the ways of motherhood.

It is not motherhood that keeps the housewife on her feet from dawn till dark ; it is house service, not child service. Women work longer and harder than most men, and not solely in maternal duties. The savage mother carries the burdens, and does all menial service for the tribe. The peasant mother toils in the fields, and the workingman's wife in the home. Many mothers, even now, are wage-earners for the family, as well as bearers and rearers of it. And the women who are not so occupied, the women who belong to rich men,— here perhaps is the exhaustive devotion to maternity which is supposed to justify an admitted economic dependence. But we do not find it even among these. Women of ease and wealth provide for their children better care than the poor woman can ; but they do not spend more time upon it themselves, nor more care and effort. They have other occupation.

In spite of her supposed segregation to maternal duties, the human female, the world over, works at extra-maternal duties for hours enough to provide her with an independent living, and then is denied independence on the ground that motherhood prevents her working!

If this ground were tenable, we should find a world full of women who never lifted a finger save in the service of their children, and of men who did *all* the work besides, and waited on the women whom motherhood prevented from waiting on themselves. The ground is not tenable. A human female, healthy, sound, has twenty-five years of life before she is a mother, and should have twenty-five years more after the period of such maternal service as is expected of her has been given. The duties of grandmotherhood are surely not alleged as preventing economic independence.

The working power of the mother has always been a prominent factor in human life. She is the worker *par excellence*, but her work is not such as to affect her economic status. Her living, all that she gets,— food, clothing, ornaments, amusements, luxuries,— these bear no relation to her power to produce wealth, to her services in the house, or to her motherhood. These things bear relation only to the man she marries, the man she depends on,— to how much he has and how much he is willing to give her. The women

whose splendid extravagance dazzles the world,
whose economic goods are the greatest, are often
neither houseworkers nor mothers, but simply
the women who hold most power over the men
who have the most money. The female of
genus homo is economically dependent on the
male. He is her food supply.

II.

Knowing how important a factor in the evolution of species is the economic relation, and finding in the human species an economic relation so peculiar, we may naturally look to find effects peculiar to our race. We may expect to find phenomena in the sex-relation and in the economic relation of humanity of a unique character,— phenomena not traceable to human superiority, but singularly derogatory to that superiority ; phenomena so marked, so morbid, as to give rise to much speculation as to their cause. Are these natural inferences fulfilled ? Are these peculiarities in the sex-relation and in the economic relation manifested in human life? Indisputably there are,— so plain, so prominent, so imperiously demanding attention, that human thought has been occupied from its first consciousness in trying some way to account for them. To explain and relate these phenomena, separating what is due to normal race-development from what is due to this abnormal sexuo-economic relation, is the purpose of the line of study here suggested.

As the racial distinction of humanity lies in its social relation, so we find the distinctive gains and losses of humanity to lie also in its social relation. We are more affected by our relation to each other than by our physical environment.

Disadvantages of climate, deficiencies in food supply, competition from other species,— all these conditions society, in its organic strength, is easily able to overcome or to adjust. But in our inter-human relations we are not so successful. The serious dangers and troubles of human life arise from difficulties of adjustment with our social environment, and not with our physical environment. These difficulties, so far, have acted as a continual check to social progress. The more absolutely a nation has triumphed over physical conditions, the more successful it has become in its conquest of physical enemies and obstacles, the more it has given rein to the action of social forces which have ultimately destroyed the nation, and left the long ascent to be begun again by others.

> There is the moral of all human tales:
> 'Tis but the same rehearsal of the past,—
> First Freedom, and then Glory; when that fails,
> Wealth, Vice, Corruption,— barbarism at last.
> And History, with all her volumes vast,
> Hath but *one* page. *

The path of history is strewn with fossils and faint relics of extinct races,— races which

* Childe Harold's Pilgrimage, Canto IV., cviii.

died of what the sociologist would call internal diseases rather than natural causes. This, too, has been clear to the observer in all ages. It has been easily seen that there was something in our own behavior which did us more harm than any external difficulty; but what we have not seen is the natural cause of our unnatural conduct, and how most easily to alter it.

Rudely classifying the principal fields of human difficulty, we find one large proportion lies in the sex-relation, and another in the economic relation, between the individual constituents of society. To speak broadly, the troubles of life as we find them are mainly traceable to the heart or the purse. The other horror of our lives — disease — comes back often to these causes,— to something wrong either in economic relation or in sex-relation. To be ill-fed or ill-bred, or both, is largely what makes us the sickly race we are. In this wrong breeding, this maladjustment of the sex-relation in humanity, what are the principal features? We see in social evolution two main lines of action in this department of life. One is a gradual orderly development of monogamous marriage, as the form of sex-union best calculated to advance the interests of the individual and of society. It should be clearly understood that this is a natural development, inevitable in the course of social progress; not an artificial condition, enforced by laws of our making. Monogamy is found among birds and mammals : it is just as natural a condition as polygamy or promiscuity or any other form of sex-union ; and its permanence and integrity are introduced and increased by the needs of the young and the advantage to the race, just as any other form of reproduction was introduced. Our moral concepts rest primarily on facts. The moral quality of monogamous marriage depends on its true advantage to the individual and to society. If it were not the best form of marriage for our racial good, it would not be right. All the way up, from the promiscuous horde of savages, with their miscellaneous matings, to the lifelong devotion of romantic love, social life has been evolving a type of sex-union best suited to develope and improve the individual and the race. This is an orderly process, and a pleasant one, involving only such comparative pain and difficulty as always attend the assumption of new processes and the extinction of the old ; but accompanied by far more joy than pain.

But with the natural process of social advancement has gone an unnatural process,— an erratic and morbid action, making the sex-relation of humanity a frightful source of evil. So prominent have been these morbid actions and evil results that hasty thinkers of all ages have assumed that the whole thing was wrong, and that celibacy was the highest virtue. Without the power of complete analysis, without knowledge of the sociological data essential to such analysis, we have sweepingly condemned as a whole what we could easily see was so allied with pain and loss. But, like all natural phenomena, the phenomena of sex may be studied, both the normal and the abnormal, the physiological and the pathological; and we are quite capable of understanding why we are in such evil case, and how we may attain more healthful conditions.

So far, the study of this subject has rested on the assumption that man must be just as we find him, that man behaves just as he chooses, and that, if he does not choose to behave as he does, he can stop. Therefore, when we discovered that human behavior in the sex-relation was productive of evil, we exhorted the human creature to stop so behaving, and have continued so to exhort for many centuries. By law and religion, by education and custom, we have sought to enforce upon the human individual the kind of behavior which our social sense so clearly showed was right.

But always there has remained the morbid action. Whatever the external form of sex-

27

union to which we have given social sanction,
however Bible and Koran and Vedas have offered
instruction, some hidden cause has operated
continuously against the true course of social
evolution, to pervert the natural trend toward
a higher and more advantageous sex-relation ;
and to maintain lower forms, and erratic phases,
of a most disadvantageous character.

Every other animal works out the kind of sex-
union best adapted to the reproduction of his
species, and peacefully practises it. We have
worked out the kind that is best for us,— best
for the individuals concerned, for the young resultant, and for society as a whole ; but we do
not peacefully practise it. So palpable is this
fact that we have commonly accepted it, and
taken it for granted that this relation must be
a continuous source of trouble to humanity.
"Marriage is a lottery," is a common saying
among us. " The course of true love never
did run smooth." And we quote with unction
Punch's advice to those about to marry,—
" Don't ! " That peculiar sub-relation which
has dragged along with us all the time that
monogamous marriage has been growing to be
the accepted form of sex-union — prostitution —
we have accepted, and called a " social necessity." We also call it "the social evil." We
have tacitly admitted that this relation in the

human race must be more or less uncomfortable and wrong, that it is part of our nature to have it so.

Now let us examine the case fairly and calmly, and see whether it is as inscrutable and immutable as hitherto believed. What are the conditions? What are the natural and what the unnatural features of the case? To distinguish these involves a little study of the evolution of the processes of reproduction.

Very early in the development of species it was ascertained by nature's slow but sure experiments that the establishment of two sexes in separate organisms, and their differentiation, was to the advantage of the species. Therefore, out of the mere protoplasmic masses, the floating cells, the amorphous early forms of life, grew into use the distinction of the sexes,— the gradual development of masculine and feminine organs and functions in two distinct organisms. Developed and increased by use, the distinction of sex increased in the evolution of species. As the distinction increased, the attraction increased, until we have in all the higher races two markedly different sexes, strongly drawn together by the attraction of sex, and fulfilling their use in the reproduction of species. These are the natural features of sex-distinction and sex-union, and they are found in the human

species as in others. The unnatural feature
by which our race holds an unenviable distinction
consists mainly in this,— a morbid excess in the
exercise of this function.

It is this excess, whether in marriage or out,
which makes the health and happiness of humanity in this relation so precarious. It is this
excess, always easily seen, which law and religion
have mainly striven to check. Excessive sex-
indulgence is the distinctive feature of humanity
in this relation.

To define "excess" in this connection is not
difficult. All natural functions that require our
conscious co-operation for their fulfilment are
urged upon our notice by an imperative desire.
We do not have to desire to breathe or to digest
or to circulate the blood, because that is done
without our volition ; but we do have to desire
to eat and drink, because the stomach cannot
obtain its supplies without in some way spur-
ring the whole organism to secure them. So
hunger is given us as an essential factor in our
process of nutrition. In the same manner sex-
attraction is an essential factor in the fulfilment
of our processes of reproduction. In a normal
condition the amount of hunger we feel is
exactly proportioned to the amount of food we
need. It tells us when to eat and when to stop.
In some diseased conditions "an unnatural

appetite " sets in ; and we are impelled to eat far beyond the capacity of the stomach to digest, of the body to assimilate. This is an excessive hunger.

We, as a race, manifest an excessive sex-attraction, followed by its excessive indulgence, and the inevitable evil consequence. It urges us to a degree of indulgence which bears no relation to the original needs of the organism, and which is even so absurdly exaggerated as to react unfavorably on the incidental gratification involved ; an excess which tends to pervert and exhaust desire as well as to injure reproduction.

The human animal manifests an excess in sex-attraction which not only injures the race through its morbid action on the natural processes of reproduction, but which injures the happiness of the individual through its morbid reaction on his own desires.

What is the cause of this excessive sex-attraction in the human species ? The immediately acting cause of sex-attraction is sex-distinction. The more widely the sexes are differentiated, the more forcibly they are attracted to each other. The more highly developed becomes the distinction of sex in either organism, the more intense is its attraction for the other. In the human species we find sex-distinction carried to

an excessive degree. Sex-distinction in humanity is so marked as to retard and confuse race-
distinction, to check individual distinction, seriously to injure the race. Accustomed as we
are simply to accept the facts of life as we find
them, to consider people as permanent types
instead of seeing them and the whole race in
continual change according to the action of
many forces, it seems strange at first to differ-
entiate between familiar manifestations of sex-
distinction, and to say: "This is normal, and
should not be disturbed. This is abnormal, and
should be removed." But that is precisely what
must be done.

Normal sex-distinction manifests itself in all
species in what are called primary and secondary sex-characteristics. The primary are those
organs and functions essential to reproduction;
the secondary, those modifications of structure
and function which subserve the uses of reproduction ultimately, but are not directly essential,—
such as the horns of the stag, of use in sex-combat; the plumage of the peacock, of use in sex-
competition. All the minor characteristics of
beard or mane, comb, wattles, spurs, gorgeous
color or superior size, which distinguish the male
from the female,— these are distinctions of sex.
These distinctions are of use to the species
through reproduction only, the processes of race-

preservation. They are not of use in self-preservation. The creature is not profited personally by his mane or crest or tail-feathers: they do not help him get his dinner or kill his enemies.

On the contrary, they react unfavorably upon his personal gains, if, through too great development, they interfere with his activity or render him a conspicuous mark for enemies. Such development would constitute excessive sex-distinction, and this is precisely the condition of the human race. Our distinctions of sex are carried to such a degree as to be disadvantageous to our progress as individuals and as a race. The sexes in our species are differentiated not only enough to perform their primal functions; not only enough to manifest all sufficient secondary sexual characteristics and fulfil their use in giving rise to sufficient sex-attraction; but so much as seriously to interfere with the processes of self-preservation on the one hand; and, more conspicuous still, so much as to react unfavorably upon the very processes of race-preservation which they are meant to serve. Our excessive sex-distinction, manifesting the characteristics of sex to an abnormal degree, has given rise to a degree of attraction which demands a degree of indulgence that directly injures motherhood and fatherhood. We are not better as parents, nor better as people, for our existing degree of sex-distinction, but visibly worse. To what conditions are we to look for the developing cause of these phenomena?

Let us first examine the balance of forces by which these two great processes, self-preservation and race-preservation, are conducted in the world. Self-preservation involves the expenditure of energy in those acts, and their ensuing modifications of structure and function, which tend to the maintenance of the individual life. Race-preservation involves the expenditure of energy in those acts, and their ensuing modifications of structure and function, which tend to the maintenance of the racial life, even to the complete sacrifice of the individual. This primal distinction should be clearly held in mind. Self-preservation and race-preservation are in no way identical processes, and are often directly opposed. In the line of self-preservation, natural selection, acting on the individual, developes those characteristics which enable it to succeed in "the struggle for existence," increasing by use those organs and functions by which it directly profits. In the line of race-preservation, sexual selection, acting on the individual, developes those characteristics which enable it to succeed in what Drummond[1] has called "the struggle for the existence of others," increasing by use those organs and functions

34

by which its young are to profit, directly or indirectly. The individual has been not only modified to its environment, under natural selection, but modified to its mate, under sexual selection, each sex developing the qualities desired by the other by the simple process of choice, those best sexed being first chosen, and transmitting their sex-development as well as their racial development.

The order mammalia is the resultant of a primary sex-distinction developed by natural selection; but the gorgeous plumage of the peacock's tail is a secondary sex-distinction developed by sexual selection. If the peacock's tail were to increase in size and splendor till it shone like the sun and covered an acre,— if it tended so to increase, we will say,— such excessive sex-distinction would be so inimical to the personal prosperity of that peacock that he would die, and his tail-tendency would perish with him. If the pea-hen, conversely, whose sex-distinction attracts in the opposite direction, not by being large and splendid, but small and dull,— if she should grow so small and dull as to fail to keep herself and her young fed and defended, then she would die; and there would be another check to excessive sex-distinction. In herds of deer and cattle the male is larger and stronger, the female smaller and weaker;

but, unless the latter is large and strong enough to keep up with the male in the search for food or the flight from foes, one is taken and the other left, and there is no more of that kind of animal. Differ as they may in sex, they must remain alike in species, equal in race-development, else destruction overtakes them. The force of natural selection, demanding and producing identical race-qualities, acts as a check on sexual selection, with its production of different sex-qualities. As sexes, they perform different functions, and therefore tend to develope differently. As species, they perform the same functions, and therefore tend to develope equally.

And as sex-functions are only used occasionally, and race-functions are used all the time,— as they mate but yearly or tri-monthly, but eat daily and hourly,— the processes of obtaining food or of opposing constant enemies act more steadily than the processes of reproduction, and produce greater effect.

We find the order mammalia accordingly producing and suckling its young in the same manner through a wide variety of species which obtain their living in a different manner. The calf and colt and cub and kitten are produced by the same process ; but the cow and horse, the bear and cat, are produced by different

36

processes. And, though cow and bull, mare and stallion, differ as to sex, they are alike in species; and the likeness in species is greater than the difference in sex. Cow, mare, and cat are all females of the order mammalia, and so far alike; but how much more different they are than similar!

Natural selection develops race. Sexual selection develops sex. Sex-development is one throughout its varied forms, tending only to reproduce what is. But race-development rises ever in higher and higher manifestation of energy. As sexes, we share our distinction with the animal kingdom almost to the beginning of life, and with the vegetable world as well. As races, we differ in ascending degree; and the human race stands highest in the scale of life so far.

When, then, it can be shown that sex-distinction in the human race is so excessive as not only to affect injuriously its own purposes, but to check and pervert the progress of the race, it becomes a matter for most serious consideration. Nothing could be more inevitable, however, under our sexuo-economic relation. By the economic dependence of the human female upon the male, the balance of forces is altered. Natural selection no longer checks the action of sexual selection, but co-operates with it. Where both sexes obtain their food through the same exertions, from the same sources, under the same conditions, both sexes are acted upon alike, and developed alike by their environment. Where the two sexes obtain their food under different conditions, and where that difference consists in one of them being fed by the other, then the feeding sex becomes the environment of the fed. Man, in supporting woman, has become her economic environment. Under natural selection, every creature is modified to its environment, developing perforce the qualities needed to obtain its livelihood under that environment. Man, as the feeder of woman, becomes the strongest modifying force in her economic condition. Under sexual selection the human creature is of course modified to its mate, as with all creatures. When the mate becomes also the master, when economic necessity is added to sex-attraction, we have the two great evolutionary forces acting together to the same end; namely, to develope sex-distinction in the human female. For, in her position of economic dependence in the sex-relation, sex-distinction is with her not only a means of attracting a mate, as with all creatures, but a means of getting her livelihood, as is the case with no other creature under heaven. Because of the economic dependence of the human female on her

38

mate, she is modified to sex to an excessive degree. This excessive modification she transmits to her children ; and so is steadily implanted in the human constitution the morbid tendency to excess in this relation, which has acted so universally upon us in all ages, in spite of our best efforts to restrain it. It is not the normal sex-tendency, common to all creatures, but an abnormal sex-tendency, produced and maintained by the abnormal economic relation which makes one sex get its living from the other by the exercise of sex-functions. This is the immediate effect upon individuals of the peculiar sexuo-economic relation which obtains among us.

III.

In establishing the claim of excessive sex-distinction in the human race, much needs to be said to make clear to the general reader what is meant by the term. To the popular mind, both the coarsely familiar and the over-refined, "sexual" is thought to mean "sensual"; and the charge of excessive sex-distinction seems to be a reproach. This should be at once dismissed, as merely showing ignorance of the terms used. A man does not object to being called "masculine," nor a woman to being called "feminine." Yet whatever is masculine or feminine is sexual. To be distinguished by femininity is to be distinguished by sex. To be over-feminine is to be over-sexed. To manifest in excess any of the distinctions of sex, primary or secondary, is to be over-sexed. Our hypothetical peacock, with his too large and splendid tail, would be over-sexed, and no offence to his moral character!

The primary sex-distinctions in our race as in others consist merely in the essential organs and functions of reproduction. The secondary distinctions, and this is where we are to look for our largest excess — consist in all those differences in organ and function, in look and action, in habit, manner, method, occupation, behavior, which distinguish men from women. In a troop of horses, seen at a distance, the sexes are indistinguishable. In a herd of deer the males are distinguishable because of their antlers. The male lion is distinguished by his mane, the male cat only by a somewhat heavier build. In certain species of insects the male and female differ so widely in appearance that even naturalists have supposed them to belong to separate species. Beyond these distinctions lies that of conduct. Certain psychic attributes are manifested by either sex. The intensity of the maternal passion is a sex-distinction as much as the lion's mane or the stag's horns. The belligerence and dominance of the male is a sex-distinction: the modesty and timidity of the female is a sex-distinction. The tendency to "sit" is a sex-distinction of the hen: the tendency to strut is a sex-distinction of the cock. The tendency to fight is a sex-distinction of males in general: the tendency to protect and provide for, is a sex-distinction of females in general.

With the human race, whose chief activities are social, the initial tendency to sex-distinction is carried out in many varied functions. We have differentiated our industries, our responsibilities, our very virtues, along sex lines. It will therefore be clear that the claim of excessive sex-distinction in humanity, and especially in woman, does not carry with it any specific "moral" reproach, though it does in the larger sense prove a decided evil in its effect on human progress.

In primary distinctions our excess is not so marked as in the farther and subtler development; yet, even here, we have plain proof of it. Sex-energy in its primal manifestation is exhibited in the male of the human species to a degree far greater than is necessary for the processes of reproduction,— enough, indeed, to subvert and injure those processes. The direct injury to reproduction from the excessive indulgence of the male, and the indirect injury through its debilitating effect upon the female, together with the enormous evil to society produced by extra-marital indulgence,— these are facts quite generally known. We have recognized them for centuries, and sought to check the evil action by law, civil, social, moral. But we have treated it always as a field of voluntary action, not as a condition of morbid development. We have held it as right that man should be so, but wrong that man should do so. Nature does not work in that way. What it is right to be, it is right to do. What it is wrong to do, it is wrong to be. This inordinate demand in the human male is an excessive sex-distinction. In

42

this, in a certain over-coarseness and hardness, a too great belligerence and pride, a too great subservience to the power of sex-attraction, we find the main marks of excessive sex-distinction in men. It has been always checked and offset in them by the healthful activities of racial life. Their energies have been called out and their faculties developed along all the lines of human progress. In the growth of industry, commerce, science, manufacture, government, art, religion, the male of our species has become human, far more than male. Strong as this passion is in him, inordinate as is his indulgence, he is a far more normal animal than the female of his species,— far less over-sexed. To him this field of special activity is but part of life,— an incident. The whole world remains besides. To her it is the world. This has been well stated in the familiar epigram of Madame de Staël,— "Love with man is an episode, with woman a history."[2] It is in woman that we find most fully expressed the excessive sex-distinction of the human species,— physical, psychical, social. See first the physical manifestation.

To make clear by an instance the difference between normal and abnormal sex-distinction, look at the relative condition of a wild cow and a "milch cow," such as we have made. The wild cow is a female. She has healthy calves, and

43

milk enough for them ; and that is all the femininity she needs. Otherwise than that she is
bovine rather than feminine. She is a light,
strong, swift, sinewy creature, able to run, jump,
and fight, if necessary. We, for economic uses,
have artificially developed the cow's capacity for
producing milk. She has become a walking
milk-machine, bred and tended to that express
end, her value measured in quarts. The secretion of milk is a maternal function,— a sex-
function. The cow is over-sexed. Turn her
loose in natural conditions, and, if she survive
the change, she would revert in a very few
generations to the plain cow, with her energies
used in the general activities of her race, and
not all running to milk.

Physically, woman belongs to a tall, vigorous,
beautiful animal species, capable of great and
varied exertion. In every race and time when
she has opportunity for racial activity, she developes accordingly, and is no less a woman for
being a healthy human creature. In every race
and time where she is denied this opportunity,
— and few, indeed, have been her years of freedom,— she has developed in the lines of action
to which she was confined ; and those were always lines of sex-activity. In consequence the
body of woman, speaking in the largest generalization, manifests sex-distinction predominantly.

44

Woman's femininity — and "the eternal feminine" means simply the eternal sexual — is more apparent in proportion to her humanity than the femininity of other animals in proportion to their caninity or felinity or equinity. "A feminine hand" or "a feminine foot" is distinguishable anywhere. We do not hear of "a feminine paw" or "a feminine hoof." A hand is an organ of prehension, a foot an organ of locomotion : they are not secondary sexual characteristics. The comparative smallness and feebleness of woman is a sex-distinction. We have carried it to such an excess that women are commonly known as "the weaker sex." There is no such glaring difference between male and female in other advanced species. In the long migrations of birds, in the ceaseless motion of the grazing herds that used to swing up and down over the continent each year, in the wild, steep journeys of the breeding salmon, nothing is heard of the weaker sex. And among the higher carnivora, where longer maintenance of the young brings their condition nearer ours, the hunter dreads the attack of the female more than that of the male. The disproportionate weakness is an excessive sex-distinction. Its injurious effect may be broadly shown in the Oriental nations, where the female in curtained harems is confined most exclusively to sex-functions and denied most fully the exercise of race-functions. In such peoples the weakness, the tendency to small bones and adipose tissue of the over-sexed female, is transmitted to the male, with a retarding effect on the development of the race. Conversely, in early Germanic tribes the comparatively free and humanly developed women — tall, strong, and brave — transmitted to their sons a greater proportion of human power and much less of morbid sex-tendency.

The degree of feebleness and clumsiness common to women, the comparative inability to stand, walk, run, jump, climb, and perform other race-functions common to both sexes, is an excessive sex-distinction ; and the ensuing transmission of this relative feebleness to their children, boys and girls alike, retards human development. Strong, free, active women, the sturdy, field-working peasant, the burden-bearing savage, are no less good mothers for their human strength. But our civilized " feminine delicacy," which appears somewhat less delicate when recognized as an expression of sexuality in excess,— makes us no better mothers, but worse. The relative weakness of women is a sex-distinction. It is apparent in her to a degree that injures motherhood, that injures wifehood, that injures the individual. The sex-usefulness and the human usefulness of women, their general duty to their kind, are greatly injured by this degree of distinction. In every way the over-sexed condition of the human female reacts unfavorably upon herself, her husband, her children, and the race.

In its psychic manifestation this intense sex-distinction is equally apparent. The primal instinct of sex-attraction has developed under social forces into a conscious passion of enormous power, a deep and lifelong devotion, overwhelming in its force. This is excessive in both sexes, but more so in women than in men,— not so commonly in its simple physical form, but in the unreasoning intensity of emotion that refuses all guidance, and drives those possessed by it to risk every other good for this one end. It is not at first sight easy, and it may seem an irreverent and thankless task, to discriminate here between what is good in the "master passion" and what is evil, and especially to claim for one sex more of this feeling than for the other; but such discrimination can be made.

It is good for the individual and for the race to have developed such a degree of passionate and permanent love as shall best promote the happiness of individuals and the reproduction of species. It is not good for the race or for the individual that this feeling should have become so intense as to override all other human faculties, to make a mock of the accumulated wisdom of the ages, the stored power of the will; to drive the individual — against his own plain conviction — into a union sure to result in evil, or to hold the individual helpless in such an evil union, when made.

Such is the condition of humanity, involving most evil results to its offspring and to its own happiness. And, while in men the immediate dominating force of the passion may be more conspicuous, it is in women that it holds more universal sway. For the man has other powers and faculties in full use, whereby to break loose from the force of this; and the woman, specially modified to sex and denied racial activity, pours her whole life into her love, and, if injured here, she is injured irretrievably. With him it is frequently light and transient, and, when most intense, often most transient. With her it is a deep, all-absorbing force, under the action of which she will renounce all that life offers, take any risk, face any hardships, bear any pain. It is maintained in her in the face of a lifetime of neglect and abuse. The common instance of the police court trials — the woman cruelly abused who will not testify against her husband — shows this. This devotion, carried to such a degree as to lead to the mismating of individuals with its personal and social injury, is an excessive sex-distinction.

But it is in our common social relations that the predominance of sex-distinction in women is made most manifest. The fact that, speaking broadly, women have, from the very beginning, been spoken of expressively enough as "the sex," demonstrates clearly that this is the main impression which they have made upon observers and recorders. Here one need attempt no farther proof than to turn the mind of the reader to an unbroken record of facts and feelings perfectly patent to every one, but not hitherto looked at as other than perfectly natural and right. So utterly has the status of woman been accepted as a sexual one that it has remained for the woman's movement of the nineteenth century to devote much contention to the claim that women are persons! That women are persons as well as females,— an unheard of proposition!

In a " Handbook of Proverbs of All Nations," a collection comprising many thousands, these facts are to be observed : first, that the proverbs concerning women are an insignificant minority compared to those concerning men ; second, that the proverbs concerning women almost invariably apply to them in general,— to the sex.

Those concerning men qualify, limit, describe, specialize. It is "a lazy man," "a violent man," "a man in his cups." Qualities and actions are predicated of man individually, and not as a sex, unless he is flatly contrasted with woman, as in "A man of straw is worth a woman of gold," "Men are deeds, women are words," or "Man, woman, and the devil are the three degrees of comparison." But of woman it is always and only "a woman," meaning simply a female, and recognizing no personal distinction : "As much pity to see a woman weep as to see a goose go barefoot." "He that hath an eel by the tail and a woman by her word hath a slippery handle." "A woman, a spaniel, and a walnut-tree,— the more you beat 'em, the better they be." Occasionally a distinction is made between "a fair woman" and "a black woman" ; and Solomon's "virtuous woman," who commanded such a high price, is familiar to us all. But in common thought it is simply "a woman" always. The boast of the profligate that he knows "the sex," so recently expressed by a new poet,— "The things you will learn from the Yellow and Brown, they'll 'elp you an' 'eap with the White"; the complaint of the angry rejected that "all women are just alike!"— the consensus of public opinion of all time goes to show that the characteristics common to the sex have predominated over the characteristics distinctive of the individual,— a marked excess in sex-distinction.

From the time our children are born, we use every means known to accentuate sex-distinction in both boy and girl; and the reason that the boy is not so hopelessly marked by it as the girl is that he has the whole field of human expression open to him besides. In our steady insistence on proclaiming sex-distinction we have grown to consider most human attributes as masculine attributes, for the simple reason that they were allowed to men and forbidden to women.

A clear and definite understanding of the difference between race-attributes and sex-attributes should be established. Life consists of action. The action of a living thing is along two main lines,— self-preservation and race-preservation. The processes that keep the individual alive, from the involuntary action of his internal organs to the voluntary action of his external organs,— every act, from breathing to hunting his food, which contributes to the maintenance of the individual life,— these are the processes of self-preservation. Whatever activities tend to keep the race alive, to reproduce the individual, from the involuntary action of the internal organs to the voluntary action of the external organs;

every act from the development of germ-cells to the taking care of children, which contributes to the maintenance of the racial life,— these are the processes of race-preservation. In race-preservation, male and female have distinctive organs, distinctive functions, distinctive lines of action. In self-preservation, male and female have the same organs, the same functions, the same lines of action. In the human species our processes of race-preservation have reached a certain degree of elaboration; but our processes of self-preservation have gone farther, much farther.

All the varied activities of economic production and distribution, all our arts and industries, crafts and trades, all our growth in science, discovery, government, religion,— these are along the line of self-preservation : these are, or should be, common to both sexes. To teach, to rule, to make, to decorate, to distribute,— these are not sex-functions : they are race-functions. Yet so inordinate is the sex-distinction of the human race that the whole field of human progress has been considered a masculine prerogative. What could more absolutely prove the excessive sex-distinction of the human race? That this difference should surge over all its natural boundaries and blazon itself across every act of life, so that every step of the human creature is marked "male" or "female,"— surely, this is enough to show our over-sexed condition.

Little by little, very slowly, and with most unjust and cruel opposition, at cost of all life holds most dear, it is being gradually established by many martyrdoms that human work is woman's as well as man's. Harriet Martineau must conceal her writing under her sewing when callers came, because "to sew" was a feminine verb, and "to write" a masculine one. Mary Somerville must struggle to hide her work from even relatives, because mathematics was a "masculine" pursuit. Sex has been made to dominate the whole human world,— all the main avenues of life marked "male," and the female left to be a female, and nothing else.

But while with the male the things he fondly imagined to be "masculine" were merely human, and very good for him, with the female the few things marked "feminine" were feminine, indeed; and her ceaseless reiterance of one short song, however sweet, has given it a conspicuous monotony. In garments whose main purpose is unmistakably to announce her sex; with a tendency to ornament which marks exuberance of sex-energy, with a body so modified to sex as to be grievously deprived of its natural activities; with a manner and behavior wholly attuned to sex-advantage, and frequently most

53

disadvantageous to any human gain ; with a field of action most rigidly confined to sex-relations ; with her overcharged sensibility, her prominent modesty, her " eternal femininity," — the female of genus homo is undeniably oversexed.

This excessive distinction shows itself again in a marked precocity of development. Our little children, our very babies, show signs of it when the young of other creatures are serenely asexual in general appearance and habit. We eagerly note this precocity. We are proud of it. We carefully encourage it by precept and example, taking pains to develope the sex-instinct in little children, and think no harm. One of the first things we force upon the child's dawning consciousness is the fact that he is a boy or that she is a girl, and that, therefore, each must regard everything from a different point of view. They must be dressed differently, not on account of their personal needs, which are exactly similar at this period, but so that neither they, nor any one beholding them, may for a moment forget the distinction of sex.

Our peculiar inversion of the usual habit of species, in which the male carries ornament and the female is dark and plain, is not so much a proof of excess indeed, as a proof of the peculiar reversal of our position in the matter of sex-selection. With the other species the males compete in ornament, and the females select. With us the females compete in ornament, and the males select. If this theory of sex-ornament is disregarded, and we prefer rather to see in masculine decoration merely a form of exuberant sex-energy, expending itself in non-productive excess, then, indeed, the fact that with us the females manifest such a display of gorgeous adornment is another sign of excessive sex-distinction. In either case the forcing upon girl-children of an elaborate ornamentation which interferes with their physical activity and unconscious freedom, and fosters a premature sex-consciousness, is as clear and menacing a proof of our condition as could be mentioned. That the girl-child should be so dressed as to require a difference in care and behavior, resting wholly on the fact that she is a girl,— a fact not otherwise present to her thought at that age,— is a precocious insistence upon sex-distinction, most unwholesome in its results. Boys and girls are expected, also, to behave differently to each other, and to people in general,—a behavior to be briefly described in two words. To the boy we say, " Do " ; to the girl, " Don't." The little boy must " take care " of the little girl, even if she is larger than he is. " Why ? "

he asks. Because he is a boy. Because of sex. Surely, if she is the stronger, she ought to take care of him, especially as the protective instinct is purely feminine in a normal race. It is not long before the boy learns his lesson. He is a boy, going to be a man ; and that means all. " I thank the Lord that I was not born a woman," runs the Hebrew prayer. She is a girl, " only a girl," "nothing but a girl," and going to be a woman,— only a woman. Boys are encouraged from the beginning to show the feelings supposed to be proper to their sex. When our infant son bangs about, roars, and smashes things, we say proudly that he is "a regular boy!" When our infant daughter coquettes with visitors, or wails in maternal agony because her brother has broken her doll, whose sawdust remains she nurses with piteous care, we say proudly that "she is a perfect little mother already!" What business has a little girl with the instincts of maternity? No more than the little boy should have with the instincts of paternity. They are sex-instincts, and should not appear till the period of adolescence. The most normal girl is the "tom-boy,"— whose numbers increase among us in these wiser days,— a healthy young creature, who is human through and through, not feminine till it is time to be. The most normal boy has calmness and gentleness as well as vigor and courage. He is a human creature as well as a male creature, and not aggressively masculine till it is time to be. Childhood is not the period for these marked manifestations of sex. That we exhibit them, that we admire and encourage them, shows our over-sexed condition.

IV.

HAVING seen the disproportionate degree of sex - distinction in humanity and its greater manifestation in the female than in the male, and having seen also the unique position of the human female as an economic dependant on the male of her species, it is not difficult to establish a relation between these two facts. The general law acting to produce this condition of exaggerated sex-development was briefly referred to in the second chapter. It is as follows: the natural tendency of any function to increase in power by use causes sex-activity to increase under the action of sexual selection. This tendency is checked in most species by the force of natural selection, which diverts the energies into other channels and developes race-activities. Where the female finds her economic environment in the male, and her economic advantage is directly conditioned upon the sex-relation, the force of natural selection is added to the force of sexual selection, and both together operate to develope sex-activity. In any animal species, free from any other condition, such a relation would have inevitably developed sex to an inordinate degree, as may be readily seen in the comparatively similar cases of those insects where the female, losing economic activity and modified entirely to sex, becomes a mere egg-sac, an organism with no powers of self-preservation, only those of race-preservation. With these insects the only race-problem is to maintain and reproduce the species, and such a condition is not necessarily evil; but with a race like ours, whose development as human creatures is but comparatively begun, it is evil because of its check to individual and racial progress. There are other purposes before us besides mere maintenance and reproduction.

It should be clear to any one accustomed to the working of biological laws that all the tendencies of a living organism are progressive in their development, and are held in check by the interaction of their several forces. Each living form, with its dominant characteristics, represents a balance of power, a sort of compromise. The size of earth's primeval monsters was limited by the tensile strength of their material. Sea monsters can be bigger, because the medium in which they move offers more support. Birds must be smaller for the opposite reason. The cow requires many stomachs of a liberal size, because her food is of low nutritive value; and she must eat large quantities to keep her machine going. The size of arboreal animals, such as monkeys or squirrels, is limited by the nature of their habitat : creatures that live in trees cannot be so big as creatures that live on the ground. Every quality of every creature is relative to its condition, and tends to increase or decrease accordingly ; and each quality tends to increase in proportion to its use, and to decrease in proportion to its disuse. Primitive man and his female were animals, like other animals. They were strong, fierce, lively beasts ; and she was as nimble and ferocious as he, save for the added belligerence of the males in their sex-competition. In this competition, he, like the other male creatures, fought savagely with his hairy rivals ; and she, like the other female creatures, complacently viewed their struggles, and mated with the victor. At other times she ran about in the forest, and helped herself to what there was to eat as freely as he did.

There seems to have come a time when it occurred to the dawning intelligence of this amiable savage that it was cheaper and easier to fight a little female, and have it done with, than to fight a big male every time. So he instituted the custom of enslaving the female ; and she, losing freedom, could no longer get her own food nor that of her young. The mother ape, with her maternal function well fulfilled, flees leaping through the forest,— plucks her fruit and nuts, keeps up with the movement of the tribe, her young one on her back or held in one strong arm. But the mother woman, enslaved, could not do this. Then man, the father, found that slavery had its obligations : he must care for what he forbade to care for itself, else it died on his hands. So he slowly and reluctantly shouldered the duties of his new position. He began to feed her, and not only that, but to express in his own person the thwarted uses of maternity : he had to feed the children, too. It seems a simple arrangement. When we have thought of it at all, we have thought of it with admiration. The naturalist defends it on the ground of advantage to the species through the freeing of the mother from all other cares and confining her unreservedly to the duties of maternity. The poet and novelist, the painter and sculptor, the priest and teacher, have all extolled this lovely relation. It remains for the sociologist, from a biological point of view, to note its effects on the constitution of the human race, both in the individual and in society.

When man began to feed and defend woman, she ceased proportionately to feed and defend herself. When he stood between her and her physical environment, she ceased proportionately to feel the influence of that environment and respond to it. When he became her immediate and all-important environment, she began proportionately to respond to this new

influence, and to be modified accordingly. In
a free state, speed was of as great advantage to
the female as to the male, both in enabling her
to catch prey and in preventing her from being
caught by enemies; but, in her new condition,
speed was a disadvantage. She was not allowed to
do the catching, and it profited her to be caught
by her new master. Free creatures, getting
their own food and maintaining their own lives,
develope an active capacity for attaining their
ends. Parasitic creatures, whose living is obtained by the exertions of others, develope
powers of absorption and of tenacity,— the
powers by which they profit most. The human
female was cut off from the direct action of
natural selection, that mighty force which heretofore had acted on male and female alike
with inexorable and beneficial effect, developing
strength, developing skill, developing endurance, developing courage,— in a word, developing
species. She now met the influence of natural
selection acting indirectly through the male,
and developing, of course, the faculties required
to secure and obtain a hold on him. Needless
to state that these faculties were those of sex-
attraction, the one power that has made him
cheerfully maintain, in what luxury he could,
the being in whom he delighted. For many,
many centuries she had no other hold, no other

assurance of being fed. The young girl had a prospective value, and was maintained for what should follow; but the old woman, in more primitive times, had but a poor hold on life. She who could best please her lord was the favorite slave or favorite wife, and she obtained the best economic conditions.

With the growth of civilization, we have gradually crystallized into law the visible necessity for feeding the helpless female; and even old women are maintained by their male relatives with a comfortable assurance. But to this day — save, indeed, for the increasing army of women wage-earners, who are changing the face of the world by their steady advance toward economic independence — the personal profit of women bears but too close a relation to their power to win and hold the other sex. From the odalisque with the most bracelets to the débutante with the most bouquets, the relation still holds good,— woman's economic profit comes through the power of sex-attraction.

When we confront this fact boldly and plainly in the open market of vice, we are sick with horror. When we see the same economic relation made permanent, established by law, sanctioned and sanctified by religion, covered with flowers and incense and all accumulated sentiment, we think it innocent, lovely, and right.

The transient trade we think evil. The bargain for life we think good. But the biological effect remains the same. In both cases the female gets her food from the male by virtue of her sex-relationship to him. In both cases, perhaps even more in marriage because of its perfect acceptance of the situation, the female of genus homo, still living under natural law, is inexorably modified to sex in an increasing degree.

Followed in specific detail, the action of the changed environment upon women has been in given instances as follows: In the matter of mere passive surroundings she has been immediately restricted in her range. This one factor has an immense effect on man and animal alike. An absolutely uniform environment, one shape, one size, one color, one sound, would render life, if any life could be, one helpless, changeless thing. As the environment increases and varies, the development of the creature must increase and vary with it; for he acquires knowledge and power, as the material for knowledge and the need for power appear. In migratory species the female is free to acquire the same knowledge as the male by the same means, the same development by the same experiences. The human female has been restricted in range from the earliest beginning. Even among savages, she has a much more restricted knowledge of

64

the land she lives in. She moves with the camp, of course, and follows her primitive industries in its vicinity; but the war-path and the hunt are the man's. He has a far larger habitat. The life of the female savage is freedom itself, however, compared with the increasing constriction of custom closing in upon the woman, as civilization advanced, like the iron torture chamber of romance. Its culmination is expressed in the proverb: "A woman should leave her home but three times,— when she is christened, when she is married, and when she is buried." Or this: "The woman, the cat, and the chimney should never leave the house." The absolutely stationary female and the wide-ranging male are distinctly human institutions, after we leave behind us such low forms of life as the gypsy moth, whose female seldom moves more than a few feet from the pupa moth. She has aborted wings, and cannot fly. She waits humbly for the winged male, lays her myriad eggs, and dies, — a fine instance of modification to sex.

To reduce so largely the mere area of environment is a great check to race-development; but it is not to be compared in its effects with the reduction in voluntary activity to which the human female has been subjected. Her restricted impression, her confinement to the four walls of the home, have done great execution, of course, in limiting her ideas, her information, her thought-processes, and power of judgment; and in giving a disproportionate prominence and intensity to the few things she knows about; but this is innocent in action compared with her restricted expression, the denial of freedom to act. A living organism is modified far less through the action of external circumstances upon it and its reaction thereto, than through the effect of its own exertions. Skin may be thickened gradually by exposure to the weather; but it is thickened far more quickly by being rubbed against something, as the handle of an oar or of a broom. To be surrounded by beautiful things has much influence upon the human creature: to make beautiful things has more. To live among beautiful surroundings and make ugly things is more directly lowering than to live among ugly surroundings and make beautiful things. What we do modifies us more than what is done to us. The freedom of expression has been more restricted in women than the freedom of impression, if that be possible. Something of the world she lived in she has seen from her barred windows. Some air has come through the purdah's folds, some knowledge has filtered to her eager ears from the talk of men. Desdemona learned somewhat of Othello. Had she known more, she might have

66

lived longer. But in the ever-growing human impulse to create, the power and will to make, to do, to express one's new spirit in new forms,— here she has been utterly debarred. She might work as she had worked from the beginning,— at the primitive labors of the household ; but in the inevitable expansion of even those industries to professional levels we have striven to hold her back. To work with her own hands, for nothing, in direct body-service to her own family,— this has been permitted,— yes, compelled. But to be and do anything further from this she has been forbidden. Her labor has not only been limited in kind, but in degree. Whatever she has been allowed to do must be done in private and alone, the first-hand industries of savage times.

Our growth in industry has been not only in kind, but in class. The baker is not in the same industrial grade with the house-cook, though both make bread. To specialize any form of labor is a step up : to organize it is another step. Specialization and organization are the basis of human progress, the organic methods of social life. They have been forbidden to women almost absolutely. The greatest and most beneficent change of this century is the progress of women in these two lines of advance. The effect of this check in industrial development, accompanied as it was by the constant inheritance of increased racial power, has been to intensify the sensations and emotions of women, and to develope great activity in the lines allowed. The nervous energy that up to present memory has impelled women to labor incessantly at something, be it the veriest folly of fancy work, is one mark of this effect.

In religious development the same dead-line has held back the growth of women through all the races and ages. In dim early times she was sharer in the mysteries and rites ; but, as religion developed, her place receded, until Paul commanded her to be silent in the churches. And she has been silent until to-day. Even now, with all the ground gained, we have but the beginnings — the slowly forced and disapproved beginnings — of religious equality for the sexes. In some nations, religion is held to be a masculine attribute exclusively, it being even questioned whether women have souls. An early Christian council settled that important question by vote, fortunately deciding that they had. In a church whose main strength has always been derived from the adherence of women, it would have been an uncomfortable reflection not to have allowed them souls. Ancient family worship ran in the male line. It was the son who kept the sacred grandfathers in due respect, and poured libations to their shades. When the woman married, she changed her ancestors, and had to worship her husband's progenitors instead of her own. This is why the Hindu and the Chinaman and many others of like stamp must have a son to keep them in countenance,— a deep-seated sex-prejudice, coming to slow extinction as women rise in economic importance.

It is painfully interesting to trace the gradual cumulative effect of these conditions upon women : first, the action of large natural laws, acting on her as they would act on any other animal; then the evolution of social customs and laws (with her position as the active cause), following the direction of mere physical forces, and adding heavily to them ; then, with increasing civilization, the unbroken accumulation of precedent, burnt into each generation by the growing force of education, made lovely by art, holy by religion, desirable by habit ; and, steadily acting from beneath, the unswerving pressure of economic necessity upon which the whole structure rested. These are strong modifying conditions, indeed.

The process would have been even more effective and far less painful but for one important circumstance. Heredity has no Salic law. Each girl child inherits from her father a cer-

tain increasing percentage of human development, human power, human tendency; and
each boy as well inherits from his mother the
increasing percentage of sex-development, sex-
power, sex-tendency. The action of heredity
has been to equalize what every tendency of
environment and education made to differ.
This has saved us from such a female as the
gypsy moth. It has held up the woman, and
held down the man. It has set iron bounds to
our absurd effort to make a race with one sex
a million years behind the other. But it has
added terribly to the pain and difficulty of
human life,— a difficulty and a pain that should
have taught us long since that we were living
on wrong lines. Each woman born, re-human-
ized by the current of race activity carried on
by her father and re-womanized by her traditional position, has had to live over again in her
own person the same process of restriction, repression, denial; the smothering "no" which
crushed down all her human desires to create,
to discover, to learn, to express, to advance.
Each woman has had, on the other hand, the
same single avenue of expression and attainment; the same one way in which alone she
might do what she could, get what she might.
All other doors were shut, and this one always
open; and the whole pressure of advancing

humanity was upon her. No wonder that young Daniel in the apocryphal tale proclaimed: "The king is strong! Wine is strong! But women are stronger!"

To the young man confronting life the world lies wide. Such powers as he has he may use, must use. If he chooses wrong at first, he may choose again, and yet again. Not effective or successful in one channel, he may do better in another. The growing, varied needs of all mankind call on him for the varied service in which he finds his growth. What he wants to be, he may strive to be. What he wants to get, he may strive to get. Wealth, power, social distinction, fame,— what he wants he can try for.

To the young woman confronting life there is the same world beyond, there are the same human energies and human desires and ambition within. But all that she may wish to have, all that she may wish to do, must come through a single channel and a single choice. Wealth, power, social distinction, fame,— not only these, but home and happiness, reputation, ease and pleasure, her bread and butter,— all, must come to her through a small gold ring. This is a heavy pressure. It has accumulated behind her through heredity, and continued about her through environment. It has been subtly

trained into her through education, till she herself has come to think it a right condition, and
pours its influence upon her daughter with increasing impetus. Is it any wonder that women
are over-sexed? But for the constant inheritance from the more human male, we should
have been queen bees, indeed, long before this.
But the daughter of the soldier and the sailor,
of the artist, the inventor, the great merchant,
has inherited in body and brain her share of his
development in each generation, and so stayed
somewhat human for all her femininity.

All morbid conditions tend to extinction.
One check has always existed to our inordinate
sex-development,—nature's ready relief, death.
Carried to its furthest excess, the individual has
died, the family has become extinct, the nation
itself has perished, like Sodom and Gomorrah.
Where one function is carried to unnatural excess, others are weakened, and the organism
perishes. We are familiar with this in individual cases,— at least, the physician is. We can
see it somewhat in the history of nations.
From younger races, nearer savagery, nearer the
healthful equality of pre-human creatures, has
come each new start in history. Persia was
older than Greece, and its highly differentiated
sexuality had produced the inevitable result of
enfeebling the racial qualities. The Greek

commander stripped the rich robes and jewels from his Persian captives, and showed their unmanly feebleness to his men. "You have such bodies as these to fight for such plunder as this," he said. In the country, among peasant classes, there is much less sex-distinction than in cities, where wealth enables the women to live in absolute idleness; and even the men manifest the same characteristics. It is from the country and the lower classes that the fresh blood pours into the cities, to be weakened in its turn by the influence of this unnatural distinction until there is none left to replenish the nation.

The inevitable trend of human life is toward higher civilization; but, while that civilization is confined to one sex, it inevitably exaggerates sex-distinction, until the increasing evil of this condition is stronger than all the good of the civilization attained, and the nation falls. Civilization, be it understood, does not consist in the acquisition of luxuries. Social development is an organic development. A civilized State is one in which the citizens live in organic industrial relation. The more full, free, subtle, and easy that relation; the more perfect the differentiation of labor and exchange of product, with their correlative institutions,—the more perfect is that civilization. To eat, drink, sleep, and keep warm,—these are common to all animals,

whether the animal couches in a bed of leaves
or one of eiderdown, sleeps in the sun to avoid
the wind or builds a furnace-heated house, lies
in wait for game or orders a dinner at a hotel.
These are but individual animal processes.
Whether one lays an egg or a million eggs,
whether one bears a cub, a kitten, or a baby,
whether one broods its chickens, guards its
litter, or tends a nursery full of children, these
are but individual animal processes. But to
serve each other more and more widely; to live
only by such service; to develope special
functions, so that we depend for our living on
society's return for services that can be of no
direct use to ourselves,— this is civilization, our
human glory and race-distinction.

All this human progress has been accomplished by men. Women have been left behind, outside, below, having no social relation
whatever, merely the sex-relation, whereby they
lived. Let us bear in mind that all the tender
ties of family are ties of blood, of sex-relationship. A friend, a comrade, a partner,— this is a
human relative. Father, mother, son, daughter,
sister, brother, husband, wife,— these are sex-
relatives. Blood is thicker than water, we say.
True. But ties of blood are not those that ring
the world with the succeeding waves of progressive religion, art, science, commerce, education,

all that makes us human. Man is the human creature. Woman has been checked, starved, aborted in human growth; and the swelling forces of race-development have been driven back in each generation to work in her through sex-functions alone.

This is the way in which the sexuo-economic relation has operated in our species, checking race-development in half of us, and stimulating sex-development in both.

V.

THE facts stated in the foregoing chapters are familiar and undeniable, the argument seems clear; yet the mind reacts violently from the conclusions it is forced to admit, and tries to find relief in the commonplace conditions of every-day life. From this looming phantom of the over-sexed female of genus homo we fly back in satisfaction to familiar acquaintances and relatives,— to Mrs. John Smith and Miss Imogene Jones, to mothers and sisters and daughters and sweethearts and wives. We feel that such a dreadful state of things cannot be true, or we should surely have noticed it. We may even perform that acrobatic feat so easy to most minds,— admit that the statement may be theoretically true, but practically false!

Two simple laws of brain action are responsible for the difficulty of convincing the human race of any large general truths concerning itself. One is common to all brains, to all nerve sensations indeed, and is cheerfully admitted to have nothing to do with the sexuo-economic relation. It is this simple fact, in popular phrase,— that what we are used to we do not notice. This rests on the law of adaptation, the steady, ceaseless pressure that tends to fit the organism to the environment. A nerve touched for the first time with a certain impression feels this first impression far more than the hundredth or thousandth, though the thousandth be far more violent than the first. If an impression be constant and regular, we become utterly insensitive to it, and only respond under some special condition, as the ticking of a clock, the noise of running water or waves on the beach, even the clatter of railroad trains, grows imperceptible to those who hear it constantly. It is perfectly possible for an individual to become accustomed to the most disadvantageous conditions, and fail to notice them.

It is equally possible for a race, a nation, a class, to become accustomed to most disadvantageous conditions, and fail to notice them. Take, as an individual instance, the wearing of corsets by women. Put a corset, even a loose one, on a vigorous man or woman who never wore one, and there is intense discomfort, and a vivid consciousness thereof. The healthy muscles of the trunk resent the pressure, the action of the whole body is checked in the middle, the stomach is choked, the process of digestion interfered with; and the victim says, "How can you bear such a thing?"

But the person habitually wearing a corset does not feel these evils. They exist, assuredly, the facts are there, the body is not deceived;

but the nerves have become accustomed to these disagreeable sensations, and no longer respond to them. The person "does not feel it." In fact, the wearer becomes so used to the sensations that, when they are removed,— with the corset,— there is a distinct sense of loss and discomfort. The heavy folds of the cravat, stock, and neckcloth of earlier men's fashions, the heavy horse-hair peruke, the stiff high collar of to-day, the kind of shoes we wear,— these are perfectly familiar instances of the force of habit in the individual.

This is equally true of racial habits. That a king should rule because he was born, passed unquestioned for thousands of years. That the eldest son should inherit the titles and estates was a similar phenomenon as little questioned. That a debtor should be imprisoned, and so entirely prevented from paying his debts, was common law. So glaring an evil as chattel slavery was an unchallenged social institution from earliest history to our own day among the most civilized nations of the earth. Christ himself let it pass unnoticed. The hideous injustice of Christianity to the Jew attracted no attention through many centuries. That the serf went with the soil, and was owned by the lord thereof, was one of the foundations of society in the Middle Ages.

Social conditions, like individual conditions, become familiar by use, and cease to be observed. This is the reason why it is so much easier to criticise the customs of other persons or other nations than our own. It is also the reason why we so naturally deny and resent the charges of the critic. It is not necessarily because of any injustice on the one side or dishonesty on the other, but because of a simple and useful law of nature. The Englishman coming to America is much struck by America's political corruption; and, in the earnest desire to serve his brother, he tells us all about it. That which he has at home he does not observe, because he is used to it. The American in England finds also something to object to, and omits to balance his criticism by memories of home.

When a condition exists among us which began in those unrecorded ages back of tradition even, which obtains in varying degree among every people on earth, and which begins to act upon the individual at birth, it would be a miracle past all belief if people should notice it. The sexuo - economic relation is such a condition. It began in primeval savagery. It exists in all nations. Each boy and girl is born into it, trained into it, and has to live in it. The world's progress in matters like these is attained by a slow and painful process, but one which works to good ends.

In the course of social evolution there are developed individuals so constituted as not to fit existing conditions, but to be organically adapted to more advanced conditions. These advanced individuals respond in sharp and painful consciousness to existing conditions, and cry out against them according to their lights. The history of religion, of political and social reform, is full of familiar instances of this. The heretic, the reformer, the agitator, these feel what their compeers do not, see what they do not, and, naturally, say what they do not. The mass of the people are invariably displeased by the outcry of these uneasy spirits. In simple primitive periods they were promptly put to death. Progress was slow and difficult in those days. But this severe process of elimination developed the kind of progressive person known as a martyr; and this remarkable sociological law was manifested: that the strength of a current of social force is increased by the sacrifice of individuals who are willing to die in the effort to promote it. "The blood of the martyrs is the seed of the church." This is so commonly known to-day, though not formulated, that power hesitates to persecute, lest it intensify the undesirable heresy. A policy of "free speech" is found to let pass most of the uneasy pushes and spurts of these stirring forces, and lead to more orderly action. Our great anti-slavery agitation, the heroic efforts of the "women's rights" supporters, are fresh and recent proofs of these plain facts: that the mass of the people do not notice existing conditions, and that they are not pleased with those who do. This is one strong reason why the sexuo-economic relation passes unobserved among us, and why any statement of it will be so offensive to many.

The other law of brain action which tends to prevent our perception of general truth is this: it is easier to personalize than to generalize. This is due primarily to the laws of mental development, but it is greatly added to by the very relation under discussion. As a common law of mental action, the power to observe and retain an individual impression marks a lower degree of development than the power to classify and collate impressions and make generalizations therefrom. There are savages who can say "hot fire," "hot stone," "hot water," but cannot say "heat," cannot think it. Similarly, they can say "good man," "good knife," "good meat"; but they cannot say "goodness," they cannot think it. They have observed specific instances, but are unable to collate them, to generalize therefrom. So, in our common life, individual instances of injustice or cruelty are observed long before the popular mind is able to see that it is a condition which causes these things, and that the condition must be altered before the effects can be removed. A bad priest, a bad king, a bad master, were long observed and pointedly objected to before it began to be held that the condition of monarchy or the condition of slavery must needs bear fruit, and that, if we did not like the fruit, we might better change the tree. Any slaveholder would admit that there were instances of cruelty, laziness, pride, among masters, and of deceit, laziness, dishonesty, among slaves. What the slaveholder did not see was that, given the relation of chattel slavery, it inevitably tended to produce these evils, and did produce them, in spite of all the efforts of the individual to the contrary. To see the individual instance is easy. To see the general cause is harder, requires a further brain development. We, as a race, have long since reached the degree of general intelligence which ought to enable us to judge more largely and wisely of social questions; but here the deteriorating effect of the sexuo-economic relation is shown.

The sex relation is intensely personal. All the functions and relations ensuing are intensely personal. The spirit of "me and my wife, my son John and his wife, us four, and no more," is the natural spirit of this phase of life. By confining half the world to this one set of functions, we have confined it absolutely to the personal. And man that is born of woman is reared by her in this same atmosphere of concentrated personality, and afterward spends a large part of his life in it. This condition tends to magnify the personal and minimize the general in our minds, with results that are familiar to us all. The difficulty of enforcing sanitary laws, where personal convenience must be sacrificed to general safety, the size of the personal grievance as against the general, the need of "having it brought home to us," which hinders every step of public advancement, and our eager response when it is "brought home to us,"— these are truisms. So far as a comparison can be made, women are in this sense more personal than men, more personally sensitive, less willing to "stand in line" and "take turns," less able to see why a general restriction is just when it touches them or their children. This is natural enough, inevitable enough, and only mentioned here as partially explaining why people do not see the general facts as to our over-sexed condition. Yet they are patent everywhere, not only patent, but painful. Being used to them, we do not notice them, or, forced to notice them, we attribute the pain we feel to the evil behavior of some individual, and never think of it as being the result of a condition common to us all.

If we have among us such a condition as has been stated,— a state of morbid and excessive sex-development,— it must, of course, show itself in daily life in a thousand ways. The non-observer, not having seen any such manifestation, concludes that there is none, and so denies the alleged condition,— says it sounds all right, but he does not see any proof of it! Having clearly in mind that, if such proof exists, such commensurate evil in common life as would naturally result from an abnormal sex-distinction, these evils must be so common and habitual as to pass unobserved; and, farther, that, when forced upon our notice, we only see them as matters of personal behavior,— let us, in spite of these hindrances, see if the visible results among us are not such as must follow such a cause, and let us seek them merely in the phenomena of every-day life as we know it, not in the deeper sexual or social results.

A concrete instance, familiar as the day, and unbelievable in its ill effects, is the attitude of the mother toward her children in regard to the sex-relation. With very few exceptions, the mother gives her daughter no warning or prevision of what life holds for her, and so lets innocence and ignorance go on perpetuating sickness and sin and pain through ceaseless generations. A normal motherhood wisely and effectively guards its young from evil. An abnormal motherhood, over-anxious and under-wise, hovers the child to its harm, and turns it out defenceless to the worst of evils. This is known to millions and millions personally. Only very lately have we thought to consider it generally. And not yet do we see that it is not the fault of the individual mother, but of her economic status. Because of our abnormal sex-development, the whole field has become something of an offence,— a thing to be hidden and ignored, passed over without remark or explanation. Hence this amazing paradox of mothers ashamed of motherhood, unable to explain it, and — measure this well — lying to their children about the primal truths of life,— mothers lying to their own children about motherhood!

The pressure under which this is done is an economic one. The girl must marry: else how live? The prospective husband prefers the girl to know nothing. He is the market, the demand. She is the supply. And with the best intentions the mother serves her child's economic advantage by preparing her for the market. This is an excellent instance. It is common. It is most evil. It is plainly traceable to our sexuo-economic relation.

Another instance of so grossly unjust, so palpable, so general an evil that it has occasionally aroused some protest even from our dull consciousness is this: the enforced attitude of the woman toward marriage. To the young girl, as has been previously stated, marriage is the one road to fortune, to life. She is born highly specialized as a female: she is carefully educated and trained to realize in all ways her sex-limitations and her sex-advantages. What she has to gain even as a child is largely gained by feminine tricks and charms. Her reading, both in history and fiction, treats of the same position for women; and romance and poetry give it absolute predominance. Pictorial art, music, the drama, society, everything, tells her that she is *she*, and that all depends on whom she marries. Where young boys plan for what they will achieve and attain, young girls plan for whom they will achieve and attain. Little Ellie and her swan's nest among the reeds is a familiar illustration. It is the lover on the red roan steed she planned for. It is Lancelot riding through the sheaves that called the Lady from her loom at Shalott: "he" is the coming world.

With such a prospect as this before her; with an organization specially developed to this end; with an education adding every weight of precept and example, of wisdom and virtue, to the natural instincts; with a social environment the whole machinery of which is planned to give the girl a chance to see and to be seen, to provide her with "opportunities"; and with all the pressure of personal advantage and self-interest added to the sex-instinct,— what one would logically expect is a society full of desperate and eager husband-hunters, regarded with popular approval.

Not at all! Marriage is the woman's proper sphere, her divinely ordered place, her natural end. It is what she is born for, what she is trained for, what she is exhibited for. It is, moreover, her means of honorable livelihood and advancement. *But*—she must not even look as if she wanted it! She must not turn her hand over to get it. She must sit passive as the seasons go by, and her "chances" lessen with each year. Think of the strain on a highly sensitive nervous organism to have so much hang on one thing, to see the possibility of attaining it grow less and less yearly, and to be forbidden to take any step toward securing it! This she must bear with dignity and grace to the end.

To what end? To the end that, if she does not succeed in being chosen, she becomes a thing of mild popular contempt, a human being with no further place in life save as an attachée, a dependant upon more fortunate relatives, an old maid. The open derision and scorn with which unmarried women used to be treated is lessening each year in proportion to their advance in economic independence. But it is not very long since the popular proverb, "Old maids lead apes in hell," was in common use; since unwelcome lovers urged their suit with the awful argument that they might be the last askers; since the hapless lady in the wood prayed for a husband, and, when the owl answered, "Who? who?" cried, "Anybody, good Lord!" There is still a pleasant ditty afloat as to the "Three Old Maids of Lynn," who did not marry when they could, and could not when they would.

The cruel and absurd injustice of blaming

the girl for not getting what she is allowed no effort to obtain seems unaccountable; but it becomes clear when viewed in connection with the sexuo-economic relation. Although marriage is a means of livelihood, it is not honest employment where one can offer one's labor without shame, but a relation where the support is given outright, and enforced by law in return for the functional service of the woman, the "duties of wife and mother." Therefore no honorable woman can ask for it. It is not only that the natural feminine instinct is to retire, as that of the male is to advance, but that, because marriage means support, a woman must not ask a man to support her. It is economic beggary as well as a false attitude from a sex point of view.

Observe the ingenious cruelty of the arrangement. It is just as humanly natural for a woman as for a man to want wealth. But, when her wealth is made to come through the same channels as her love, she is forbidden to ask for it by her own sex-nature and by business honor. Hence the millions of mismade marriages with "anybody, good Lord!" Hence the million broken hearts which must let all life pass, unable to make any attempt to stop it. Hence the many "maiden aunts," elderly sisters and daughters, unattached women everywhere, who are a burden on their male relatives and society at large. This is changing for the better, to be sure, but changing only through the advance of economic independence for women. A "bachelor maid" is a very different thing from "an old maid."

This, then, is the reason for the Andromeda position of the possibly-to-be-married young woman, and for the ridicule and reproach meted out to her. Since women are viewed wholly as creatures of sex even by one another, and since everything is done to add to their young powers of sex-attraction; since they are marriageable solely on this ground, unless, indeed, "a fortune" has been added to their charms,— failure to marry is held a clear proof of failure to attract, a lack of sex-value. And, since they have no other value, save in a low order of domestic service, they are quite naturally despised. What else is the creature good for, failing in the functions for which it was created? The scorn of male and female alike falls on this sexless thing: she is a human failure.

It is not strange, therefore, though just as pitiful,— this long chapter of patient, voiceless, dreary misery in the lives of women; and it is not strange, either, to see the marked and steady change in opinion that follows the development of other faculties in woman besides those of sex. Now that she is a person as well as a female, filling economic relation to society, she is welcomed and accepted as a human creature, and need not marry the wrong man for her bread and butter. So sharp is the reaction from this unlovely yoke that there is a limited field of life to-day wherein women choose not to marry, preferring what they call "their independence,"—a new-born, hard-won, dear-bought independence. That any living woman should prefer it to home and husband, to love and motherhood, throws a fierce light on what women must have suffered for lack of freedom before.

This tendency need not be feared, however. It is merely a reaction, and a most natural one. It will pass as naturally, as more and more women become independent, when marriage is not the price of liberty. The fear exhibited that women generally, once fully independent, will not marry, is proof of how well it has been known that only dependence forced them to marriage as it was. There will be needed neither bribe nor punishment to force women to true marriage with independence.

Along this line it is most interesting to mark the constant struggle between natural instinct and natural law, and social habit and social law, through all our upward course. Beginning with the natural functions and instincts of sex, holding her great position as selecter of the best among competing males, woman's beautiful work is to improve the race by right marriage. The feeling by which this is accomplished, growing finer as we become more civilized, developes into that wide, deep, true, and lasting love which is the highest good to individual human beings. Following its current, we have always reverenced and admired "true love"; and our romances, from the earliest times, abound in praise of the princess who marries the page or prisoner, venerating the selective power in woman, choosing "the right man" for his own sake. Directly against this runs the counter-current, resulting in the marriage of convenience, a thing which the true inner heart of the world has always hated. Young Lochinvar is not an eternal hero for nothing. The personified type of a great social truth is sure of a long life. The poor young hero, handsome, brave, good, but beset with difficulties, stands ever against the wealth and power of the bad man. The woman is pulled hither and thither between them, and the poor hero wins in the end. That he is heaped with honor and riches, after all, merely signifies our recognition that he is the higher good. This is better than a sun-myth. It is a race-myth, and true as truth.

So we have it among us in life to-day, endlessly elaborated and weakened by profuse detail, as is the nature of that life, but there yet. The girl who marries the rich old man or the titled profligate is condemned by the popular voice; and the girl who marries the poor young man, and helps him live his best, is still approved by the same great arbiter. And yet why should we blame the woman for pursuing her vocation? Since marriage is her only way to get money, why should she not try to get money in that way? Why cast the weight of all self-interest on the "practical" plane so solidly against the sex-interest of the individual and of the race? The mercenary marriage is a perfectly natural consequence of the economic dependence of women.

On the other hand, note the effect of this dependence upon men. As the excessive sex-distinction and economic dependence of women increase, so do the risk and difficulty of marriage increase, so is marriage deferred and avoided, to the direct injury of both sexes and society at large. In simpler relations, in the country, wherever women have a personal value in economic relation as well

93

as a feminine value in sex-relation, an early
marriage is an advantage. The young farmer
gets a profitable servant when he marries.
The young business man gets nothing of the
kind,— a pretty girl, a charming girl, ready
for "wifehood and motherhood"— so far as
her health holds out,— but having no economic
value whatever. She is merely a consumer,
and he must wait till he can "afford to marry."
These are instances frequent everywhere, and
familiar to us all, of the palpable effects in
common life of our sexuo-economic relation.

If there is one unmixed evil in human life,
it is that known to us in all ages, and popularly
called "the social evil," consisting of promiscuous and temporary sex-relations. The inherent wrong in these relations is sociological
before it is legal or moral. The recognition
by the moral sense of a given thing as wrong
requires that it be wrong, to begin with. A
thing is not wrong merely because it is called
so. The wrongness of this form of sex-relation in an advanced social state rests solidly
on natural laws. In the evolution of better
and better means of reproducing the species,
a longer period of infancy was developed.
This longer period of infancy required longer
care, and it was accordingly developed that
the best care during this time was given by

both parents. This induced a more perma‚ nent mating. And the more permanent mat‚ ing, bound together by the common interests and duties, developed higher psychic attributes in the parents by use, in the children by heredity. That is why society is right in demanding of its constituent individuals the virtue of chastity, the sanctity of marriage. Society is perfectly right, because social evolution is as natural a process as individual evolution; and the permanent parent is proven an advantageous social factor. But social evolution, deep, unconscious, slow, is one thing; and self-conscious, loud-voiced society is another.

The deepest forces of nature have tended to evolve pure, lasting, monogamous marriage in the human race. But our peculiar arrangement of feeding one sex by the other has tended to produce a very different thing, and has produced it. In no other animal species is the female economically dependent on the male. In no other animal species is the sex-relation for sale. A coincidence. Where, on the one hand, every condition of life tends to develope sex in women, to crush out the power and the desire for economic production and exchange, and to develope also the age-long habit of seeking all earthly good at a man's hands and of making but one return; where, on the other hand, man inherits the excess in sex-energy, and is never blamed for exercising it, and where he developes also the age-long habit of taking what he wants from women, for whose helpless acquiescence he makes an economic return, — what should naturally follow? Precisely what has followed. We live in a world of law, and humanity is no exception to it. We have produced a certain percentage of females with inordinate sex-tendencies and inordinate greed for material gain. We have produced a certain percentage of males with inordinate sex-tendencies and a cheerful willingness to pay for their gratification. And, as the percentage of such men is greater than the percentage of such women, we have worked out most evil methods of supplying the demand. But always in the healthy social heart we have known that it was wrong, a racial wrong, productive of all evil. Being a man's world, it was quite inevitable that he should blame woman for their mutual misdoing. There is reason in it, too. Bad as he is, he is only seeking gratification natural in kind, though abnormal in degree. She is not only in some cases doing this, but in most cases showing the falseness of the deed by doing it for hire, — physical falsehood, — a sin against nature.

It is a true instinct that revolts against obtaining bread by use of the sex-functions. Why, then, are we so content to do this in marriage? Legally and religiously, we say that it is right; but in its reactionary effect on the parties concerned and on society at large it is wrong. The physical and psychical effects are evil, though modified by our belief that it is right. The physical and psychical effects of prostitution were still evil when the young girls of Babylon earned their dowries thereby in the temple of Bela, and thought it right. What we think and feel alters the moral quality of an act in our consciousness as we do it, but does not alter its subsequent effect. We justify and approve the economic dependence of women upon the sex-relation in marriage. We condemn it unsparingly out of marriage. We follow it with our blame and scorn up to the very doors of marriage, — the mercenary bride, — but think no harm of the mercenary wife, filching her husband's pockets in the night. Love sanctifies it, we say: love must go with it.

Love never yet went with self-interest. The deepest antagonism lies between them: they are diametrically opposed forces. In the beautiful progress of evolution we find constant opposition between the instincts and processes

of self-preservation and the instinct and processes of race-preservation. From those early
forms where birth brought death, as in the
flowering aloe, the ephemeral may-fly, up to
the highest glory of self-effacing love; these
two forces work in opposition. We have tied
them together. We have made the woman,
the mother,— the very source of sacrifice
through love,— get gain through love,— a hideous paradox. No wonder that our daily lives
are full of the flagrant evils produced by this
unnatural state. No wonder that men turn
with loathing from the kind of women they
have made.

VI.

THE peculiar combination of functions which we are studying has not only an immediate effect on individuals through sex-action, and through the sex-affected individuals upon society, but also an effect upon society through economic action, and through the economically affected society upon the individual.

The economic aspect of the question brings it prominently forward to-day as influencing not only our private health and happiness and the processes of reproduction, but our public health and happiness and the processes of social economics as well. Society is confronted in this age with most pressing problems in economics, and we need the fullest understanding of the factors involved. These problems are almost wholly social rather than physical, and concern not the capacity of a given society to produce and distribute enough wealth for its maintenance, but some maladjustment of internal processes which checks that production and distribution, and developes such irregular and morbid processes of innutrition, malnutrition, and over-nutrition as continually to injure the health and activity of the social organism. Our difficulty about wealth is not in getting it out of the earth,

but in getting it away from one another. We
have phenomena before us in the development
of social economic relations analogous to those
accompanying our development in sex-relation.

In the original constituents of society, the
human animal in its primitive state, economic processes were purely individual. The
amount of food obtained by a given man bore
direct relation to his own personal exertions.
Other men were to him merely undesirable
competitors for the same goods; and, the fewer
these competitors were, the more goods remained for him. Therefore, he killed as many
of his rivals as possible. Given a certain
supply of needed food, as the edible beasts
or fruits in a forest, and a certain number of
individuals to get this food, each by his own
exertions, it follows that, the more numerous
the individuals, the less food to be obtained by
each; and, conversely, the fewer the individuals, the more food to be obtained by each.
Wherefore, the primitive savage slew his fel-
low-man at sight, on good economic grounds.
This is the extreme of individual competition,
perfectly logical, and, in its time, economically
right. That time is forever past. The basic
condition of human life is union; the organic
social relation, the interchange of functional
service, wherein the individual is most advan-

taged, not by his own exertions for his own goods, but by the exchange of his exertions with the exertions of others for goods produced by them together. We are not treating here of any communistic theory as to the equitable division of the wealth produced, but of a clear truth in social economics,— that wealth is a social product. Whatever one may believe as to what should be done with the wealth of the world, no one can deny that the production of this wealth requires the combined action of many individuals. From the simplest combination of strength that enables many men to overcome the mammoth or to lift the stone — an achievement impossible to one alone — to the subtle and complex interchange of highly specialized skilled labor which makes possible our modern house; the progress of society rests upon the increasing collectivity of human labor.

The evolution of organic life goes on in geometrical progression: cells combine, and form organs; organs combine, and form organisms; organisms combine, and form organizations. Society is an organization. Society is the fourth power of the cell. It is composed of individual animals of genus homo, living in organic relation. The course of social evolution is the gradual establish-

ment of organic relation between individuals,
and this organic relation rests on purely economic grounds.   In the simplest combination
of primordial cells the force that drew and
held them together was that of economic necessity.   It profited them to live in combination.   Those that did so survived, and those
that did not perished.   So with the appearance
of the most elaborate organisms : it profited
them to become a complex bundle of members
and organs in indivisible relation.   A creature so constructed survived, where the same
amount of living matter unorganized would
have perished.   And so it is, literally and exactly, in a complex society, with all its elaborate specialization of individuals in arts and
crafts, trades and professions.   A society so
constructed survives, where the same number
of living beings, unorganized, would perish.
The specialization of labor and exchange of
product in a social body is identical in its
nature with the specialization and exchange of
function in an individual body.   This process,
on orderly lines of evolution, involves the
gradual subordination of individual effort for
individual good to the collective effort for the
collective good, — not from any so-called "altruism," but from the economic necessities of
the case.   It is as natural, as "selfish," for

society so to live, the individual citizens working together for the social good, as for one's own body to live by the hands and feet, teeth and eyes, heart and lungs, working together for the individual good. Social evolution tends to an increasing specialization in structure and function, and to an increasing interdependence of the component parts, with a correlative decrease through disuse of the once valuable process of individual struggle for success; and this is based absolutely on the advantage to the individual as well as to the social body.

But, as we study this process of development, noting with admiration the progressive changes in human relation, the new functions, the extended structure, the increase of sensation in the socialized individuals with its enormous possibilities of joy and healthful sensitiveness to pain, we are struck by the visible presence of some counter-force, acting against the normal development and producing most disadvantageous effects. As in our orderly progress in social sex-development we are checked by the tenacious hold of rudimentary impulses artificially maintained by false conditions, so in our orderly progress in social economic development we see the same peculiar survival of rudimentary impulses, which should have been long since easily outgrown. It is no longer of advantage to the individual to struggle for his own gain at the expense of others: his gain now requires the co-ordinate efforts of these others; yet he continues so to struggle.

In this lack of adjustment between the individual and the social interest lies our economic trouble. An illustration of this may be seen in the manufacture of prepared foods. This is a process impossible to the individual singly, and of great advantage to the individual in collective relation, — a perfectly natural economic process, advantageous in proportion to the amount and quality of the food manufactured. This we constantly find accompanied by a morbid process of dilution and adulteration, by which society is injured, in order that the individual concerned in the manufacture may be benefited. This is as though one of the organs of the body — the liver, for instance — should deliberately weaken or poison its quota of secretion, in order that by giving less it might retain more, and become large and fat individually. An organ can do so, does do so; but such action is morbid action, and constitutes disease. The body is injured, weakened, destroyed, and so ultimately the organ perishes also. It is a false conception of gain, and the falsehood lies in not recognizing the true relation between individual and social interests. This failure to recognize or, at least, to act up to a recognition of social interests, owing to the disproportionate pressure of individual interests, is the underlying cause of our economic distress. As society is composed of individuals, we must look to them for the action causing these morbid social processes; and, as individuals act under the pressure of conditions, we must look to the conditions affecting the individuals for the causes of their action.

In general, under social law, men develope right action; but some hidden spring seems to force them continually into wrong action. We have our hand upon this hidden spring in the sexuo-economic relation. If we had remained on an individual economic basis, the evil influence would have had far less ill effect; but, as we grow into the social economic relation, it increases with our civilization. The sex-relation is primarily and finally individual. It is a physical relation between individual bodies; and, while it may also extend to a psychical relation between individual souls, it does not become a social relation, though it does change its personal development to suit social needs.

In all its processes, to all its results, the sex-relation is personal, working through individuals upon individuals, and developing individual traits and characteristics, to the great advantage of society. The qualities developed by social relation are built into the race through the sex-relation, but the sex-relation itself is wholly personal. Our economic relation, on the contrary, though originally individual, becomes through social evolution increasingly collective. By combining the human sex-relation with the human economic relation, we have combined a permanently individual process with a progressively collective one. This involves a strain on both, which increases in direct proportion to our socialization, and, so far, has resulted in the ultimate destruction of the social organism acted upon by such irreconcilable forces.

As has been shown, this combination has affected the sex-relation of individuals by bringing into it a tendency to collectivism with economic advantage, best exhibited in our distinctive racial phenomenon of prostitution. On the other hand, it has affected the economic relation of society by bringing into it a tendency to individualism with sex-advantage, best exhibited in the frequent practice of sacrificing public good to personal gain, that the

individual may thereby "support his family."
We are so used to considering it the first duty
of a man to support his family that it takes a
very glaring instance of bribery and corruption
in their interests to shake our conviction; but,
as a sociological law, every phase of the prostitution of public service to private gain, from
the degradation of the artist to the exploita-
tion of the helpless unskilled laborer, marks
a diseased social action. Our social status
rests upon our common consent, common
action, common submission to the common
will. No individual interests can stand for
a moment against the interests of the common
weal, either when war demands the last sacrifice of individual property and life or when
peace requires the absolute submission of individual property and life to common law,—
the fixed expression of the people's will. The
maintenance of "law and order" involves the
very spirit of socialism,— the sinking of personal interest in common interest. All this
rests upon the evolution of the social spirit,
the keen sense of social duty, the conscientious fulfilment of social service; and it is
here that the excessive individualism maintained by our sexuo-economic relation enters
as a strong and increasingly disadvantageous
social factor. We have dimly recognized the

irreconcilability of the sex-relation with economic relations on both sides,— in our sharp condemnation of making the sex-functions openly commercial, and in the drift toward celibacy in collective institutions. Bodies of men or women, actuated by the highest religious impulses, desiring to live nobly and to serve society, have always recognized something antagonistic in the sex-relation. They have thought it inherent in the relation itself, not seeing that it was the economic side which made it reactionary. Yet this action was practically admitted by the continued existence of communal societies where the sex-relation did exist, in an unacknowledged form, and without the element of economic exchange. It is admitted also by the noble and self-sacrificing devotion of married missionaries of the Protestant Church, who are supported by contributions. If the missionary were obliged to earn his wife's living and his own, he could do little mission work.

The highest human attributes are perfectly compatible with the sex-relation, but not with the sexuo-economic relation. We see this opposition again in the tendency to collectivity in bodies of single men,— their comradeship, equality, and mutual helpfulness as compared with the attitude of the same men toward one another, when married. This is why the quality of "organizability" is stronger in men than in women; their common economic interests force them into relation, while the isolated and even antagonistic economic interests of women keep them from it. The condition of individual economic dependence in which women live resembles that of the savage in the forest. They obtain their economic goods by securing a male through their individual exertions, all competing freely to this end. No combination is possible. The numerous girls at a summer resort, in their attitude toward the scant supply of young men, bear an unconscious resemblance to the emulous savages in a too closely hunted forest. And here may be given an economic reason for the oft-noted bitterness with which the virtuous women regard the vicious. The virtuous woman stands in close ranks with her sisters, refusing to part with herself — her only economic goods — until she is assured of legal marriage, with its lifelong guarantee of support. Under equal proportions of birth in the two sexes, every woman would be tolerably sure of obtaining her demands. But here enters the vicious woman, and offers the same goods — though of inferior quality, to be sure — for a far less price. Every one of such illegitimate competitors lowers the chances of the unmarried women and the income of the married. No wonder those who hold themselves highly should be moved to bitterness at being undersold in this way. It is the hatred of the trade-unionist for "scab labor."

On the woman's side we are steadily maintaining the force of primitive individual competition in the world as against the tendency of social progress to develope co-operation in its place, and this tendency of course is inherited by their sons. On the man's side the same effect is produced through another feature of the relation. The tendency to individualism with sex-advantage is developed in man by an opposite process to that operating on the woman. She gets her living by getting a husband. He gets his wife by getting a living. It is to her individual economic advantage to secure a mate. It is to his individual sex-advantage to secure economic gain. The sex-functions to her have become economic functions. Economic functions to him have become sex-functions. This has confounded our natural economic competition, inevitably growing into economic co-operation, with the element of sex-competition, — an entirely different force.

Competition among males, with selection by

the female of the superior male, is the process
of sexual selection, and works to racial improvement. So far as the human male com-
petes freely with his peers in higher and
higher activities, and the female chooses the
winner, so far we are directly benefited. But
there is a radical distinction between sex-competition and marriage by purchase. In the
first the male succeeds by virtue of what he
can do; in the second, by virtue of what he
can get. The increased power to do, transmitted to the young, is of racial advantage.
But mere possessions, with no question as to
the method of their acquisition, are not necessarily of advantage to the individual as a
father. To make the sexual gain of the male
rest on his purchasing power puts the immense force of sex-competition into the field
of social economics, not only as an incentive
to labor and achievement, which is good, but
as an incentive to individual gain, however
obtained, which is bad; thus accounting for
our multiplied and intensified desire to get, —
the inordinate greed of our industrial world.
The tournament of the Middle Ages was a
brutal sport perhaps, with its human injury,
pain, and death, under the cry of: "Fight on,
brave knights! Fair eyes are looking on
you!" but it represents a healthier process

than our modern method of securing the
wherewithal to maintain the sex-relation.   As
so beautifully phrased by Jean Ingelow : —[4]

> " I worked afar that I might rear
>   A happy home on English soil;
>   I labored for the gold and gear,
>   I loved my toil.

> " Forever in my spirit spake
>   The natural whisper, ' Well 'twill be
>   When loving wife and children break
>   Their bread with thee ! ' "

Or, put more broadly by Kipling : —

> " But since our women must walk gay,
>   And money buys their gear,
>   The sealing vessels filch this way
>   At hazard, year by year."

The contest in every good man's heart
to-day between the "ought to" and the
"must," between his best work and the "pot-
boiler," is his personal share of this incessant
struggle between social interest and self-interest.   For himself and by himself he would be
glad to do his best work, to be true to his
ideals, to be brave in meeting loss for that
truth's sake.   But as the compromising capi-
talist says in "Put Yourself in His Place,"[5]
when his sturdy young friend — a bachelor —
wonders at his giving in to unjust demands,

"Marriage makes a mouse of a man." To the young business man who falls into evil courses in the sex-relation the open greed of his fair dependant is a menace to his honesty, to his business prospects. On the same man married the needs of his wife often operate in the same way. The sense of the dependence of the helpless creature whose food must come through him does not stimulate courage, but compels submission.

The foregoing distinction should be clearly held in mind. Legitimate sex-competition brings out all that is best in man. To please her, to win her, he strives to do his best. But the economic dependence of the female upon the male, with its ensuing purchasability, does not so affect a man: it puts upon him the necessity for getting things, not for doing them. In the lowest grades of labor, where there is no getting without doing and where the laborer always does more than he gets, this works less palpable evil than in the higher grades, the professions and arts, where the most valuable work is always ahead of the market, and where to work for the market involves a lowering of standards. The young artist or poet or scientific student works for his work's sake, for art, for science, and so for the best good of society. But the artist or

student married must get gain, must work for
those who will pay; and those who will pay
are not those who lift and bear forward the
standard of progress. Community of interest
is quite possible with those who are working
most disinterestedly for the social good; but
bring in the sex-relation, and all such soli-
darity disintegrates,—resolves itself into the
tiny groups of individuals united on a basis of
sex-union, and briskly acting in their own
immediate interests at anybody's or every-
body's expense.

The social perception of the evil resultant
from the intrusion of sex-influence upon racial
action has found voice in the heartless proverb,
"There is no evil without a woman at the
bottom of it." When a man's work goes
wrong, his hopes fail, his ambitions sink,
cynical friends inquire, "Who is she?" It
is not for nothing that a man's best friends
sigh when he marries, especially if he is a
man of genius. This judgment of the world
has obtained side by side with its equal faith
in the ennobling influence of woman. The
world is quite right. It does not have to
be consistent. Both judgments are correct.
Woman affecting society through the sex-
relation or through her individual economic
relation is an ennobling influence. Woman

affecting society through our perverse combination of the two becomes a strange influence, indeed.

One of the amusing minor results of these conditions is that, while we have observed the effect of marriage upon social economic relation and the effect of social economic relation upon marriage,— seeing that the devoted servant of the family was a poor servant of society and that the devoted servant of society was a poor servant of the family, seeing the successful collectivity of celibate institutions, — we have jumped to the conclusion that collective prosperity was conditioned upon celibacy, and that we did not want it. That is why the popular mind is so ready to associate socialistic theories with injury to marriage. Having seen that marriage makes us less collective, we infer conversely that collectivity will make us less married,— that it will " break up the home," "strike at the roots of the family."

When we make plain to ourselves that a pure, lasting, monogamous sex-union can exist without bribe or purchase, without the manacles of economic dependence, and that men and women so united in sex-relation will still be free to combine with others in economic relation, we shall not regard devotion to hu-

manity as an unnatural sacrifice, nor collective
prosperity as a thing to fear.

Besides this maintenance of primeval individualism in the growing collectivity of social
economic process and the introduction of the
element of sex-combat into the narrowing field
of industrial competition, there is another side
to the evil influence of the sexuo-economic
relation upon social development. This is in
the attitude of woman as a non-productive consumer.

In the industrial evolution of the human
race, that marvellous and subtle drawing out
and interlocking of special functions which
constitute the organic life of society, we find
that production and consumption go hand in
hand; and production comes first. One cannot consume what has not been produced.
Economic production is the natural expression
of human energy,— not sex-energy at all, but
race-energy,— the unconscious functioning of
the social organism. Socially organized human beings tend to produce, as a gland to
secrete: it is the essential nature of the relation. The creative impulse, the desire to
make, to express the inner thought in outer
form, "just for the work's sake, no use at all
i' the work!" this is the distinguishing character of humanity. "I want to mark!" cries

the child, demanding the pencil. He does not want to eat. He wants to mark. He is not seeking to get something into himself, but to put something out of himself. He generally wants to do whatever he sees done, — to make pie-crust or to make shavings, as it happens. The pie he may eat, the shavings not; but he likes to make both. This is the natural process of production, and is followed by the natural process of consumption, where practicable. But consumption is not the main end, the governing force. Under this organic social law, working naturally, we have the evolution of those arts and crafts in the exercise of which consists our human living, and on the product of which we live. So does society evolve within itself — secrete as it were — the social structure with all its complex machinery; and we function therein as naturally as so many glands, other things being equal.

But other things are not equal. Half the human race is denied free productive expression, is forced to confine its productive human energies to the same channels as its reproductive sex-energies. Its creative skill is confined to the level of immediate personal bodily service, to the making of clothes and preparing of food for individuals. No social service is possible. While its power of production is checked, its power of consumption is inordinately increased by the showering upon it of the "unearned increment"[6]of masculine gifts. For the woman there is, first, no free production allowed; and, second, no relation maintained between what she does produce and what she consumes. She is forbidden to make, but encouraged to take. Her industry is not the natural output of creative energy, not the work she does because she has the inner power and strength to do it; nor is her industry even the measure of her gain. She has, of course, the natural desire to consume; and to that is set no bar save the capacity or the will of her husband.

Thus we have painfully and laboriously evolved and carefully maintain among us an enormous class of non-productive consumers, — a class which is half the world, and mother of the other half. We have built into the constitution of the human race the habit and desire of taking, as divorced from its natural precursor and concomitant of making. We have made for ourselves this endless array of "horse-leech's daughters, crying, Give! give!" To consume food, to consume clothes, to consume houses and furniture and decorations and ornaments and amusements, to take and take and take forever,—from one man if they are virtuous, from many if they are vicious, but always to take and never to think of giving anything in return except their womanhood,—this is the enforced condition of the mothers of the race. What wonder that their sons go into business "for what there is in it"! What wonder that the world is full of the desire to get as much as possible and to give as little as possible! What wonder, either, that the glory and sweetness of love are but a name among us, with here and there a strange and beautiful exception, of which our admiration proves the rarity!

Between the brutal ferocity of excessive male energy struggling in the market-place as in a battlefield and the unnatural greed generated by the perverted condition of female energy, it is not remarkable that the industrial evolution of humanity has shown peculiar symptoms. One of the minor effects of this last condition—this limiting of female industry to close personal necessities, and this tendency of her over-developed sex-nature to overestimate the so-called "duties of her position"—has been to produce an elaborate devotion to individuals and their personal needs,—not to the understanding and developing of their higher natures, but to the intensification of their bodily tastes and pleasure. The wife and mother, pouring the rising tide of racial power into the same old channels that were allowed her primitive ancestors, constantly ministers to the physical needs of her family with a ceaseless and concentrated intensity. They like it, of course. But it maintains in the individuals of the race an exaggerated sense of the importance of food and clothes and ornaments to themselves, without at all including a knowledge of their right use and value to us all. It developes personal selfishness.

Again, the consuming female, debarred from any free production, unable to estimate the labor involved in the making of what she so lightly destroys, and her consumption limited mainly to those things which minister to physical pleasure, creates a market for sensuous decoration and personal ornament, for all that is luxurious and enervating, and for a false and capricious variety in such supplies, which operates as a most deadly check to true industry and true art. As the priestess of the temple of consumption, as the limitless demander of things to use up, her economic influence is reactionary and injurious. Much, very much, of the current of useless production in which our economic energies run waste

— man's strength poured out like water on the sand — depends on the creation and careful maintenance of this false market, this sink into which human labor vanishes with no return. Woman, in her false economic position, reacts injuriously upon industry, upon art, upon science, discovery, and progress. The sexuo-economic relation in its effect on the constitution of the individual keeps alive in us the instincts of savage individualism which we should otherwise have well outgrown. It sexualizes our industrial relation and commercializes our sex-relation. And, in the external effect upon the market, the over-sexed woman, in her unintelligent and ceaseless demands, hinders and perverts the economic development of the world.

VII.

A CONDITION so long established, so wide-spread, so permanent as the sexuo-economic relation in the human species could not have been introduced and maintained in the course of social evolution without natural causes and uses. No wildest perversion of individual will could permanently maintain a condition wholly injurious to society. Church and State and social forms move and change with our growth, and we cannot hinder them long after the time has come for further progress. Once it was of advantage to society that the sexuo-economic relation should be established. Now that it is no longer of advantage to society, the "woman's movement" has set in; and the relation is changing under our eyes from year to year, from day to day, in spite of our traditional opposition. The change considered in these pages is not one merely to be prophesied and recommended: it is already taking place under the forces of social evolution; and only needs to be made clear to our conscious thought, that we may withdraw the futile but irritating resistance of our misguided will.

The original necessity for this distinctive human phenomenon lies very deep among the

primal forces of social life. The relations required to develope individual organisms failed
in the further development of the social organism of organization. Co-ordination requires
first a common interest, and then the establishment of a common consciousness. It was
for the common interest of the individual cells
to obtain food easily, and this drew them into
closer relation. That relation being established, their co-existence became a unit, an
entity, a thing with a conscious life of its
own. In the fullest development of the most
elaborate organisms, this holds good. There
must be a common interest to be served by all
this co-ordinate activity; and there must be a
common consciousness established, whereby
to serve most easily the common interest.
When the component cells in our tissues
shrink and fail for lack of nutrition, when the
several organs weary of inaction and fretfully
demand their natural exercise, the man does
not say, "My tissues need replenishment" or
"My organs need exercise": he says, "I am
hungry." And that "I," the personal consciousness directing the smooth interaction of
all its parts, goes to work to get food. Social
evolution rests on this common interest. Individual men are profited by social relation;
and, therefore, they enter into social relation.

Such relation requires a common consciousness, through which the co-ordinate action may
take place; and the whole course of social development is marked by the constant extension
of this social consciousness and its necessary
vehicles. Language is our largest common
medium, and leads on into literature, which is
but preserved speech. The brain of man is
the social organ, the organ of communication.
Through it flows the current of thought,
whereby we are enabled to work together. By
so much as our brains hold in common, we can
understand each other; and, therefore, some
degree of common education is essential to
free social development.

At the very beginning of this process, when
the human animal was still but an animal,—
but an individual, — came the imperative
demand for the establishment of a common
consciousness between these hitherto irreconcilable individuals. The first step in nature
toward this end is found in the relation between mother and child. Where the young,
after birth, are still dependent on the mother,
the functions of the one separate living body
needing the service of another separate living
body, we have the overlapping of personality,
the mutual need, which brings with it the
essential instinct that holds together these in-

teracting personalities. That instinct we call love. The child must have the mother's breast. The mother's breast must have the child. Therefore, between mother and child was born love, long before fatherhood was anything more than a momentary incident. But the common consciousness, the mutual attraction between mother and child, stopped there absolutely. It was limited in range to this closest relation; in duration, to the period of infancy.

The common interest of human beings must be served by racial faculties, not merely by the sex-functions of the female, or the duties of mother to child. As the male, acting through his natural instincts, steadily encroached upon the freedom of the female until she was reduced to the state of economic dependence, he thereby assumed the position of provider for this creature no longer able to provide for herself. He was not only compelled to serve her needs, but to fulfil in his own person the thwarted uses of maternity. He became, and has remained, a sort of man-mother, alone in creation in his remarkable position. By this common interest, existing now not only between mother and child, but between father, mother, and child, grew up a wider common consciousness. And, as the father served the child not through sex-function,

but through race-function, this service was open
to far wider development and longer duration
than the mother's alone could ever have reached.
Maternal energy is the force through which
have come into the world both love and industry.   It is through the tireless activity of this
desire, the mother's wish to serve the young,
that she began the first of the arts and crafts
whereby we live.   While the male savage was
still a mere hunter and fighter, expressing
masculine energy, the katabolic force, along
its essential line, expanding, scattering, the
female savage worked out in equally natural
ways the conserving force of female energy.
She gathered together and saved nutrition for
the child, as the germ-cell gathers and saves
nutrition in the unconscious silences of nature.   She wrapped it in garments and built a
shelter for its head as naturally as the same
maternal function had loved, clothed, and
sheltered the unborn.   Maternal energy, working externally through our elaborate organism,
is the source of productive industry, the main
current of social life.

But not until this giant force could ally
itself with others and work co-operatively,
overcoming the destructive action of male
energy in its blind competition, could our
human life enter upon its full course of racial

evolution. This is what was accomplished through the suppression of the free action of maternal energy in the female and its irresistible expression through the male. The two forces were combined, and he was the active factor in their manifestation. It was one of nature's calm, unsmiling miracles, no more wonderful than where she makes the guileless, greedy bee, who thinks he is merely getting his dinner, serve as an agent of reproduction to countless flowers. The bee might resent it if he knew what office he performed, and that his dinner was only there that he might fulfil that office. The subjection of woman has involved to an enormous degree the maternalizing of man. Under its bonds he has been forced into new functions, impossible to male energy alone. He has had to learn to love and care for some one besides himself. He has had to learn to work, to serve, to be human. Through the sex-passion, mightily overgrown, the human race has been led and driven up the long, steep path of progress, over all obstacles, through all dangers, carrying its accompanying conditions of disease and sin (and surmounting them), up and up in spite of all, until at last a degree of evolution is reached in which the extension of human service and human love makes possible a better way.

By the action of his own desires, through all its by-products of evil, man was made part mother; and so both man and woman were enabled to become human. It was an essential step in our racial progress, a means to an end. It should not be considered as an extreme maternal sacrifice, but as a novel and thorough system of paternal sacrifice,—the male of genus homo coerced by sex-necessity into the expression of maternal energy. The naturally destructive tendencies of the male have been gradually subverted to the conservative tendencies of the female, and this so palpably that the process is plainly to be observed throughout history. Into the male have been bred, by natural selection and unbroken training, the instincts and habits of the female, to his immense improvement. The female was dependent upon the male in individual economic relation. She was in a state of helpless slavery. She was treated with unspeakable injustice and cruelty. But nature's processes go on quite undisturbed among incidents like these. To blend the opposing sex-tendencies of two animals into the fruitful powers of a triumphant race was a painful process, but that does not matter. It was essential, and it has been fulfilled. There should be an end to the bitterness of feeling which has arisen between the sexes in this century. Right as is the change of attitude in the woman of to-day, she need feel no resentment as to the past, no shame, no sense of wrong. With a full knowledge of the initial superiority of her sex and the sociological necessity for its temporary subversion, she should feel only a deep and tender pride in the long patient ages during which she has waited and suffered, that man might slowly rise to full racial equality with her. She could afford to wait. She could afford to suffer.

It is high time that women began to understand their true position, primarily and eternally, and to see how little the long years of oppression have altered it. It was not well for the race to have the conservative processes of life so wholly confined to the female, the male being merely a temporary agent in reproduction and of no further use. His size, strength, and ferocity — admirable qualities in maintaining the life of an individual animal — were not the most desirable to develope the human race. We needed most the quality of co-ordination, — the facility in union, the power to make and to save rather than to spend and to destroy. These were female qualities. Acting from his own nature, man could not manifest traits that he did not possess.

Throned as woman's master, chained as her servant, he has, through this strange combination of functions, acquired these traits under the heavy law of necessity. Originally, the two worked on divers lines, he spending and scattering, she saving and building. She was the deep, steady, main stream of life, and he the active variant, helping to widen and change that life, but rather as an adjunct than as an essential. Races there were and are which reproduce themselves without the masculine organism, — by hermaphroditism and parthenogenesis.

As the evolution of species progressed, we find a long series of practical experiments in males, — very tiny, transient, and inferior devices at first, but gradually developed into fuller and fuller equality with the female. In some of the lower forms, as in rotifers, insects, and crustaceans, are found the most inferior males, often none at all; and, where they do exist, they have no use save as an agent in reproduction. The most familiar instance of this is among the bees, where the drone, after fulfilling his functions, dies or is destroyed by the sturdy co-mothers of the hive. The common spider, too, has a tiny male, who tremblingly achieves his one brief purpose, and is then eaten up by his mate.

She is the spider, a permanent flycatcher. He is merely a fertilizing agent. The little green aphis, so numerous on our rose-bushes, can reproduce parthenogenetically so long as conditions are good,—while it is warm and there is enough to eat; but, when conditions grow hard, males are developed, and the dual method of reproduction is introduced.

In the two great activities of life, self-preservation and race-preservation, the female in these lower species is better equipped than the male for the first, and carries almost the whole burden of the second. His short period of functional use is as nothing compared to her long period of gestation, and the services she performs, in many cases, in providing for her young after their birth. Race-preservation has been almost entirely a female function, sometimes absolutely so. But it has been proven better for the race to have two highly developed parents rather than to have one. Therefore, sexual equality has been slowly evolved, not only by increasing the importance of the male element in reproduction, but by developing race-qualities in the male, so long merely a reproductive agent. The last step of this process has been the elevation of the male of genus homo to full racial equality with the female, and this has involved her temporary subjection. Both her physical and psychical tendencies have been transplanted into the organism of the male. He has been made the working mother of the world. The sexuo-economic relation was necessary to raise and broaden, to deepen and sweeten, to make more feminine, and so more human, the male of the human race. If the female had remained in full personal freedom and activity, she would have remained superior to him, and both would have remained stationary. Since the female had not the tendency to vary which distinguished the male, it was essential that the expansive forces of masculine energy be combined with the preservative and constructive forces of feminine energy. The expansive and variable male energy, struggling under its new necessity for constructive labor, has caused that labor to vary and progress more than it would have done in feminine hands alone. Out of her wealth of power and patience, liking to work, to give, she toils on forever in the same primitive industries. He, impatient of obstacles, not liking to work, desirous to get rather than to give, splits his task into a thousand specialties, and invents countless ways to lighten his labors. Male energy made to expend itself in performing female functions is what has brought our industries to their present development. Without the economic dependence of the female, the male would still be merely the hunter and fighter, the killer, the destroyer; and she would continue to be the industrious mother, without change or progress.

> "What the children of Israel delighted in making
> The children of Egypt delighted in breaking,"

runs the old rhyme; but there is small gain in such a process. In her subordinate position, under every disadvantage, through the very walls of her prison, the constructive force of woman has made man its instrument, and worked for the upbuilding of the world. As his energy was purely individualistic, and only to be controlled by the power of sex-attraction, it needed precisely this form of union, with its peculiar exaggeration of sex-faculty, to hold him to his task. Woman's abnormal development of sex, restrained and imprisoned by every law, has acted like a coiled spring upon the only free agent in society,— man. Under its intense stimulus he has moved mountains. All the world has seen it; and we have always murmured admiringly, "Oh, 'tis love, 'tis love, 'tis love that makes the world go round." It has done so, indeed, or, at least, has driven man round the world in one long range of struggle and conquest, of work and war. And every man who loves, and says, "I am yours: do with me what you will," knows the power, and honors it.

Human development thus far has proceeded in the male line, under the force of male energy, spurred by sex-stimulus, and by the vast storage battery of female energy suppressed. Women can well afford their period of subjection for the sake of a conquered world, a civilized man. In spite of the agony of the process, the black, long ages of shame and pain and horror, women should remember that they are still here; and, thanks to the blessed power of heredity, they are not so far aborted that a few generations of freedom will not set them abreast of the age. When the centuries of slavery and dishonor, of torture and death, of biting injustice and slow, suffocating repression, seem long to women, let them remember the geologic ages, the millions and millions of years when puny, pygmy, parasitic males struggled for existence, and were used or not, as it happened, like a half-tried patent medicine. What train of wives and concubines was ever so ignominiously placed as the extra husbands carried among the scales of the careful female cirriped, lest she lose one or two! What neglect of faded wives can compare with the scorned, unnoticed death of the drone bee, starved, stung, shut out, walled up in wax, kept only for his momentary sex-function, and not absolutely necessary for that! What Bluebeard tragedy or cruelty of bride-murdering Eastern king can emulate the ruthless slaughter of the hapless little male spider, used by his ferocious mate "to coldly furnish forth a marriage breakfast"! Never once in the history of humanity has any outrage upon women compared with these sweeping sacrifices of helpless males in earlier species. The female has been dominant for the main duration of life on earth. She has been easily equal always up to our own race; and in our race she has been subjugated to the male during the earlier period of development for such enormous racial gain, such beautiful and noble uses, that the sacrifice should never be mentioned nor thought of by a womanhood that knows its power. For the upbuilding of human life on earth she could afford to have her own held back; and — closer, tenderer, lovelier service — for the raising of her fierce sex-mate to a free and gentle brotherhood, for the uplifting of the human soul in her dear son, she could have borne not only this, but more, — borne it smilingly, ungrudgingly, gladly, for his sake and the world's.

And now that the long strain is over, now that the time has come when neither he nor the world is any longer benefited by her subordination, now that she is coming steadily out into direct personal expression, into the joy of racial action in full freedom, of power upon the throne instead of behind it, it is unworthy of this supreme new birth to waste one regret upon the pain that had to be.

Thus it may be seen that, even allowing for the injury to the individual and to society through the check to race-development and the increase of sex-development in woman, with its transmitted effects; allowing, further, that our highly specialized motherhood cannot be shown to be an advantage to humanity, — still it remains true that our sexuo-economic relation, with its effect of carrying on human life through the male side only, in activities driven by intensified sex-energy, has reacted to the benefit of the individual and of the race in many ways, as already suggested: in the extension of female function through the male; in the blending of faculties which have resulted in the possibility of our civilization; in the superior fighting power developed in the male, and its effects in race-conquest, military and commercial; in the increased productivity developed by his assumption of maternal function; and by the sex-relation becoming mainly proportioned to his power to pay for it. Even motherhood has been indirectly the gainer in that, although the mother herself has been checked in direct maternal service, serving the race far more through her stimulation of male activities than through any activities of her own; yet the child has ultimately profited more by the materno-paternal services than he would have done by the maternal services alone.

All this may be granted as having been true in the past. And many, reassured by this frank admission, will ask, if it is so clear that the subjection of woman was useful, that this evil-working, monstrous sexuo-economic relation was after all of racial advantage, how we know that it is time to change. Principally, because we are changing. Social development is not caused by the promulgators of theories and by the writers of books. When Rousseau wrote of equality, free France was being born, — the spirit of the times thrilled through the human mind; and those who had ears to hear heard, those who had pens to write wrote. The condition of chattel slavery, working to its natural end, roused Garrison and Phillips and Harriet Beecher Stowe. They did not make the movement. The period of women's economic dependence is drawing to a close, because its racial usefulness is wearing out. We have already reached a stage of human relation where we feel the strength of social duty pull against the sex-ties that have been for so long the only ties that we have recognized. The common consciousness of humanity, the sense of social need and social duty, is making itself felt in both men and women. The time has come when we are open to deeper and wider impulses than the sex-instinct; the social instincts are strong enough to come into full use at last. This is shown by the twin struggle that convulses the world to-day,—in sex and economics,—the "woman's movement" and the "labor movement." Neither name is wholly correct. Both make a class issue of what is in truth a social issue, a question involving every human interest. But the women naturally feel most the growing healthful pain of their position. They personally revolt, and think it is they who are most to be benefited. Similarly, since the "laboring classes" feel most the growing healthful pain of their position, they as naturally revolt under the same conviction. Sociologically, these conditions, which some find so painful and alarming, mean but one thing,—the increase of social consciousness. The progress of social organization has produced a corresponding degree of individualization, which has reached at last even to women,—even to the lowest grade of unskilled labor. This higher degree of individualization means a sharp personal consciousness of the evils of a situation hitherto little felt. With this higher growth of individual consciousness, and forming a part of it, comes the commensurate growth of social consciousness. We have grown to care for one another.

The woman's movement rests not alone on her larger personality, with its tingling sense of revolt against injustice, but on the wide, deep sympathy of women for one another. It is a concerted movement, based on the recognition of a common evil and seeking a common good. So with the labor movement. It is not alone that the individual laborer is a better educated, more highly developed man than the stolid peasant of earlier days, but also that with this keener personal consciousness has come the wider social consciousness, without which no class can better its conditions. The traits incident to our sexuo-economic relation have developed till they forbid the continuance of that relation. In the economic world, excessive masculinity, in its fierce competition and primitive individualism; and excessive femininity, in its inordinate consumption and hindering conservatism; have reached a stage where they work more evil than good.

The increasing specialization of the modern woman, acquired by inheritance from the ceaselessly specializing male, makes her growing racial faculties strain against the primitive restrictions of a purely sexual relation. The desire to produce — the distinctive human quality — is no longer satisfied with a status that allows only reproduction. In our present stage of social evolution it is increasingly difficult and painful for women to endure their condition of economic dependence, and therefore they are leaving it. This does not mean that at a given day all women will stand forth free together, but that in slowly gathering numbers, now so great that all the world can see, women in the most advanced races are so standing free. Great advances along social lines come slowly, like the many-waved progress of the tide: they are not sudden jumps over yawning chasms.

But, besides this first plain perception that our strange relation is coming to an end, we may see how in its own working it developes forces which must end it or us. The method of action of our peculiar cat's-paw combination of the sexes — the mother-father doing the work of the helpless creature he carries on his back; the parasite mate devouring even when she should most feed — has been this, as repeatedly shown: because of sex-desire the male subjugates the female. Lest he lose her, he feeds her, and, perforce, her young. She, obtaining food through the sex-relation, becomes over-sexed, and acts with constantly increasing stimulus on his sex-activities; and, as these activities are made economic by their relation, she so stimulates industry and all progress. But, — and here is the natural end of an unnatural position, a position that serves its purpose for a time, but holds in itself the seeds of its own destruction, — through the unchecked sex-energy, accumulated under the abnormal pressure of the economic side of the relation, such excess is developed as tends to destroy both individual and race; and such psychic qualities are developed as tend also to our injury and extinction.

A relation that inevitably produces abnormal development cannot be permanently maintained. The intensification of sex-energy as a social force results in such limitless exaggeration of sex-instinct as finds expression sexually in the unnatural vices of advanced civilization, and, socially, in the strained economic relation between producer and consumer which breaks society in two. The sexuo-economic relation serves to bring social development to a certain level. After that level is reached, a higher relation must be adopted, or the lifting process comes to an end; and either the race succumbs to the morbid action of its own forces or some fresher race comes in, and begins the course of social evolution anew.

Under the stimulus of the sexuo-economic relation, one civilization after another has climbed up and fallen down in weary succession. It remains for us to develope a newer, better form of sex-relation and of economic relation therewith, and so to grasp the fruits of all previous civilizations, and grow on to the beautiful results of higher ones. The true and lasting social progress, beyond that which we have yet made, is based on a spirit of inter-human love, not merely the inter-sexual; and it requires an economic machinery organized and functioned for human needs, not sexual ones. The sexuo-economic relation drives man up to where he can become fully human. It deepens and develops the human soul until it is able to conceive and fulfil the larger social uses in which our further life must find expression. But, unless the human soul sees these new forces, feels them, gives way to them in loyal service, it fails to reach

the level from which all further progress must
proceed, and falls back. Again and again
society has so risen, so failed to grasp new
duties, so fallen back.

To-day it will not so fall again, because
the social consciousness is at last so vital a
force in both men and women that we feel
clearly that our human life cannot be fully
lived on sex-lines only. We are so far individualized, so far socialized, that men can
work without the tearing spur of exaggerated
sex-stimulus, work for some one besides mate
and young; and women can love and serve
without the slavery of economic dependence,
— love better and serve more. Sex-stimulus
begins and ends in individuals. The social
spirit is a larger thing, a better thing, and
brings with it a larger, nobler life than we
could ever know on a sex-basis solely.

Moreover, it should be distinctly understood,
as it is already widely and vaguely felt, that
the higher development of social life following the economic independence of women
makes possible a higher sex-life than has ever
yet been known. As fast as the human individual rises in social progress to a certain
degree of development, so fast this primitive
form of sex-union chafes and drags: it is felt
to be unsatisfying and injurious. This is a

marked feature in modern life. The long, sure, upward trend of the human race toward monogamous marriage is no longer helped, but hindered by the economic side of the relation. The best marriage is between the best individuals; and the best individuals of both sexes to-day are increasingly injured by the economic basis of our marriage, which produces and maintains those qualities in men and women and their resultant industrial conditions which make marriage more difficult and precarious every day.

The woman's movement, then, should be hailed by every right-thinking, far-seeing man and woman as the best birth of our century. The banner advanced proclaims "equality before the law," woman's share in political freedom; but the main line of progress is and has been toward economic equality and freedom. While life exists on earth, the economic conditions must underlie and dominate each existing form and its activities; and social life is no exception. A society whose economic unit is a sex-union can no more develope beyond a certain point industrially than a society like the patriarchal, whose political unit was a sex-union, could develope beyond a certain point politically.

The last freeing of the individual makes

possible the last combination of individuals. While sons must bend to the will of a patriarchal father, no democracy is possible. Democracy means, requires, is, individual liberty. While the sexuo-economic relation makes the family the centre of industrial activity, no higher collectivity than we have to-day is possible. But, as women become free, economic, social factors, so becomes possible the full social combination of individuals in collective industry. With such freedom, such independence, such wider union, becomes possible also a union between man and woman such as the world has long dreamed of in vain.

VIII.

In the face of so vital and radical a change
in human life as this change of economic base
in the position of women, it is well to call
attention more at length to the illustrations
of every-day facts in our common lives, which
he who runs may read, if he knows how to
read.   We do not, as a rule, know how to read
the most important messages to humanity,—
the signs of the times.   Historic crises, which
have been slowly maturing, burst upon us in
sudden birth before the majority of the people
imagine that anything is going on.   The first
gun fired at Fort Sumter was an extreme surprise to most of the citizens of the Union.
The Boston Tea Party was, no doubt, an unaccountable piece of insolence to many
worthy Britons.   When "the deluge" did
pour over the *noblesse* of France, few had been
really foreseeing enough to avoid it.

Fortunately, the laws of social evolution do
not wait for our recognition or acceptance:
they go straight on.   And this greater and
more important change than the world has
ever seen, this slow emergence of the long-
subverted human female to full racial equality,
has been going on about us full long enough to
be observed.   It is seen more prominently in

this country than in any other, for many reasons.

The Anglo-Saxon blood, that English mixture of which Tennyson sings, — "Saxon and Norman and Dane though we be,"— is the most powerful expression of the latest current of fresh racial life from the north, — from those sturdy races where the women were more like men, and the men no less manly because of it. The strong, fresh spirit of religious revolt in the new church that protested against and broke loose from the old, woke and stirred the soul of woman as well as the soul of man, and in the equality of martyrdom the sexes learned to stand side by side. Then, in the daring and exposure, the strenuous labor and bitter hardship of the pioneer life of the early settlers, woman's very presence was at a premium; and her labor had a high economic value. Sexdependence was almost unfelt. She who moulded the bullets, and loaded the guns while the men fired them, was co-defender of the home and young. She who carded and dyed and wove and spun was co-provider for the family. Men and women prayed together, worked together, and fought together in comparative equality. More than all, the development of democracy has brought to us the fullest individualization that the world has ever seen. Although politically expressed by men alone, the character it has produced is inherited by their daughters. The Federal Democracy in its organic union, reacting upon individuals, has so strengthened, freed, emboldened, the human soul in America that we have thrown off slavery, and with the same impulse have set in motion the long struggle toward securing woman's fuller equality before the law.

This struggle has been carried on unflaggingly for fifty years, and fast nears its victorious end. It is not only in the four States where full suffrage is exercised by both sexes, nor in the twenty-four where partial suffrage is given to women, that we are to count progress; but in the changes legal and social, mental and physical, which mark the advance of the mother of the world toward her full place. Have we not all observed the change even in size of the modern woman, with its accompanying strength and agility? The Gibson Girl and the Duchess of Towers,[7]—these are the new women; and they represent a noble type, indeed. The heroines of romance and drama to-day are of a different sort from the Evelinas and Arabellas of the last century. Not only do they look differently, they behave differently. The false sentimentality, the false delicacy, the false modesty, the utter falseness of elaborate compliment and servile gallantry which went with the other falsehoods,—all these are disappearing. Women are growing honester, braver, stronger, more healthful and skilful and able and free, more human in all ways.

The change in education is in large part a cause of this, and progressively a consequence. Day by day the bars go down. More and more the field lies open for the mind of woman to glean all it can, and it has responded most eagerly. Not only our pupils, but our teachers, are mainly women. And the clearness and strength of the brain of the woman prove continually the injustice of the clamorous contempt long poured upon what was scornfully called " the female mind." There is no female mind. The brain is not an organ of sex. As well speak of a female liver.

Woman's progress in the arts and sciences, the trades and professions, is steady; but it is most unwise to claim from these relative advances the superiority of women to men, or even their equality, in these fields. What is more to the purpose and easily to be shown is the superiority of the women of to-day to those of earlier times, the immense new development of racial qualities in the sex. No modern proverbs, if we expressed ourselves in proverbs now, would speak with such sweeping, unbroken contumely of the women of to-day as did those unerring exhibitors of popular feeling in former times.

The popular thought of our day is voiced in fiction, fluent verse, and an incessant play of humor. By what is freely written by most authors and freely read by most people is shown our change in circumstances and change in feeling. In old romances the woman was nothing save beautiful, high-born, virtuous, and perhaps "accomplished." She did nothing but love and hate, obey or disobey, and be handed here and there among villain, hero, and outraged parent, screaming, fainting, or bursting into floods of tears as seemed called for by the occasion.

In the fiction of to-day women are continually taking larger place in the action of the story. They are given personal characteristics beyond those of physical beauty. And they are no longer content simply to *be*: they *do*. They are showing qualities of bravery, endurance, strength, foresight, and power for the swift execution of well - conceived plans. They have ideas and purposes of their own; and even when, as in so many cases described by the more reactionary novelists, the efforts of the heroine are shown to be entirely futile, and she comes back with a rush to the self-effacement of marriage with economic dependence, still the efforts were there. Disapprove as he may, use his art to oppose and contemn as he may, the true novelist is forced to chronicle the distinctive features of his time; and no feature is more distinctive of this time than the increasing individualization of women. With lighter touch, but with equally unerring truth, the wit and humor of the day show the same development. The majority of our current jokes on women turn on their "newness," their advance.

No sociological change equal in importance to this clearly marked improvement of an entire sex has ever taken place in one century. Under it all, the *crux* of the whole matter, goes on the one great change, that of the economic relation. This follows perfectly natural lines. Just as the development of machinery constantly lowers the importance of mere brute strength of body and raises that of mental power and skill, so the pressure of industrial conditions demands an ever-higher specialization, and tends to break up that relic of the patriarchal age,— the family as an economic unit.

Women have been led under pressure of

necessity into a most reluctant entrance upon fields of economic activity. The sluggish and greedy disposition bred of long ages of dependence has by no means welcomed the change. Most women still work only as they "have to," until they can marry and "be supported." Men, too, liking the power that goes with money, and the poor quality of gratitude and affection bought with it, resent and oppose the change; but all this disturbs very little the course of social progress.

A truer spirit is the increasing desire of young girls to be independent, to have a career of their own, at least for a while, and the growing objection of countless wives to the pitiful asking for money, to the beggary of their position. More and more do fathers give their daughters, and husbands their wives, a definite allowance,— a separate bank account,— something which they can play is all their own. The spirit of personal independence in the women of to-day is sure proof that a change has come.

For a while the introduction of machinery which took away from the home so many industries deprived woman of any importance as an economic factor; but presently she arose, and followed her lost wheel and loom to their new place, the mill. To-day there is hardly an industry in the land in which some women are not found. Everywhere throughout America are women workers outside the unpaid labor of the home, the last census giving three million of them. This is so patent a fact, and makes itself felt in so many ways by so many persons, that it is frequently and widely discussed. Without here going into its immediate advantages or disadvantages from an industrial point of view, it is merely instanced as an undeniable proof of the radical change in the economic position of women that is advancing upon us. She is assuming new relations from year to year before our eyes; but we, seeing all social facts from a personal point of view, have failed to appreciate the nature of the change.

Consider, too, the altered family relation which attends this movement. Entirely aside from the strained relation in marriage, the other branches of family life feel the strange new forces, and respond to them. "When I was a girl," sighs the gray-haired mother, "we sisters all sat and sewed while mother read to us. Now every one of my daughters has a different club!" She sighs, be it observed. We invariably object to changed conditions in those departments of life where we have established ethical values. For all the

daughters to sew while the mother read aloud
to them was esteemed right; and, therefore, the
radiating diffusion of daughters among clubs
is esteemed wrong, — a danger to home life.
In the period of the common sewing and reading the women so assembled were closely
allied in industrial and intellectual development as well as in family relationship. They
all could do the same work, and liked to do it.
They all could read the same book, and liked
to read it. (And reading, half a century ago,
was still considered half a virtue and the
other half a fine art.) Hence the ease with
which this group of women entered upon their
common work and common pleasure.

The growing individualization of democratic
life brings inevitable change to our daughters
as well as to our sons. Girls do not all like
to sew, many do not know how. Now to sit
sewing together, instead of being a harmonizing process, would generate different degrees
of restlessness, of distaste, and of nervous
irritation. And, as to the reading aloud, it is
not so easy now to choose a book that a well-
educated family of modern girls and their
mother would all enjoy together. As the race
become more specialized, more differentiated,
the simple lines of relation in family life draw
with less force, and the more complex lines of

relation in social life draw with more force; and this is a perfectly natural and desirable process for women as well as for men.

It may be suggested, in passing, that one of the causes of "Americanitis" is this increasing nervous strain in family relation, acting especially upon woman. As she becomes more individualized, she suffers more from the primitive and indifferentiated conditions of the family life of earlier times. What "a wife" and "a mother" was supposed to find perfectly suitable, this newly specialized wife and mother, who is also a personality, finds clumsy and ill-fitting,—a mitten where she wants a glove. The home cares and industries, still undeveloped, give no play for her increasing specialization. Where the embryonic combination of cook - nurse - laundress - chambermaid-housekeeper - waitress - governess was content to be "jack of all trades" and mistress of none, the woman who is able to be one of these things perfectly, and by so much less able to be all the others, suffers doubly from not being able to do what she wants to do, and from being forced to do what she does not want to do. To the delicately differentiated modern brain the jar and shock of changing from trade to trade a dozen times a day is a distinct injury, a waste of nervous force. With the larger socialization of the woman of to-day, the fitness for and accompanying desire for wider combinations, more general interest, more organized methods of work for larger ends, she feels more and more heavily the intensely personal limits of the more primitive home duties, interests, methods. And this pain and strain must increase with the advance of women until the new functional power makes to itself organic expression, and the belated home industries are elevated and organized, like the other necessary labors of modern life.

In the meantime, however, the very best and foremost women suffer most; and a heavy check is placed on social progress by this difficulty in enlarging old conditions to suit new powers. It should still be remembered it is not the essential relations of wife and mother which are thus injurious, but the industrial conditions born of the economic dependence of the wife and mother, and hitherto supposed to be part of her functions. The change we are making does not in any way militate against the true relations of the family, marriage, and parentage, but only against those sub-relations belonging to an earlier period and now in process of extinction. The family as an entity, an economic and social unit, does not

hold as it did. The ties between brother
and sister, cousins and relatives generally, are
gradually lessening their hold, and giving
way under pressure of new forces which tend
toward better things.

The change is more perceptible among
women than among men, because of the longer
survival of more primitive phases of family
life in them. One of its most noticeable
features is the demand in women not only for
their own money, but for their own work for
the sake of personal expression. Those who
object to women's working on the ground that
they should not compete with men or be
forced to struggle for existence look only at
work as a means of earning money. They
should remember that human labor is an exercise of faculty, without which we should cease
to be human; that to do and to make not only
gives deep pleasure, but is indispensable to
healthy growth. Few girls to-day fail to manifest some signs of this desire for individual expression. It is not only in the classes who are
forced to it: even among the rich we find
this same stirring of normal race-energy. To
carve in wood, to hammer brass, to do "art
dressmaking," to raise mushrooms in the
cellar,— our girls are all wanting to do something individually. It is a most healthy state,

and marks the development of race-distinction in women with a corresponding lowering of sex-distinction to its normal place.

In body and brain, wherever she touches life, woman is changing gloriously from the mere creature of sex, all her race-functions held in abeyance, to the fully developed human being, none the less true woman for being more truly human. What alarms and displeases us in seeing these things is our funny misconception that race-functions are masculine. Much effort is wasted in showing that women will become "unsexed" and "masculine" by assuming these human duties. We are told that a slight sex-distinction is characteristic of infancy and old age, and that the assumption of opposite traits by either sex shows either a decadent or an undeveloped condition. The young of any race are less marked by sex-distinction; and in old age the distinguishing traits are sometimes exchanged, as in the crowing of old hens and in the growing of the beard on old women. And we are therefore assured that the endeavor of women to perform these masculine economic functions marks a decadent civilization, and is greatly to be deprecated. There would be some reason in this objection if the common racial activities of humanity, into which women are now so eagerly entering, were masculine functions. But they are not. There is no more sublimated expression of our morbid ideas of sex-distinction than in this complacent claiming of all human life-processes as sex-functions of the male. "Masculine" and "feminine" are only to be predicated of reproductive functions, — processes of race-preservation. The processes of self-preservation are racial, peculiar to the species, but common to either sex.

If it could be shown that the women of to-day were growing beards, were changing as to pelvic bones, were developing bass voices, or that in their new activities they were manifesting the destructive energy, the brutal combative instinct, or the intense sex-vanity of the male, then there would be cause for alarm. But the one thing that has been shown in what study we have been able to make of women in industry is that they are women still, and this seems to be a surprise to many worthy souls. A female horse is no less female than a female starfish, but she has more functions. She can do more things, is a more highly specialized organism, has more intelligence, and, with it all, is even more feminine in her more elaborate and farther-reaching processes of reproduction. So the

" new woman " will be no less female than the
" old " woman, though she has more functions,
can do more things, is a more highly specialized organism, has more intelligence. She
will be, with it all, more feminine, in that
she will develope far more efficient processes
of caring for the young of the human race than
our present wasteful and grievous method, by
which we lose fifty per cent. of them, like a
codfish. The average married pair, says the
scientific dictator, in all sobriety, should have
four children merely to preserve our present
population, two to replace themselves and two
to die, — a pleasant method this, and redound-
ing greatly to the credit of our motherhood.

The rapid extension of function in the
modern woman has nothing to do with any
exchange of masculine and feminine traits : it
is simply an advance in human development of
traits common to both sexes, and is wholly
good in its results. No one who looks at the
life about us can fail to see the alteration
going on. It is a pity that we so fail to estimate its value. On the other hand, the
growth and kindling intensity of the social
consciousness among us all is as conspicuous
a feature of modern life as the change in
woman's position, and closely allied therewith.

Never before have people cared so much

about other people. From its first expression in greater kindliness and helpfulness toward individual human beings to its last expression in the vague, blind, groping movements toward international justice and law, the heart of the world is alive and stirring to-day. The whole social body is affected with sudden shudders of feeling over some world calamity or world rejoicing. When the message of "Uncle Tom's Cabin" ran from heart to heart around the world, kindling a streak of fire, the fire of human love and sympathy which is latent in us all and longing always for some avenue of common expression, it proved that in every civilized land of our time the people are of one mind on some subjects. Nothing could have so spread and so awakened a response in the Periclean, the Augustan, or even the Elizabethan age; for humanity was not then so far socialized and so far individualized as to be capable of such a general feeling.

Invention and the discoveries of science are steadily unifying the world to-day. The statement is frequently advanced that the minds of the men of Greece or of the great thinkers of the Middle Ages were stronger and larger than the minds of the men of to-day. Perhaps they were. So were the bodies of the megatherium and the ichthyosaurus stronger and larger than the bodies of the animals of to-day. Yet they were lower in the scale of organic evolution. The ability of the individual is not so much the criterion of social progress as that organic relation of individuals which makes the progress of each available to all. Emerson has done more for America than Plato could do for Greece. Indeed, Plato has done more for America than he could do for Greece, because the printing-press and the public school have made thought more freely and easily transmissible.

Human progress lies in the perfecting of the social organization, and it is here that the changes of our day are most marked. Whereas, in more primitive societies, injuries were only felt by the individual as they affected his own body or direct personal interests, and later his own nation or church, to-day there is a growing sensitiveness to social injuries, even to other nations. The civilized world has suffered in Armenia's agony,[8] even though the machinery of social expression is yet unable fully to carry out the social feeling or the social will. Function comes before organ always; and the human heart and mind, which are the social heart and mind, must feel and think long before the social body can act in full expression.

162

Social sympathy and thought are growing more intense and active every day. In our cumbrous efforts at international arbitration, in the half-hearted alliances and agreements between great peoples, in the linking of humanity together across ocean and mountain and desert plain by steam and electricity, in the establishment of such world-functions as the international postal service,— in these, externally, our social unity has begun to act. In the more familiar field of personal life, who has not seen how unceasingly many of us are occupied in the interests of the community, even to the injury of our own? The rising manifestations of social interest among women were covered with ridicule at first, through such characters as Mrs. Jellyby or Mrs. Pardiggle, although a few women who were so great and so identified with religion and philanthropy as to command respect, women like the saintly Elizabeth Fry,[9] Florence Nightingale, and Clara Barton, escaped. But both belong to the same age, are part of the same phenomena. To-day there is hardly a woman of intelligence in all America, to say nothing of other countries, who is not definitely and actively concerned in some social interest, who does not recognize some duty besides those incident to her own blood relationship.

The woman's club movement is one of the most important sociological phenomena of the century,— indeed, of all centuries,— marking as it does the first timid steps toward social organization of these so long unsocialized members of our race. Social life is absolutely conditioned upon organization. The military organizations which promote peace, the industrial organizations which maintain life, and all the educational, religious, and charitable organizations which serve our higher needs constitute the essential factors of that social activity in which, as individuals, we live and grow; and it is plain, therefore, that while women had no part in these organizations they had no part in social life. Their main relation to society was an individual one, an animal one, a sexual one. They produced the people of whom society was made, but they were not society. Of course, they were indispensable in this capacity; but one might as well call food a part of society because people could not exist without eating as to call women a social factor because people could not exist without being born. Women have made the people who made the world, and will always continue so to do. But they have heretofore had a most insignificant part in the world their sons have made.

The only form of organization possible to
women was for long the celibate religious
community. This has always been dear to
them; and, as to-day many avoid undesired
marriage for the sake of "independence," so
in earlier times many fled from undesired
marriage to the communal independence of the
convent. The fondness of women for the
church has been based, not only on religious
feeling, but on the force of the human longing
for co-ordinate interest and activities; and
only here could this be gratified. In the
church at least they could be together. They
could feel in common and act in common,—
the deepest human joy. As the church has
widened its activities, it has found everywhere
in women its most valuable and eager workers.
To labor together, together to raise funds for
a common end, for a new building or a new
minister, for local charities or for foreign
missions,— but to labor together, and for
other needs than those of the family relation,
— this has always met glad response from the
struggling human soul in woman. When it
became possible to work together for other
than religious ends,— when large social service
was made possible to women, as in our sanitary
commission during the last war,— women
everywhere rose to meet the need. The rise

and spread of that greatest of women's organizations, the Woman's Christian Temperance Union, has shown anew how ready is the heart of woman to answer the demands of other than personal relations.

And now the whole country is budding into women's clubs. The clubs are uniting and federating by towns, States, nations: there are even world organizations. The sense of human unity is growing daily among women. Not to see it is impossible. Not to watch with pleasure and admiration this new growth in social life, this sudden and enormous re-enforcement of our best forces from the very springs of life, only shows how blind we are to true human advantage, how besotted in our fondness for sex-distinction in excess.

One of the most valuable features of this vast line of progress is the new heroism it is pouring into life. The crumbling and flattening of ambitions and ideals under pressure of our modern business life is a patent fact. We are growing to surrender taste and conscience and honor itself to the demands of business success, prostituting the noblest talents to the most ignoble uses with that last excuse of cowardice, —"A man must live." Into this phase of life comes a new spirit, — the spirit of such women as Elizabeth Cady

Stanton and Susan B. Anthony; of Dr. Elizabeth Blackwell and her splendid sisterhood; of all the women who have battled and suffered for half a century, forcing their way, with sacrifices never to be told, into the field of freedom so long denied them,— not for themselves alone, but for one another. We have loudly cried out at the injury to the home and family which are supposed to follow such a course. We have unsparingly ridiculed the unattractive and unfeminine among these vanguard workers. But few have thought what manner of spirit it must take to leave the dear old easy paths so long trodden by so many feet, and go to hew out new ones alone. The nature of the effort involved and the nature of the opposition incurred conduced to lessen the soft charms and graces of the ultra-feminine state; but the women who follow and climb swiftly up the steps which these great leaders so laboriously built may do the new work in the new places, and still keep much of what these strenuous heroes had to lose.

It is not being a doctor that makes a woman unwomanly, but the treatment which the first women medical students and physicians received was such as to make even men unmanly. That time is largely past. The gates are nearly all open, at least in some places; and the racial activities of women are free to develope as rapidly as the nature of the case will allow. The main struggle now is with the distorted nature of the creature herself. Grand as are the women who embody at whatever cost the highest spirit of the age, there still remains to us the heavy legacy of the years behind,— the innumerable weak and little women, with the aspirations of an affectionate guinea pig. The soul of woman must speak through the long accumulations of her intensified sex-nature, through the uncertain impulses of a starved and thwarted class. She must recognize that she is handicapped. She must understand her difficulty, and meet it bravely and firmly.

But this is a matter for personal volition, for subjective consciousness. The thing to see and to rejoice in is that, with and without their conscious volition, with or without the approval and assistance of men, in spite of that crowning imbecility of history,— the banded opposition of some women to the advance of the others,— the female of our race is making sure and rapid progress in human development.

IX

THE main justification for the subjection of women, which is commonly advanced, is the alleged advantage to motherhood resultant from her extreme specialization to the uses of maternity under this condition.

There are two weak points in this position. One is that the advantage to motherhood cannot be proved: the other, that it is not the uses of maternity to which she is specialized, but the uses of sex-indulgence. So far from the economic dependence of women working in the interests of motherhood, it is the steadily acting cause of a pathological maternity and a decreasing birth-rate.

In simple early times there was a period when women were economically profited by child-bearing; when, indeed, that was their sole use, and, failing it, they were entitled to no respect or profit whatever. Such a condition tended to increase the quantity of children, if not the quality. With industrial development and the increasing weight of economic cares upon the shoulders of the man, children come to be looked upon as a burden, and are dreaded instead of desired by the hard-worked father. They subtract from the family income; and the mother, absolutely dependent

upon that income and also overworked in her
position of unpaid house-servant, is not impelled to court maternity by any economic
pressure. In the working classes — to which
the great majority of people belong — the
woman is by no means "segregated to the
uses of maternity." Among the most intelligent and conscientious workingmen to-day
there is a strong feeling against large families,
and a consistent effort is made to prevent
them.

Lest this be considered as not bearing directly upon the economic position of women,
but rather on the general status of the working classes, let us examine the same condition
among the wealthy. It is here that the economic dependence of women is carried to its
extreme. The daughters and wives of the rich
fail to perform even the domestic service expected of the women of poorer families. They
are from birth to death absolutely non-productive in goods or labor of economic value, and
consumers of such goods and labor to an extent
limited only by the purchasing power of their
male relatives. In this condition the economic advantage of the woman, married or
unmarried, not merely in food and clothes,
but in such social advantage as she desires, lies
in her power to attract and hold the devotion

of men; and this power is not the power of maternity. On the contrary, maternity, by lowering the personal charms and occupying the time of the mother, fails to bring her the pleasure and profit obtainable by the woman who is not a mother. It is through the sex-relation minus its natural consequence that she profits most; and, therefore, the force of economic advantage acts against maternity instead of toward it.

In the last extreme this is clear to all in the full flower of the sexuo-economic relation, — prostitution, than which nothing runs more absolutely counter to the improvement of the race through maternity. Specialization to uses of maternity, as in the queen bee, is one thing. Specialization to uses of sex without maternity is quite another. Yet this popular opinion, that we as a race are greatly benefited by having all our women saved from direct economic activity, and so allowed to concentrate all their energies on the beautiful work of motherhood, remains strong among us.

In *The Forum* for November, 1888, Lester F. Ward published a paper called "Our Better Halves," in which was clearly shown the biological supremacy of the female sex. This naturally aroused much discussion; and in an answering article, "Woman's Place in Nat-

ure" (*The Forum*, May, 1889), Mr. Grant
Allen very thoroughly states the general view
on this subject. He says of woman: "I believe it to be true that she is very much less
the race than man; that she is, indeed, not
even half the race at present, but rather a part
of it told specially off for the continuance of
the species, just as truly as drones or male
spiders are parts of their species told off for
the performance of male-functions, or as 'ro-
tund' honey ants are individual insects told
off to act as living honey jars to the community. She is the sex sacrificed to reproductive necessities."

Since biological facts point to the very
gradual introduction and development of the
male organism solely as a reproductive necessity, and since women are sacrificed not to
reproductive necessities, but to a most unnecessary and injurious degree of sex-indulgence
under economic necessity, such a statement as
Mr. Grant Allen's has elements of humor.
The opinion is held, however, not only by the
special students of biology and sociology, but
by the general public, and demands most careful attention. Those holding such a view may
admit the over-development of sex consequent
upon the economic relation between men and
women, and the train of evils, individual

172

and social, following that over-development. They may even admit, further, something of the alleged injury to economic evolution. But they will claim in answer that these morbid conditions are essential to human progress, and that the good to humanity through the segregation of the female to the uses of maternity overbalances the evil, great as this is; also, conversely, that the gain to the individual and to society to be obtained by the economic freedom of the female would be more than offset by the loss to the race caused by the removal of our highly specialized motherhood.

To meet this, it is necessary to show that our highly specialized motherhood is not so advantageous as believed; that it is below rather than above the efficacy of motherhood in other species; that its deficiency is due to the sexuo-economic relation; that the restoration of economic freedom to the female will improve motherhood; and, finally, to indicate in some sort the lines of social and individual development along which this improvement may be "practically" manifested.

In approaching this subject, we need something of special mental preparation. We need to realize that our ideas upon this theme are peculiarly colored by prejudice, that in no other field of thought are we so blinded by our emotions. We have felt more on this subject than on any other, and thought less. We have also felt much on the relation of the sexes; but it has been made a subject of study, of comparison, of speculation. There are differences of feeling on the sex question, but as to motherhood none. Here and there, to be sure, some isolated philosopher, a Plato, a Rousseau, dares advance some thought on this ground; but, on the whole, no theme of commensurate importance has been so little studied. More sacred than religion, more binding than the law, more habitual than methods of eating, we are each and all born into the accepted idea of motherhood and trained in it; and in maturity we hand it down unquestioningly. A man may question the purposes and methods of his God with less danger of outcry against him than if he dare to question the purposes and methods of his mother. This matriolatry is a sentiment so deep-seated, wide-spread, and long-established as to be dominant in every class of minds. It is so associated with our religious instincts, on the one hand, and our sex-instincts, on the other, both of which we have long been forbidden to discuss, — the one being too holy and the other too unholy, —

that it is well-nigh impossible to think clearly
and dispassionately on the subject. It is easy
to understand why we are so triple-plated with
prejudice in the case.

The instinct that draws the child to its
mother is exactly as old as the instinct that
draws the mother to her child; and that dates
back to the period when the young first needed
care,— among the later reptiles, perhaps.
This tie has lasted unbroken through the
whole line of progression, and is stronger with
us than with any other creature, because in
our social evolution the parent is of advantage
to the child not only through its entire life,
but even after death, by our laws of inheritance. So early, so radically important, so
long accumulated an animal instinct, added
to by social law, is a great force. Besides this, we must reckon with our long
period of ancestor worship. This finally
changed the hideous concepts of early idola-
ters into the idea of parental divinity; for,
having first made a god of their father, they
then made a father of God, and this deep
religious feeling has added much to the heavy
weight of instinct. Parental government,
too, absolute in the patriarchal period, has
added further to our devout, blind faith in
parenthood until it is *lèse-majesté* to ques-

tion its right fulfilment. Two most interesting developments are to be noted along this line. One is that the height of filial devotion was reached in the patriarchal age; when the father was the sole governor and feeder of the family, and could slay or sell his child at will; and that this relic of ancestor worship has steadily declined with the extension of government, until, in our democracy, with the fullest development of individual liberty and responsibility, is found the lowest degree of filial reverence and submission. Its place is taken, to our great gain, by such familiar, loving intercourse between parent and child as was utterly incompatible with the grovelling attitude of children in earlier times.

The other is the gradual swing from supreme devotion to the father, "the author of my being," as the child used to consider him, to our modern mother-worship. The dying soldier on the battlefield thinks of his mother, longs for her, not for his father. The traveller and exile dreams of his mother's care, his mother's doughnuts. The pathos of the popular tale to-day is in bringing the prodigal back to his mother, not to his father. If the original prodigal had a mother, she was probably busy in cooking the fatted calf. If to-day's prodigal has a father, he is merely engaged in paying for the veal. Our tenderest love, our deepest reverence, our fiercest resentment of insult, all centre about the mother to-day rather than about the father; and this is a strong proof that the recognition of woman's real power and place in life grow upon us just as our minds grow able to perceive it. Nothing can ever exceed the truth as to the value of the mother. Our instinct is a right one, as all deep-seated social instincts are; but about it has grown up a mass of falsehoods and absurdities such as always tend to confuse and impede the progress of great truths.

As the main agent in reproduction, the mother is most to be venerated on basic physiological grounds. As the main agent in developing love, the great human condition, she is the fountain of all our growth. As the beginner of industry, she is again a source of progress. As the first and final educator, she outwardly moulds what she has inwardly made; and, as she is the visible, tangible, lovable, living type of all this, the being in whose person is expressed the very sum of good to the individual, it is no wonder that our strongest, deepest, tenderest feelings cluster about the great word "mother."

Fully recognizing all this, it yet remains

177

open to us to turn the light of science and the honest labor of thought upon this phase of human life as upon any other; to lay aside our feelings, and use our reason; to discover if even here we are justified in leaving the most important work of individual life to the methods of primitive instinct. Motherhood is but a process of life, and open to study as all processes of life are open. Among unconscious, early forms it fulfils its mission by a simple instinct. In the consciousness and complexity of human life it demands far more numerous and varied forces for its right fulfilment. It is with us a conscious process, — a process rife with consequences for good or evil. With this voluntary power come new responsibility and a need for new methods, — a need not merely to consider whether or not we will enter upon the duties of maternity, but how best we can fulfil them.

Motherhood, like every other natural process, is to be measured by its results. It is good or evil as it serves its purpose. Human motherhood must be judged as it serves its purpose to the human race. Primarily, its purpose is to reproduce the race by reproducing the individual; secondarily, to improve the race by improving the individual. The mere office of reproduction is as well performed by the laying of eggs to be posthumously hatched as by many years of exquisite devotion; but in the improvement of the species we come to other requirements. The functions of motherhood have been evolved as naturally as the functions of nutrition, and each stage of development has brought new duties to the mother. The mother bird must brood her young, the mother cow must suckle them, the mother cat must hunt for them; and, in every varied service which the mother gives, its value is to be measured by its effect upon the young. To perform that which is most good for the young of the species is the measure of right motherhood, and that which is most good for the young is what will help them to a better maturity than that of their parents. To leave in the world a creature better than its parent. this is the purpose of right motherhood.

In the human race this purpose is served by two processes: first, by the simple individual function of reproduction, of which all care and nursing are but an extension; and, second, by the complex social function of education. This was primarily a maternal process, and therefore individual; but it has long since become a racial rather than an individual function, and bears no relation to sex or other personal limitation. The young of the human race require for their best development not only the love and care of the mother, but the care and instruction of many besides their mother. So largely is this true that it may be said' in extreme terms that it would be better for a child to-day to be left absolutely without mother or family of any sort, in the city of Boston, for instance, than to be supplied with a large and affectionate family and be planted with them in Darkest Africa.

Human functions are race-functions, social functions; and education is one of them. The duty of the human mother, and the measure of its right or wrong fulfilment, are to be judged along these two main lines, reproduction and education. As we have no species above us with which to compare our motherhood, we must measure by those below us. We must show improvement upon them in this function which we all hold in common.

Does the human mother succeed better than others of her order, mammalia, in the reproduction of the species? Does she bring forth and rear her young more perfectly than lower mothers? They, being less conscious, act simply under instinct, mating in their season, bringing forth young in their season, nursing, guarding, defending as best they may; and they leave in the world behind them creatures as good, or better, than their mothers. Of wild animals we have few reliable statistics, and of tame ones it is difficult to detach their natural processes from our interference therewith. But in both the simple maintenance of species shows that motherhood at least reproduces fairly well; and in those we breed for our advantage the wonderful possibilities of race-development through this process are made apparent. How do we, with the human brain and the human conscience, rich in the power and wisdom of our dominant race, — how do we, as mothers, compare with our forerunners?

Human motherhood is more pathological than any other, more morbid, defective, irregular, diseased. Human childhood is similarly pathological. We, as animals, are very inferior animals in this particular. When we take credit to ourselves for the sublime devotion with which we face ''the perils of maternity,'' and boast of ''going down to the gates of death '' for our children, we should rather take shame to ourselves for bringing these perils upon both mother and child. The gates of death? They are the gates of life to the unborn; and there is no death there save what we, the mothers, by our unnatural lives, have brought upon our own children. Gates of death, indeed, to the thousands of babies late-born, prematurely born, misborn, and still-born for lack of right motherhood. In the primal physical functions of maternity the human female cannot show that her supposed specialization to these uses has improved her fulfilment of them, rather the opposite. The more freely the human mother mingles in the natural industries of a human creature, as in the case of the savage woman, the peasant woman, the working-woman everywhere who is not overworked, the more rightly she fulfils these functions.

The more absolutely woman is segregated to sex-functions only, cut off from all economic use and made wholly dependent on the sex-relation as means of livelihood, the more pathological does her motherhood become. The over-development of sex caused by her economic dependence on the male reacts unfavorably upon her essential duties. She is too female for perfect motherhood! Her excessive specialization in the secondary sexual characteristics is a detrimental element in heredity. Small, weak, soft, ill-proportioned women do not tend to produce large, strong, sturdy, well-made men or women. When Frederic the Great wanted grenadiers of great size, he married big men to big women,— not to little ones. The female segregated to the uses of sex alone naturally deteriorates in racial development, and naturally transmits that deterioration to her offspring. The human mother, in the processes of reproduction, shows no gain in efficiency over the lower animals, but rather a loss, and so far presents no evidence to prove that her specialization to sex is of any advantage to her young. The mother of a dead baby or the baby of a dead mother; the sick baby, the crooked baby, the idiot baby; the exhausted, nervous, prematurely aged mother,— these are not uncommon among us; and they do not show much progress in our motherhood.

Since we cannot justify the human method of maternity in the physical processes of reproduction, can we prove its advantages in the other branch, education? Though the mother be sickly and the child the same, will not her loving care more than make up for it? Will not the tender devotion of the mother, and her unflagging attendance upon the child, render human motherhood sufficiently successful in comparison with that of other species to justify our peculiar method? We must now show that our motherhood, in its usually accepted sense, the "care" of the child (more accurately described as education), is of a superior nature.

Here, again, we lack the benefit of comparison. No other animal species is required to care for its young so long, to teach it so much. So far as they have it to do, they do it well. The hen with her brood is an accepted model of motherhood in this respect. She not only lays eggs and hatches them, but educates and protects her young so far as it is necessary. But beyond such simple uses as this we have no standard of comparison for educative motherhood. We can only study it among ourselves, comparing the child left motherless with the child mothered, the child with a mother and nothing else with the child whose mother is helped by servants and teachers, the child with what we recognize as a superior mother to the child with an inferior mother. This last distinction, a comparison between mothers, is of great value. We have tacitly formulated a certain vague standard of human motherhood, and loosely apply it, especially in the epithets "natural" and "unnatural" mother.

But these terms again show how prone we still are to consider the whole field of maternal action as one of instinct rather than of reason, as a function rather than a service.

We do have a standard, however, loose and vague as it is; and even by that standard it is painful to see how many human mothers fail. Ask yourselves honestly how many of the mothers whose action toward their children confronts you in street and shop and car and boat, in hotel and boarding-house and neighboring yard, — how many call forth favorable comment compared with those you judge unfavorably? Consider not the rosy ideal of motherhood you have in your mind, but the coarse, hard facts of motherhood as you see them, and hear them, in daily life.

Motherhood in its fulfilment of educational duty can be measured only by its effects. If we take for a standard the noble men and women whose fine physique and character we so fondly attribute to "a devoted mother," what are we to say of the motherhood which has filled the world with the ignoble men and women, of depraved physique and character? If the good mother makes the good man, how about the bad ones? When we see great men and women, we give credit to their mothers. When we see inferior men and women, — and that is a common circumstance, — no one presumes to question the motherhood which has produced them. When it comes to congenital criminality, we are beginning to murmur something about "heredity"; and, to meet gross national ignorance, we do demand a better system of education. But no one presumes to suggest that the mothering of mankind could be improved upon; and yet there is where the responsibility really lies. If our human method of reproduction is defective, let the mother answer. She is the main factor in reproduction. If our human method of education is defective, let the mother answer. She is the main factor in education.

To this it is bitterly objected that such a claim omits the father and his responsibility. When the mother of the world is in her right place and doing her full duty, she will have no ground of complaint against the father. In the first place, she will make better men. In the second, she will hold herself socially responsible for the choice of a right father for her children. In the third place, as an economic free agent, she will do half duty in providing for the child. Men who are not equal to good fatherhood under such conditions will have no chance to become fathers, and will die with general pity instead of living with general condemnation. In his position, doing all the world's work, all the father's, and half the mother's, man has made better shift to achieve the impossible than woman has in hers. She has been supposed to have no work or care on earth save as mother. She has really had the work of the mother and that of the world's house service besides. But she has surely had as much time and strength to give to motherhood as man to fatherhood; and not until she can show that the children of the world are as well mothered as they are well fed can she cast on him the blame for our general deficiency.

There is no personal blame to be laid on either party. The sexuo-economic relation has its inevitable ill-effects on both motherhood and fatherhood. But it is to the mother that the appeal must be made to change this injurious relation. Having the deeper sense of duty to the young, the larger love, she must come to feel how her false position hurts her motherhood, and for her children's sake break away from it. Of man and his fatherhood she can make what she will.

The duty of the mother is first to produce children as good as or better than herself; to hand down the constitution and character of those behind her the better for her stewardship; to build up and improve the human race through her enormous power as mother; to make better people. This being done, it is then the duty of the mother, the human mother, so to educate her children as to complete what bearing and nursing have only begun. She carries the child nine months in her body, two years in her arms, and as long as she lives in her heart and mind. The education of the young is a tremendous factor in human reproduction. A right motherhood should be able to fulfil this great function perfectly. It should understand with an ever-growing power the best methods of developing, strengthening, and directing the child's faculties of body and mind, so that each generation, reaching maturity, would start clear of the last, and show a finer, fuller growth, both physically and mentally, than the preceding. That humanity does slowly improve is not here denied; but, granting our gradual improvement, is it all that we could make? And is the gain due to a commensurate improvement in motherhood?

To both we must say no. When we see how some families improve, while others deteriorate, and how uncertain and irregular is such improvement as appears, we know that we could make better progress if all children had the same rich endowment and wise care that some receive. And, when we see how much of our improvement is due to gains made in hygienic knowledge, in public provision for education and sanitary regulation, none of which has been accomplished by mothers, we are forced to see that whatever advance the race has made is not exclusively attributable to motherhood. The human mother does less for her young, both absolutely and proportionately, than any kind of mother on earth. She does not obtain food for them, nor covering, nor shelter, nor protection, nor defence. She does not educate them beyond the personal habits required in the family circle and in her limited range of social life. The necessary knowledge of the world, so indispensable to every human being, she cannot give, because she does not possess it. All this provision and education are given by other hands and brains than hers. Neither does the amount of physical care and labor bestowed on the child by its mother warrant her claims to superiority in motherhood : this is but a part of our idealism of the subject.

The poor man's wife has far too much of other work to do to spend all her time in waiting on her children. The rich man's wife could do it, but does not, partly because she hires some one to do it for her, and partly because she, too, has other duties to occupy her time. Only in isolated cases do we find a mother deputing all other service to others, and concentrating her energies on feeding, clothing, washing, dressing, and, as far as may be, educating her own child. When such cases are found, it remains to be shown that the child so reared is proportionately benefited by this unremittent devotion of its mother. On the contrary, the best service and education a child can receive involve the accumulated knowledge and exchanged activities of thousands upon thousands besides his mother,—the fathers of the race.

There does not appear, in the care and education of the child as given by the mother, any special superiority in human maternity. Measuring woman first in direct comparison of her reproductive processes with those of other animals, she does not fulfil this function so easily or so well as they. Measuring her educative processes by inter-personal comparison, the few admittedly able mothers with the many painfully unable ones, she seems more lacking, if possible, than in the other branch. The gain in human education thus far has not been acquired or distributed through the mother, but through men and single women; and there is nothing in the achievements of human motherhood to prove that it is for the advantage of the race to have women give all their time to it. Giving all their time to it does not improve it either in quantity or quality. The woman who works is usually a better reproducer than the woman who does not. And the woman who does not work is not proportionately a better educator.

An extra-terrestrial sociologist, studying human life and hearing for the first time of our so-called "maternal sacrifice" as a means of benefiting the species, might be touched and impressed by the idea. "How beautiful!" he would say. "How exquisitely pathetic and tender! One-half of humanity surrendering all other human interests and activities to concentrate its time, strength, and devotion upon the functions of maternity! To bear and rear the majestic race to which they can never fully belong! To live vicariously forever, through their sons, the daughters being only another vicarious link! What a supreme and magnificent martyrdom!" And he would direct his researches toward discovering what system was used to develope and perfect this sublime consecration of half the race to the perpetuation of the other half. He would view with intense and pathetic interest the endless procession of girls, born human as their brothers were, but marked down at once as "female — abortive type — only use to produce males." He would expect to see this "sex sacrificed to reproductive necessities," yet gifted with human consciousness and intelligence, rise grandly to the occasion, and strive to fit itself in every way for its high office. He would expect to find society commiserating the sacrifice, and honoring above all the glorious creature whose life was to be sunk utterly in the lives of others, and using every force properly to rear and fully to fit these functionaries for their noble office. Alas for the extra-terrestrial sociologist and his natural expectations! After exhaustive study, finding nothing of these things, he would return to Mars or Saturn or wherever he came from, marvelling within himself at the vastness of the human paradox.

If the position of woman is to be justified by the doctrine of maternal sacrifice, surely society, or the individual, or both, would make some preparation for it. No such preparation is made. Society recognizes no such function. Premiums have been sometimes paid for large numbers of children, but they were paid to the fathers of them. The elaborate social machinery which constitutes our universal marriage market has no department to assist or advance motherhood. On the contrary, it is directly inimical to it, so that in our society life motherhood means direct loss, and is avoided by the social devotee. And the individual? Surely here right provision will be made. Young women, glorying in their prospective duties, their sacred and inalienable office, their great sex-martyrdom to race-advantage, will be found solemnly preparing for this work. What do we find? We find our young women reared in an attitude which is absolutely unconscious of and often injurious to their coming motherhood,— an irresponsible, indifferent, ignorant class of beings, so far as motherhood is concerned. They are fitted to attract the other sex for economic uses or, at most, for mutual gratification, but not for motherhood. They are reared in unbroken ignorance of their supposed principal duties, knowing nothing of these duties till they enter upon them.

This is as though all men were to be soldiers with the fate of nations in their hands; and no man told or taught a word of war or military service until he entered the battle-field!

The education of young women has no department of maternity. It is considered indelicate to give this consecrated functionary any previous knowledge of her sacred duties. This most important and wonderful of human functions is left from age to age in the hands of absolutely untaught women. It is tacitly supposed to be fulfilled by the mysterious working of what we call "the divine instinct of maternity." Maternal instinct is a very respectable and useful instinct common to most animals. It is "divine" and "holy" only as all the laws of nature are divine and holy; and it is such only when it works to the right fulfilment of its use. If the race-preservative processes are to be held more sacred than the self-preservative processes, we must admit all the functions and faculties of reproduction to the same degree of reverence, —the passion of the male for the female as well as the passion of the mother for her young. And if, still further, we are to honor the race-preservative processes most in their highest and latest development, which is the only comparison to be made on a natural basis, we should place the great, disinterested, social function of education far above the second-selfishness of individual maternal functions. Maternal instinct, merely as an instinct, is unworthy of our superstitious reverence. It should be measured only as a means to an end, and valued in proportion to its efficacy.

Among animals, which have but a low degree of intelligence, instinct is at its height, and works well. Among savages, still incapable of much intellectual development, instinct holds large place. The mother beast can and does take all the care of her young by instinct; the mother savage, nearly all, supplemented by the tribal traditions, the educative influences of association, and some direct instruction. As humanity advances, growing more complex and varied, and as human intelligence advances to keep pace with new functions and new needs, instinct decreases in value. The human creature prospers and progresses not by virtue of his animal instinct, but by the wisdom and force of a cultivated intelligence and will, with which to guide his action and to control and modify the very instincts which used to govern him.

The human female, denied the enlarged activities which have developed intelligence in man, denied the education of the will which only comes by freedom and power, has maintained the rudimentary forces of instinct to the present day. With her extreme modification to sex, this faculty of instinct runs mainly along sex-lines, and finds fullest vent in the processes of maternity, where it has held unbroken sway. So the children of humanity are born into the arms of an endless succession of untrained mothers, who bring to the care and teaching of their children neither education for that wonderful work nor experience therein: they bring merely the intense accumulated force of a brute instinct,—the blind devoted passion of the mother for the child. Maternal love is an enormous force, but force needs direction. Simply to love the child does not serve him unless specific acts of service express this love. What these acts of service are and how they are performed make or mar his life forever.

Observe the futility of unaided maternal love and instinct in the simple act of feeding the child. Belonging to order mammalia, the human mother has an instinctive desire to suckle her young. (Some ultra-civilized have lost even that.) But this instinct has not taught her such habits of life as insure her ability to fulfil this natural function. Failing in the natural method, of what further use is instinct in the nourishment of the child? Can maternal instinct discriminate between Marrow's Food and Bridge's Food, Hayrick's Food and Pestle's Food, Pennywhistle's Sterilized Milk, and all the other infants' foods which are prepared and put upon the market by—men! These are not prepared by instinct, maternal or paternal, but by chemical analysis and physiological study; and their effect is observed and the diet varied by physicians, who do not do their work by instinct, either.

If the bottle-baby survive the loss of mother's milk, when he comes to the table, does maternal instinct suffice then to administer a proper diet for young children? Let the doctor and the undertaker answer. The wide and varied field of masculine activity in the interests of little children, from the peculiar human phenomenon of masculine assistance in parturition (there is one animal, the obstetric frog, where it also appears) to the manufacture of articles for feeding, clothing, protecting, amusing, and educating the baby, goes to show the utter inadequacy of maternal instinct in the human female. Another thing it shows also,— the criminal failure of that human female to supply by intelligent effort what instinct can no longer accomplish. For a reasoning, conscious being deliberately to undertake the responsibility of maintaining human life without making due preparation for the task is more than carelessness.

Before a man enters a trade, art, or profession, he studies it. He qualifies himself for the duties he is to undertake. He would be held a presuming impostor if he engaged in work he was not fitted to do, and his failure would mark him instantly with ridicule and reproach. In the more important professions, especially in those dealing with what we call "matters of life and death," the shipmaster or pilot, doctor or druggist, is required not only to study his business, but to pass an examination under those who have already become past masters, and obtain a certificate or a diploma or some credential to show that he is fit to be intrusted with the direct responsibility for human life.

Women enter a position which gives into their hands direct responsibility for the life or death of the whole human race with neither study nor experience, with no shadow of preparation or guarantee of capability. So far as they give it a thought, they fondly imagine that this mysterious "maternal instinct" will see them through. Instruction, if needed, they will pick up when the time comes: experience they will acquire as the children appear. "I guess I know how to bring up children!" cried the resentful old lady who was being advised: "I've buried seven!" The record of untrained instinct as a maternal faculty in the human race is to be read on the rows and rows of little gravestones which crowd our cemeteries. The experience gained by practising on the child is frequently buried with it.

No, the maternal sacrifice theory will not bear examination. As a sex specialized to reproduction, giving up all personal activity, all honest independence, all useful and progressive economic service for her glorious consecration to the uses of maternity, the human female has little to show in the way of results which can justify her position. Neither the enormous percentage of children lost by death nor the low average health of those who survive, neither physical nor mental progress, give any proof of race advantage from the maternal sacrifice.

X.

ALTHOUGH the superior maternity of the human female is so difficult to prove, so open to heavy charges of inadequacy, so erratic and pathological, there remain intact our devout belief in it, our reverence, our unshaken conviction that it is the one perfect thing. The facts as to our carelessness and ignorance in the fulfilment of this function are undeniable: the rate of infant mortality and children's diseases,—those classed by physicians as "preventable diseases," namely,—these mortal errors and failures confront us everywhere; but we ignore them all, or attribute them to any and every reason save deficient motherhood.

One of the most frequent excuses, among those who have gone far enough to admit that excuse is needed, is that the father is to blame for these conditions. His vices, it is alleged, weaken the constitution of the race. His failure to provide prevents the mother from giving the proper care. He is held responsible for what evil we see in our children; and still we worship the mother for the physical process of bearing a child,—now considered an act of heroism,—and for the "devotion" with which she clings to it afterward, irrespective of the wisdom or effectiveness of this devotion. A healthy and independent mother-hood would no more think of taking credit to itself for the right fulfilment of its natural functions than would a cat for bringing forth her kittens or a sheep her lambs. The common fact that the women of the lower social grades bear more children and bear them more easily than the women of higher classes ought to give pause to this ridiculous assumption, but it does not. The more women weaken themselves and their offspring, and imperil their very lives by anti-maternal habits, the more difficulty, danger, and expense are associated with this natural process, the more do women solemnly take credit to themselves and receive it from others for the glorious self-sacrifice with which they risk their lives (and their babies' lives!) for the preservation of humanity. As to the father and his share in the evil results, nothing that he has ever done or can do removes from motherhood its primal responsibility.

Suppose the female of some other species, ignoring her racial duty of right selection, should mate with mangy, toothless cripples, — if there were such among her kind, — and so produce weak, malformed young, and help exterminate her race. Should she then blame him for the result? An entire sex, sacredly set apart for maternal functions so superior as to justify their lack of economic usefulness, should in the course of ages have learned how to select proper fathers. If the only way in which the human mother can feed and guard her children is through another person, a provider and protector on whom their lives and safety must depend, what natural, social, or moral excuse has she for not choosing a good one?

But how can a young girl know a good prospective father, we ask. That she is not so educated as to know proves her unfitness for her great task. That she does not think or care proves her dishonorable indifference to her great duty. She can in no way shirk the responsibility for criminal carelessness in choosing a father for her children, unless indeed there were no choice, — no good men left on earth. Moreover, we are not obliged to leave this crucial choice in the hands of young girls. Motherhood is the work of grown women, not of half-children; and, when we honestly care as much for motherhood as we pretend, we shall train the woman for her duty, not the girl for her guileless manœuvres to secure a husband. We talk about the noble duties of the mother, but our maidens are educated for economically successful marriage.

Leaving this field of maternal duty through

sex-selection, there remains the far larger ground to which the popular mind flees in triumph : that the later work of the mother proves the success of our racial division of labor on sex-lines, that in the care of the child, the education of the child, the beautiful life of the home and family, it is shown how well our system works. This is the last stronghold. Solidly intrenched herein sits popular thought, safe in the sacred precincts of the home. "Every man's home is his castle," is the common saying. The windows are shut to keep out the air. The curtains are down to keep out the light. The doors are barred to keep out the stranger. Within are the hearth fire and its gentle priestess, the initial combination of human life,—the family in the home.

Our thrones have been emptied, and turned into mere chairs for passing presidents. Our churches have been opened to the light of modern life, and the odor of sanctity has been freshened with sweet sunny air. We can see room for change in these old sanctuaries, but none in the sanctuary of the home. And this temple, with its rights, is so closely interwound with the services of subject woman, its altar so demands her ceaseless sacrifices, that we find it impossible to conceive of any other basis of human living. We are chilled to the heart's

core by the fear of losing any of these ancient
and hallowed associations. Without this blessed
background of all our memories and foreground
of all our hopes, life seems empty indeed. In
homes we were all born. In homes we all die
or hope to die. In homes we all live or want to
live. For homes we all labor, in them or out of
them. The home is the centre and circumfer-
ence, the start and the finish, of most of our
lives. We love it with a love older than the
human race. We reverence it with the blind
obeisance of those crouching centuries when its
cult began. We cling to it with the tenacity
of every inmost, oldest instinct of our animal
natures, and with the enthusiasm of every latest
word in the unbroken chant of adoration which
we have sung to it since first we learned to
praise.

And since we hold that our home life, just as
we have it, is the best thing on earth, and that
our home life plainly demands one whole woman
at the least to each home, and usually more, it
follows that anything which offers to change
the position of woman threatens to "under-
mine the home," "strikes at the root of the
family," and we will none of it. If, in honest
endeavor to keep up to the modern standard of
free thought and free speech, we do listen,—
turning from our idol for a moment, and saying

to the daring iconoclast, "Come, show us anything better!" — with what unlimited derision
do we greet his proposed substitute! Yet everywhere about us to-day this inner tower, this
castle keep of vanishing tradition, is becoming
more difficult to defend or even to keep in repair.
We buttress it anew with every generation; we
love its very cracks and crumbling corners; we
hang and drape it with endless decorations;
we hide the looming dangers overhead with
fresh clouds of incense; and we demand of
the would-be repairers and rebuilders that they
prove to us the desirability of their wild plans
before they lift a hammer. But, when they
show their plans, we laugh them to scorn.

It is a difficult case to meet. To call attention to existing conditions and to establish the
relation between them and existing phenomena
is one thing. To point out how a change of
condition will produce new phenomena, and how
these phenomena will benefit us, is quite another.
Yet this is the task that is always involved in
the conscious progress of the human race.
While that progress was unconscious, it was
enough that certain individuals and classes
gradually entered into new relations in process
of social evolution, and that they forced their
conditions upon the reluctant conservatives
who failed so to evolve.

In the quite recent passage from the feudal to the monarchical system, no time was wasted in the endeavor to persuade and convince the headstrong barons of their national duty. The growing power of the king struggled with and survived the lessening power of the barons,— that was all. Had a book been written then to urge the change, it could have proved clearly enough the evils of the feudal system; but, when it tried to portray the glories of national peace and power under a single monarch, it would have had small weight. National peace and power, which had been hitherto non-existent, would have failed to appeal to the sturdy lords of the soil, whose only idea of peace and power was to sit down and rest on their prostrate neighbors. Had their strength run in the line of argument, they would have scouted the "should be's" and "will be's" of the author, and defied him to prove that the new condition would be developed by the new processes; and, indeed, he would have found it hard.

So to-day, in questioning the economic status of woman and her position in the home and in the family, it is far easier to prove present evil than future good. Yet this is what is most exactingly demanded. It is required of the advocate of social reform not only that he convince the contented followers of the present system of its wrong, but that he prove to their satisfaction the superiority of some other system. This, in the nature of the case, is impossible. When people are contented, you cannot make them feel that what is is wrong, or that something else might be better. Even the discontented are far more willing to refer their troubles to some personal factor than to admit that their condition as a whole inevitably produces the general trouble in which they share. Even if convinced that a change of condition will remove the source of injury, they, like the fox with the swarm of flies, fear to be disturbed, lest their last state be worse than their first. In the face of this inevitable difficulty, however, the task must be undertaken.

Two things let us premise and agree upon before starting. First, that the duty of human life is progress, development ; that we are here, not merely to live, but to grow,— not to be content with lean savagery or fat barbarism or sordid semi-civilization, but to toil on through the centuries, and build up the ever-nobler forms of life toward which social evolution tends. If this is not believed, if any hold that to keep alive and reproduce the species is the limit of our human duty, then they need look no farther here. That aim can be attained, and has been attained, for irrefutable centuries, through many forms of sex-relation and of economic relation. Human beings have lived and brought up children as good as their parents in free promiscuity and laziness, in forced polygamy and slavery, in willing polyandry and industry, and in monogamy *plus* prostitution and manufactures. Just to live and bear children does not prove the relative superiority of any system, either in sex or economics. But, when we believe that life means progress, then each succeeding form of sex-relation or economic relation is to be measured by its effect on that progress.

It may be necessary here to agree on a definition of human progress. According to the general law of organic evolution, it may be defined as follows : such progress in the individual and in his social relations as shall maintain him in health and happiness and increase the organic development of society.

If we accept such a definition of human progress, if we agree that progress is the duty of society, and that all social institutions are to be measured by it, we may proceed to our second premise. This is not to be ranked with the first in importance : it should be too commonly understood and accepted to be dragged into such a prominent position. But it is not commonly understood and accepted. In fact, it is misunderstood and denied to so general a degree that no apology is needed for insisting on it here.

The second premise is this : our enjoyment of a thing does not prove that it is right. Even our love, admiration, and reverence for a thing does not prove that it is right ; and, even from an evolutionary point of view, our belief that a thing is "natural" does not prove that it is right. A thing may be right in one stage of evolution which becomes wrong in another. For instance, promiscuity is "natural" ; the human animal, like many others, is quite easily inclined thereto. Monogamy is proven right by social evolution : it is the best way to carry on the human race in social relation ; but it is not yet as "natural" as could be desired.

So, to return to our second premise, which is admittedly rather a large one, to show that any custom or status of ours is "natural" and enjoyable does not prove that it is right. It does not of course prevent its being right. Right things may be enjoyed, may be loved, admired, and reverenced, may even be "natural" ; but so may wrong things. Even that subhuman faculty called instinct is only a true guide to conduct when the conditions are present which originally developed that instinct. The instinct that makes a modern house-dog turn around three times before he lies down is not worthy of much admiration to-day, though it served its purpose on the grassy plains and in the leafy hollows where it was formed. If these two premises are granted, that the duty of human life is progress, and that a given condition is not necessarily right because we like it, we may go on.

Is our present method of home life, based on the economic dependence of woman in the sex-relation, the best calculated to maintain the individual in health and happiness, and develope in him the higher social faculties ? The individual is not maintained in health and happiness,— that is visible to all ; and how little he is developed in social relation is shown in the jarring irregularity and wastefulness of our present economic system.

Economic independence for women necessarily involves a change in the home and family relation. But, if that change is for the advantage of individual and race, we need not fear it. It does not involve a change in the marriage relation except in withdrawing the element of economic dependence, nor in the relation of mother to child save to improve it. But it does involve the exercise of human faculty in women, in social service and exchange rather than in domestic service solely. This will of course require the introduction of some other form of living than that which now obtains. It will render impossible the present method of feeding the world by means of millions of private servants, and bringing up children by the same hand.

It is a melancholy fact that the vast majority of our children are reared and trained by domestic servants,— generally their mothers, to be sure, but domestic servants by trade. To become a producer, a factor in the economic activities of the world, must perforce interfere with woman's present status as a private servant. House mistress she may still be, in the sense of owning and ordering her home, but housekeeper or house-servant she may not be — and be anything else. Her position as mother will alter, too. Mother in the sense of bearer and rearer of noble children she will be, as the closest and dearest, the one most honored and best loved ; but mother in the sense of exclusive individual nursery-maid and nursery-governess she may not be — and be anything else.

It is precisely here that the world calls a halt. Nothing, it says, can be better than our homes with their fair priestesses. Nothing can be better for children than the hourly care of their own mothers. It is the position of the feudal baron over again. We can perhaps be made to see the evils of existing conditions : we cannot be made to see any possibility of improving on them. Nevertheless, it may be tried.

Let us deliberately set ourselves to imagine, by sheer muscular effort as it were, a better kind of motherhood than that of the private nursery governess, a better way to feed and clean and clothe the world than by the private house servant.

Here is felt the need of our second premise; for we enjoy things as they are (that is, some of us do, sometimes, and the rest of us think that we do). We love, admire, and reverence them; and it is "natural" to have them so. If it can be shown that human progress is better served by other methods, then other methods will be proven right; and we must grow to enjoy and honor them as fast as we can, and in due course of time we shall find them natural. If it can be shown that our babies would be better off if part of their time was passed in other care than their mothers', then such other care would be right; and it would be the duty of motherhood to provide it. If it can be shown that we could all be better provided for in our personal needs of nutrition, cleanliness, warmth, shelter, privacy, by some other method than that which requires the labor of one woman or more to each family, then it would be the duty of womanhood to find such method and to practise it.

Perhaps it is worth while to examine the nature of our feeling toward that social institution called "the family," and the probable effect upon it of the change in woman's economic status.

Marriage and "the family" are two institutions, not one, as is commonly supposed. We confuse the natural result of marriage in children, common to all forms of sex-union, with the family,— a purely social phenomenon. Marriage is a form of sex-union recognized and sanctioned by society. It is a relation between two or more persons, according to the custom of the country, and involves mutual obligations. Although made by us an economic relation, it is not essentially so, and will exist in much higher fulfilment after the economic phase is outgrown.

The family is a social group, an entity, a little state. It holds an important place in the evolution of society quite aside from its connection with marriage. There was a time when the family was the highest form of social relation,— indeed, the only form of social relation,— when to the minds of pastoral, patriarchal tribes there was no conception so large as "my country," no State, no nation. There was only a great land spotted with families, each family its own little world, of which Grandpa was priest and king. The family was a social unit. Its interests were common to its members, and inimical to those of other families. It moved over the earth, following its food supply, and fighting occasionally with stranger families for the grass or water on which it depended. Indissoluble common interests are what make organic union, and those interests long rested on blood relationship.

While the human individual was best fed and guarded by the family, and so required the prompt, correlative action of all the members of that family, naturally the family must have a head; and that form of government known as the patriarchal was produced. The natural family relation, as seen in parents and young of other species, or in ourselves in later forms, involves no such governmental development: that is a feature of the family as a social entity alone.

One of the essentials of the patriarchal family life was polygamy, and not only polygamy, but open concubinage, and a woman slavery which was almost the same thing. The highest period of the family as a social institution was a very low period for marriage as a social institution,— a period, in fact, when marriage was but partially evolved from the early promiscuity of the primitive savage. The family seems indeed to be a gradually disappearing survival of the still looser unit of the horde, which again is more closely allied to the band or pack of gregarious carnivora than to an organic social relation. A loose, promiscuous group of animals is not a tribe; and the most primitive savage groups seem to have been no more than this.

The tribe in its true form follows the family, — is a natural extension of it, and derives its essential ties from the same relationship. These social forms, too, are closely related to economic conditions. The horde was the hunting unit; the family, and later the tribe, the pastoral unit. Agriculture and its resultant, commerce and manufacture, gradually weaken these crude blood ties, and establish the social relationship which constitutes the State. Before the pastoral era the family held no important position, and since that era it has gradually declined. With social progress we find human relations resting less and less on a personal and sex basis, and more and more on general economic independence. As individuals have become more highly specialized, they have made possible a higher form of marriage.

The family is a decreasing survival of the earliest grouping known to man. Marriage is an increasing development of high social life, not fully evolved. So far from being identical with the family, it improves and strengthens in inverse ratio to the family, as is easily seen by the broad contrast between the marriage relations of Jacob and the unquenchable demand for lifelong single mating that grows in our hearts to-day. There was no conception of marriage as a personal union for life of two well-matched individuals during the patriarchal era. Wives were valued merely for child-bearing. The family needed numbers of its own blood, especially males ; and the man-child was the price of favor to women then. It was but a few degrees beyond the horde, not yet become a tribe in the full sense. Its bonds of union were of the loosest,— merely common paternity, with a miscellaneous maternity of inimical interests. Such a basis forever forbade any high individualization, and high individualization with its demands for a higher marriage forbids any numerical importance to the family. Marriage has risen and developed in social importance as the family has sunk and decreased.

It is most interesting to note that, under the comparatively similar conditions of the settlement of Utah, the numerical strength and easily handled common interests of many people under one head, which distinguish the polygamous family, were found useful factors in that great pioneering enterprise. In the further development of society a relation of individuals more fluent, subtle, and extensive was needed. The family as a social unit makes a ponderous body of somewhat irreconcilable constituents, requiring a sort of military rule to make it work at all ; and it is only useful while the ends to be attained are of a simple nature, and allow of the slowest accomplishment. It is easy to see the family extending to the tribe by its own physical increase ; and, similarly, the father hardening into the chief, under the necessities of larger growth. Then, as the steadily enlarging forces of national unity make the chief an outgrown name and the tribe an outgrown form, the family dwindles to a monogamic basis, as the higher needs of the sex-relation become differentiated from the more primitive economic necessities of the family.

And now, further, when our still developing social needs call for an ever-increasing delicacy and freedom in the inter-service and common service of individuals, we find that even what economic unity remains to the family is being rapidly eliminated. As the economic relation becomes rudimentary and disappears, the sex-relation asserts itself more purely ; and the demand in the world to-day for a higher and nobler sex-union is as sharply defined as the growing objection to the existing economic union.

Strange as it may seem to us, so long accustomed to confound the two, it is precisely the outgrown relics of a previously valuable family relation which so painfully retard the higher development of the monogamic marriage relation.

Each generation of young men and women comes to the formation of sex-union with higher and higher demands for a true marriage, with ever-growing needs for companionship. Each generation of men and women need and ask more of each other. A woman is no longer content and grateful to have "a kind husband": a man is no longer content with a patient Griselda; and, as all men and women, in marrying, revert to the economic status of the earlier family, they come under conditions which steadily tend to lower the standard of their mutual love, and make of the average marriage only a sort of compromise, borne with varying ease or difficulty according to the good breeding and loving-kindness of the parties concerned. This is not necessarily, to their conscious knowledge, an "unhappy marriage." It is as happy as those they see about them, as happy perhaps as we resignedly expect "on earth"; and in heaven we do not expect marriages. But it is not what they looked forward to when they were young.

When two young people love each other, in

the long hours which are never long enough for them to be together in, do they dwell in ecstatic forecast on the duties of housekeeping? They do not. They dwell on the pleasure of having a home, in which they can be "at last alone"; on the opportunity of enjoying each other's society; and, always, on what they will *do* together. To act with those we love,— to walk together, work together, read together, paint, write, sing, anything you please, so that it be together,— that is what love looks forward to.

Human love, as it rises to an ever higher grade, looks more and more for such companionship. But the economic status of marriage rudely breaks in upon love's young dream. On the economic side, apart from all the sweetness and truth of the sex-relation, the woman in marrying becomes the house-servant, or at least the housekeeper, of the man. Of the world we may say that the intimate personal necessities of the human animal are ministered to by woman. Married lovers do not work together. They may, if they have time, rest together: they may, if they can, play together; but they do not make beds and sweep and cook together, and they do not go down town to the office together. They are economically on entirely different social planes, and these constitute a bar to any higher, truer union than such as we see about us.

Marriage is not perfect unless it is between class equals. There is no equality in class between those who do their share in the world's work in the largest, newest, highest ways and those who do theirs in the smallest, oldest, lowest ways.

Granting squarely that it is the business of women to make the home life of the world true, healthful, and beautiful, the economically dependent woman does not do this, and never can. The economically independent woman can and will. As the family is by no means identical with marriage, so is the home by no means identical with either.

A home is a permanent dwelling-place, whether for one, two, forty, or a thousand, for a pair, a flock, or a swarm. The hive is the home of the bees as literally and absolutely as the nest is the home of mating birds in their season. Home and the love of it may dwindle to the one chamber of the bachelor or spread to the span of a continent, when the returning traveller sees land and calls it "home." There is no sweeter word, there is no dearer fact, no feeling closer to the human heart than this.

On close analysis, what are the bases of our feelings in this connection? and what are their supporting facts? Far down below humanity, where "the foxes have holes, and the birds of the air have nests," there begins the deep home feeling. Maternal instinct seeks a place to shelter the defenceless young, while the mother goes abroad to search for food. The first sharp impressions of infancy are associated with the sheltering walls of home, be it the swinging cradle in the branches, the soft dark hollow in the trunk of a tree, or the cave with its hidden lair. A place to be safe in; a place to be warm and dry in; a place to eat in peace and sleep in quiet; a place whose close, familiar limits rest the nerves from the continuous hail of impressions in the changing world outside; the same place over and over,— the restful repetition, rousing no keen response, but healing and soothing each weary sense,— that "feels like home." All this from our first consciousness. All this for millions and millions of years. No wonder we love it.

Then comes the gradual addition of tenderer associations, family ties of the earliest. Then, still primitive, but not yet outgrown, the groping religious sentiment of early ancestor-worship, adding sanctity to safety, and driving deep our sentiment for home. It was the place in which to pray, to keep alight the sacred fire, and pour libations to departed grandfathers. Following this, the slow-dying era of paternal government gave a new sense of honor to the place of comfort and the place of prayer. It became the seat of government also,— the palace and the throne. Upon this deep foundation we have built a towering superstructure of habit, custom, law; and in it dwell together every deepest, oldest, closest, and tenderest emotion of the human individual. No wonder we are blind and deaf to any suggested improvement in our lordly pleasure-house.

But look farther. Without contradicting any word of the above, it is equally true that the highest emotions of humanity arise and live outside the home and apart from it. While religion stayed at home, in dogma and ceremony, in spirit and expression, it was a low and narrow religion. It could never rise till it found a new spirit and a new expression in human life outside the home, until it found a common place of worship, a ceremonial and a morality on a human basis, not a family basis. Science, art, government, education, industry,— the home is the cradle of them all, and their grave, if they stay in it. Only as we live, think, feel, and work outside the home, do we become humanly developed, civilized, socialized.

The exquisite development of modern home life is made possible only as an accompaniment and result of modern social life. If the reverse were true, as is popularly supposed, all nations that have homes would continue to evolve a noble civilization. But they do not. On the contrary, those nations in which home and family worship most prevail, as in China, present a melancholy proof of the result of the domestic virtues without the social. A noble home life is the product of a noble social life. The home does not produce the virtues needed in society. But society does produce the virtues needed in such homes as we desire to-day. The members of the freest, most highly civilized and individualized nations, make the most delightful members of the home and family. The members of the closest and most highly venerated homes do not necessarily make the most delightful members of society.

In social evolution as in all evolution the tendency is from "indefinite, incoherent homogeneity to definite, coherent heterogeneity";[10] and the home, in its rigid maintenance of a permanent homogeneity, constitutes a definite limit to social progress. What we need is not less home, but more; not a lessening of the love of human beings for a home, but its extension through new and more effective expression. And, above all, we need the complete disentanglement in our thoughts of the varied and often radically opposed interests and industries so long supposed to be component parts of the home and family.

The change in the economic position of woman from dependence to independence must bring with it a rearrangement of these home interests and industries, to our great gain.

XI.

As a natural consequence of our division of labor on sex-lines, giving to woman the home and to man the world in which to work, we have come to have a dense prejudice in favor of the essential womanliness of the home duties, as opposed to the essential manliness of every other kind of work. We have assumed that the preparation and serving of food and the removal of dirt, the nutritive and excretive processes of the family, are feminine functions; and we have also assumed that these processes must go on in what we call the home, which is the external expression of the family. In the home the human individual is fed, cleaned, warmed, and generally cared for, while not engaged in working in the world.

Human nutrition is a long process. There's many a ship 'twixt the cup and the lip, to paraphrase an old proverb. Food is produced by the human race collectively,— not by individuals for their own consumption, but by interrelated groups of individuals, all over the world, for the world's consumption. This collectively produced food circulates over the earth's surface through elaborate processes of transportation, exchange, and preparation, before it reaches the mouths of the consumers; and the final processes of selection and preparation are in the hands of woman. She is the final purchaser : she is the final handler in that process of human nutrition known as cooking, which is a sort of extra-organic digestion proven advantageous to our species. This department of human digestion has become a sex-function, supposed to pertain to women by nature.

If it is to the advantage of the human race that its food supply should be thus handled by a special sex, this advantage should be shown in superior health and purity of habit. But no such advantage is visible. In spite of all our power and skill in the production and preparation of food we remain "the sickest beast alive" in the matter of eating. Our impotent outcries against adulteration prove that part of the trouble is in the food products as offered for purchase, the pathetic reiteration of our numerous cook-books proves that part of the trouble is in the preparation of those products, and the futile exhortations of physicians and mothers prove that part of the trouble is in our morbid tastes and appetites. It would really seem as if the human race after all its long centuries had not learned how to prepare good food, nor how to cook it, nor how to eat it,— which is painfully true.

This great function of human nutrition is

confounded with the sex-relation, and is considered a sex-function : it is in the helpless hands of that amiable but abortive agent, the economically dependent women ; and the essential incapacity of such an agent is not hard to show. In her position as private house-steward she is the last purchaser of the food of the world, and here we reach the governing factor in our incredible adulteration of food products.

All kinds of deceit and imposition in human service are due to that desire to get without giving, which, as has been shown in previous chapters, is largely due to the training of women as non-productive consumers. But the particular form of deceit and imposition practised by a given dealer is governed by the intelligence and power of the buyer. The dilution and adulteration of food products is a particularly easy path to profit, because the ultimate purchaser has almost no power and very little intelligence. The individual housewife must buy at short intervals and in small quantities. This operates to her pecuniary disadvantage, as is well known ; but its effect on the quality of her purchases is not so commonly observed. Not unless she becomes the head of a wealthy household, and so purchases in quantity for family, servants, and guests, is her trade of sufficient value to have force in the market.

The dealer who sells to a hundred poor women can and does sell a much lower quality of food than he who sells an equal amount to one purchaser. Therefore, the home, as a food agency, holds an essentially and permanently unfavorable position as a purchaser; and it is thereby the principal factor in maintaining the low standard of food products against which we struggle with the cumbrous machinery of legislation.

Most housekeepers will innocently prove their ignorance of these matters by denying that the standard of food products is so low. Let such offended ladies but examine the statutes and ordinances of their own cities,— of any civilized city,— and see how the bread, the milk, the meat, the fruit, are under a steady legislative inspection which endeavors to protect the ignorance and helplessness of the individual purchaser. If the private housekeeper had the technical intelligence as purchaser which is needed to discriminate in the selection of foods, if she were prepared to test her milk, to detect the foreign substance in her coffee and spices, rightly to estimate the quality of her meat and the age of her fruit and vegetables, she would then be able at least to protest against her supply, and to seek, as far as time, distance, and funds allowed, a better market. This technical intelligence, however, is only to be obtained by special study and experience ; and its attainment only involves added misery and difficulty to the private purchaser, unless accompanied by the power to enforce what the intelligence demands.

As it is, woman brings to her selection from the world's food only the empirical experience gained by practising upon her helpless family, and this during the very time when her growing children need the wise care which she is only able to give them in later years. This experience, with its pitiful limitation and its practical check by the personal taste and pecuniary standing of the family, is lost where it was found. Each mother slowly acquires some knowledge of her business by practising it upon the lives and health of her family and by observing its effect on the survivors ; and each daughter begins again as ignorant as her mother was before her. This "rule of thumb" is not transmissible. It is not a genuine education such as all important work demands, but a slow animal process of soaking up experience,— hopelessly ineffectual in protecting the health of society. As the ultimate selecting agent in feeding humanity, the private housewife fails, and this not by reason of any lack of effort on her part, but by the essential defect of her position as individual purchaser. Only organization can oppose such evils as the wholesale adulteration of food; and woman, the house-servant, belongs to the lowest grade of unorganized labor.

Leaving the selection of food, and examining its preparation, one would naturally suppose that the segregation of an entire sex to the fulfilment of this function would insure most remarkable results. It has, but they are not so favorable as might be expected. The art and science of cooking involve a large and thorough knowledge of nutritive value and of the laws of physiology and hygiene. As a science, it verges on preventive medicine. As an art, it is capable of noble expression within its natural bounds. As it stands among us to-day, it is so far from being a science and akin to preventive medicine, that it is the lowest of amateur handicrafts and a prolific source of disease; and, as an art, it has developed under the peculiar stimulus of its position as a sex-function into a voluptuous profusion as false as it is evil. Our innocent proverb, "The way to a man's heart is through his stomach," is a painfully plain comment on the way in which we have come to deprave our bodies and degrade our souls at the table.

On the side of knowledge it is permanently impossible that half the world, acting as amateur cooks for the other half, can attain any high degree of scientific accuracy or technical skill. The development of any human labor requires specialization, and specialization is forbidden to our cook-by-nature system. What progress we have made in the science of cooking has been made through the study and experience of professional men cooks and chemists, not through the Sisyphean labors of our endless generations of isolated women, each beginning again where her mother began before her.

Here, of course, will arise a pained outcry along the "mother's doughnuts" line, in answer to which we refer to our second premise in the last chapter. The fact that we like a thing does not prove it to be right. A Missouri child may regard his mother's saleratus biscuit with fond desire, but that does not alter their effect upon his spirits or his complexion. Cooking is a matter of law, not the harmless play of fancy. Architecture might be more sportive and varied if every man built his own house, but it would not be the art and science that we have made it ; and, while every woman prepares food for her own family, cooking can never rise beyond the level of the amateur's work.

But, low as is the status of cooking as a science, as an art it is lower. Since the wife-cook's main industry is to please,— that being her chief means of getting what she wants or of expressing affection, — she early learned to cater to the palate instead of faithfully studying and meeting the needs of the stomach. For uncounted generations the grown man and the growing child have been subject to the constant efforts of her who cooked from affection, not from knowledge,— who cooked to please. This is one of the widest pathways of evil that has ever been opened. In every field of life it is an evil to put the incident before the object, the means before the end ; and here it has produced that familiar result whereby we live to eat instead of eating to live.

This attitude of the woman has developed the rambling excess called "fancy cookery," — a thing as far removed from true artistic development as a swinging ice-pitcher from a Greek vase. Through this has come the limitless unhealthy folly of high living, in which human labor and time and skill are wasted in producing what is neither pure food nor pure pleasure, but an artificial performance, to be appreciated only by the virtuoso. Lower living could hardly be imagined than that which results from this unnatural race between artifice and appetite, in which body and soul are both corrupted.

In the man, the subject of all this dining-room devotion, has been developed and maintained that cultivated interest in his personal tastes and their gratification,— that demand for things which he likes rather than for things which he knows to be good, wherein lies one of the most dangerous elements in character known to the psychologist. The sequences of this affectionate catering to physical appetites may be traced far afield to its last result in the unchecked indulgence in personal tastes and desires, in drug habits and all intemperance. The temperament which is unable to resist these temptations is constantly being bred at home.

As the concentration of woman's physical energies on the sex-functions, enforced by her economic dependence, has tended to produce and maintain man's excess in sex-indulgence, to the injury of the race; so the concentration of woman's industrial energies on the close and constant service of personal tastes and appetites has tended to produce and maintain an excess in table indulgence, both in eating and drinking, which is also injurious to the race. It is not here alleged that this is the only cause of our habits of this nature; but it is one of primal importance, and of ceaseless action.

We can perhaps see its working better by a light-minded analogy than by a bold statement. Suppose two large, healthy, nimble apes. Suppose that the male ape did not allow the female

ape to skip about and pluck her own cocoanuts,
but brought to her what she was to have. Suppose that she was then required to break the
shell, pick out the meat, prepare for the male
what he wished to consume; and suppose, further, that her share in the dinner, to say nothing of her chance of a little pleasure excursion
in the treetops afterward, was dependent on his
satisfaction with the food she prepared for him.
She, as an ape of intelligence, would seek,
by all devices known to her, to add stimulus
and variety to the meals she arranged, to select
the bits he specially preferred to please his taste
and to meet his appetite; and he, developing
under this agreeable pressure, would gradually
acquire a fine discrimination in foods, and would
look forward to his elaborate feasts with increas
ing complacency. He would have a new force
to make him eat,— not only his need of food,
with its natural and healthy demands, but her
need of — everything, acting through his need
of food.

This sounds somewhat absurd in a family of
apes, but it is precisely what has occurred in
the human family. To gratify her husband has
been the woman's way of obtaining her own
ends, and she has of necessity learned how to do
it; and, as she has been in general an uneducated and unskilled worker, she could only seek

to please him through what powers she had,—mainly those of house service. She has been set to serve two appetites, and to profit accordingly. She has served them well, but the profit to either party is questionable.

On lines of social development we are progressing from the gross gorging of the savage on whatever food he could seize, toward the discriminating selection of proper foods, and an increasing delicacy and accuracy in their use. Against this social tendency runs the cross-current of our sexuo-economic relation, making the preparation of food a sex-function, and confusing all its processes with the ardor of personal affection and the dragging weight of self-interest. This method is applied, not only to the husband, but, in a certain degree, to the children; for, where maternal love and maternal energy are forced to express themselves mainly in the preparation of food, the desire properly to feed the child becomes confounded with an unwise desire to please, and the mother degrades her high estate by catering steadily to the lower tastes of humanity instead of to the higher.

Our general notion is that we have lifted and ennobled our eating and drinking by combining them with love. On the contrary, we have lowered and degraded our love by combining it with eating and drinking; and, what is more, we have lowered these habits also. Some progress has been made, socially ; but this unhappy mingling of sex-interest and self-interest with normal appetites, this Cupid-in-the-kitchen arrangement, has gravely impeded that progress. Professional cooking has taught us much. Commerce and manufacture have added to our range of supplies. Science has shown us what we need, and how and when we need it. But the affectionate labor of wife and mother is little touched by these advances. If she goes to the cooking school, it is to learn how to make the rich delicacies that will please rather than to study the nutritive value of food in order to guard the health of the household. From the constantly enlarging stores opened to her through man's activities she chooses widely, to make "a variety" that shall kindle appetite, knowing nothing of the combination best for physical needs. As to science, chemistry, hygiene,— they are but names to her. "John likes it so." "Willie won't eat it so." "Your father never could bear cabbage." She must consider what he likes, not only because she loves to please him or because she profits by pleasing him, but because he pays for the dinner, and she is a private servant.

Is it not time that the way to a man's heart through his stomach should be relinquished for some higher avenue? The stomach should be left to its natural uses, not made a thoroughfare for stranger passions and purposes; and the heart should be approached through higher channels. We need a new picture of our over-worked blind god,— fat, greasy, pampered with sweetmeats by the poor worshippers long forced to pay their devotion through such degraded means.

No, the human race is not well nourished by making the process of feeding it a sex-function. The selection and preparation of food should be in the hands of trained experts. And woman should stand beside man as the comrade of his soul, not the servant of his body.

This will require large changes in our method of living. To feed the world by expert service, bringing to that great function the skill and experience of the trained specialist, the power of science, and the beauty of art, is impossible in the sexuo-economic relation. While we treat cooking as a sex-function common to all women and eating as a family function not otherwise rightly accomplished, we can develope no farther. We are spending much earnest study and hard labor to-day on the problem of teaching and training women in the art of cooking, both the wife and the servant; for, with our usual habit of considering voluntary individual conduct **as**

the cause of conditions, we seek to modify conditions by changing individual conduct.

What we must recognize is that, while the
conditions remain, the conduct cannot be altered. Any trade or profession, the development of which depended upon the labor of
isolated individuals, assisted only by hired servants more ignorant than themselves, would
remain at a similarly low level.

So far as health can be promoted by public
means, we are steadily improving by sanitary
regulations and medical inspection, by professionally prepared "health foods" and by the
literature of hygiene, by special legislation as to
contagious diseases and dangerous trades; but
the health that lies in the hands of the housewife is not reached by these measures. The
nine-tenths of our women who do their own
work cannot be turned into proficient purchasers
and cooks any more than nine-tenths of our
men could be turned into proficient tailors
with no better training or opportunity than
would be furnished by clothing their own families. The alternative remaining to the women
who comprise the other tenth is that peculiar
survival of earlier labor methods known as
"domestic service."

As a method of feeding humanity, hired
domestic service is inferior even to the service

of the wife and mother, and brings to the art of cooking an even lower degree of training and a narrower experience. The majority of domestic servants are young girls who leave this form of service for marriage as soon as they are able; and we thus intrust the physical health of human beings, so far as cooking affects it, to the hands of untrained, immature women, of the lowest social grade, who are actuated by no higher impulse than that of pecuniary necessity. The love of the wife and mother stimulates at least her desire to feed her family well. The servant has no such motive. The only cases in which domestic cooking reaches anything like proficiency are those in which the wife and mother is "a natural-born cook," and regales her family with the products of genius, or those in which the households of the rich are able to command the service of professionals.

There was a time when kings and lords retained their private poets to praise and entertain them; but the poet is not truly great until he sings for the world. So the art of cooking can never be lifted to its true place as a human need and a social function by private service. Such an arrangement of our lives and of our houses as will allow cooking to become a profession is the only way in which to free this great art from its present limitations. It should be a reputable, well-paid profession, wherein those women or those men who were adapted to this form of labor could become cooks, as they would become composers or carpenters. Natural distinctions would be developed between the mere craftsman and the artist; and we should have large, new avenues of lucrative and honorable industry, and a new basis for human health and happiness.

This does not involve what is known as "co-operation." Co-operation, in the usual sense, is the union of families for the better performance of their supposed functions. The process fails because the principle is wrong. Cooking and cleaning are not family functions. We do not have a family mouth, a family stomach, a family face to be washed. Individuals require to be fed and cleaned from birth to death, quite irrespective of their family relations. The orphan, the bachelor, the childless widower, have as much need of these nutritive and excretive processes as any patriarchal parent. Eating is an individual function. Cooking is a social function. Neither is in the faintest degree a family function. That we have found it convenient in early stages of civilization to do our cooking at home proves no more than the allied fact that we have also found it convenient in such stages to do our weaving and spinning at home, our soap and candle making, our butchering and pickling, our baking and washing.

As society developes, its functions specialize; and the reason why this great race-function of cooking has been so retarded in its natural growth is that the economic dependence of women has kept them back from their share in human progress. When women stand free as economic agents, they will lift and free their arrested functions, to the much better fulfilment of their duties as wives and mothers and to the vast improvement in health and happiness of the human race.

Co-operation is not what is required for this, but trained professional service and such arrangement of our methods of living as shall allow us to benefit by such service. When numbers of people patronize the same tailor or baker or confectioner, they do not co-operate. Neither would they co-operate in patronizing the same cook. The change must come from the side of the cook, not from the side of the family. It must come through natural functional development in society, and it is so coming. Woman, recognizing that her duty as feeder and cleaner is a social duty, not a sexual one, must face the requirements of the situation, and prepare herself to meet them. A hundred years ago this could not have been done. Now it is being done, because the time is ripe for it.

If there should be built and opened in any of our large cities to-day a commodious and well-served apartment house for professional women with families, it would be filled at once. The apartments would be without kitchens; but there would be a kitchen belonging to the house from which meals could be served to the families in their rooms or in a common dining-room, as preferred. It would be a home where the cleaning was done by efficient workers, not hired separately by the families, but engaged by the manager of the establishment; and a roof-garden, day nursery, and kindergarten, under well-trained professional nurses and teachers, would insure proper care of the children. The demand for such provision is increasing daily, and must soon be met, not by a boarding-house or a lodging-house, a hotel, a restaurant, or any makeshift patching together of these; but by a permanent provision for the needs of women and children, of family privacy with collective advantage. This must be offered on a business basis to prove a substantial business success; and it will so prove, for it is a growing social need.

There are hundreds of thousands of women in New York City alone who are wage-earners, and who also have families; and the number increases. This is true not only among the poor and unskilled, but more and more among business women, professional women, scientific, artistic, literary women. Our school-teachers, who form a numerous class, are not entirely without relatives. To board does not satisfy the needs of a human soul. These women want homes, but they do not want the clumsy tangle of rudimentary industries that are supposed to accompany the home. The strain under which such women labor is no longer necessary. The privacy of the home could be as well maintained in such a building as described as in any house in a block, any room, flat, or apartment, under present methods. The food would be better, and would cost less; and this would be true of the service and of all common necessities.

In suburban homes this purpose could be accomplished much better by a grouping of adjacent houses, each distinct and having its own yard, but all kitchenless, and connected by covered ways with the eating-house. No detailed prophecy can be made of the precise forms which would ultimately prove most useful and pleasant; but the growing social need is for the specializing of the industries practised in the home and for the proper mechanical provision for them.

The cleaning required in each house would be

much reduced by the removal of the two chief elements of household dirt,— grease and ashes.

Meals could of course be served in the house as long as desired; but, when people become accustomed to pure, clean homes, where no steaming industry is carried on, they will gradually prefer to go to their food instead of having it brought to them. It is a perfectly natural process, and a healthful one, to go to one's food. And, after all, the changes between living in one room, and so having the cooking most absolutely convenient; going as far as the limits of a large house permit, to one's own dining-room; and going a little further to a dining-room not in one's own house, but near by,— these differ but in degree. Families could go to eat together, iust as they can go to bathe together or to listen to music together; but, if it fell out that different individuals presumed to develope an appetite at different hours, they could meet it without interfering with other people's comfort or sacrificing their own. Any housewife knows the difficulty of always getting a family together at meals. Why try? Then arises sentiment, and asserts that family affection, family unity, the very existence of the family, depend on their being together at meals. A family unity which is only bound together with a table-cloth is of questionable value.

There are several professions involved in our clumsy method of housekeeping. A good cook is not necessarily a good manager, nor a good manager an accurate and thorough cleaner, nor a good cleaner a wise purchaser. Under the free development of these branches a woman could choose her position, train for it, and become a most valuable functionary in her special branch, all the while living in her own home; that is, she would live in it as a man lives in his home, spending certain hours of the day at work and others at home.

This division of the labor of housekeeping would require the service of fewer women for fewer hours a day. Where now twenty women in twenty homes work all the time, and insufficiently accomplish their varied duties, the same work in the hands of specialists could be done in less time by fewer people; and the others would be left free to do other work for which they were better fitted, thus increasing the productive power of the world. Attempts at cooperation so far have endeavored to lessen the existing labors of women without recognizing their need for other occupation, and this is one reason for their repeated failure.

It seems almost unnecessary to suggest that women as economic producers will naturally choose those professions which are compatible with motherhood, and there are many professions much more in harmony with that function than the household service. Motherhood is not a remote contingency, but the common duty and the common glory of womanhood. If women did choose professions unsuitable to maternity, Nature would quietly extinguish them by her unvarying process. Those mothers who persisted in being acrobats, horse-breakers, or sailors before the mast, would probably not produce vigorous and numerous children. If they did, it would simply prove that such work did not hurt them. There is no fear to be wasted on the danger of women's choosing wrong professions, when they are free to choose. Many women would continue to prefer the very kinds of work which they are doing now, in the new and higher methods of execution. Even cleaning, rightly understood and practised, is a useful, and therefore honorable, profession. It has been amusing heretofore to see how this least desirable of labors has been so innocently held to be woman's natural duty. It is woman, the dainty, the beautiful, the beloved wife and revered mother, who has by common consent been expected to do the chamber-work and scullery work of the world. All that is basest and foulest she in the last instance must handle and remove. Grease, ashes, dust, foul linen, and sooty ironware,— among these her days must pass. As we socialize our functions, this passes from her hands into those of man. The city's cleaning is his work. And even in our houses the professional cleaner is more and more frequently a man.

The organization of household industries will simplify and centralize its cleaning processes, allowing of many mechanical conveniences and the application of scientific skill and thoroughness. We shall be cleaner than we ever were before. There will be less work to do, and far better means of doing it. The daily needs of a well-plumbed house could be met easily by each individual in his or her own room or by one who liked to do such work; and the labor less frequently required would be furnished by an expert, who would clean one home after another with the swift skill of training and experience. The home would cease to be to us a workshop or a museum, and would become far more the personal expression of its occupants — the place of peace and rest, of love and privacy — than it can be in its present condition of arrested industrial development. And woman will fill her place in those industries with far better results than are now provided by her ceaseless struggles, her conscientious devotion, her pathetic ignorance and inefficiency.

XII.

As self-conscious creatures, to whom is always open the easy error of mistaking feeling for fact, to whose consciousness indeed the feeling is the fact,— a further process of reasoning being required to infer the fact from the feeling,— we are not greatly to be blamed for laying such stress on sentiment and emotion. We may perhaps admit, in the light of cold reasoning, that the home is not the best place in which to do so much work in, nor the wife and mother the best person to do it. But this intellectual conviction by no means alters our feeling on the subject. Feeling, deep, long established, and over-stimulated, lies thick over the whole field of home life. Not what we think about it (for we never have thought about it very much), but what we feel about it, constitutes the sum of our opinion. Many of our feelings are true, right, legitimate. Some are fatuous absurdities, mere dangling relics of outgrown tradition, slowly moulting from us as we grow.

Consider, for instance, that long-standing popular myth known as "the privacy of the home." There is something repugnant in the idea of food cooked outside the home, even though served within it; still more in the going out of the family to eat, and more yet in the going out of separate individuals to eat. The limitless personal taste developed by " home cooking " fears that it will lose its own particular shade of brown on the bacon, its own hottest of hot cakes, its own corner biscuit.

This objection must be honestly faced, and admitted in some degree. A *menu,* however liberally planned by professional cooks, would not allow so much play for personal idiosyncrasy as do those prepared by the numerous individual cooks now serving us. There would be a far larger range of choice in materials, but not so much in methods of preparation and service. The difference would be like that between every man's making his own coat or having his women servants make it for him, on the one hand, and his selecting one from many ready made or ordering it of his tailor, on the other.

In the regular professional service of food there would be a good general standard, and the work of specialists for special occasions. We have long seen this process going on in the steady increase of professionally prepared food, from the cheap eating-house to the fashionable caterer, from the common " cracker " to the delicate " wafer." " Home cooking," robbed of its professional adjuncts, would fall a long way. We do not realize how far we have already progressed in this line, nor how fast we are going.

One of the most important effects of a steady general standard of good food will be the elevation of the popular taste. We should acquire a cultivated appreciation of what *is* good food, far removed from the erratic and whimsical self-indulgence of the private table. Our only standard of taste in cooking is personal appetite and caprice. That we "like" a dish is enough to warrant full approval. But liking is only adaptation. Nature is forever seeking to modify the organism to the environment; and, when it becomes so modified, so adapted, the organism "likes" the environment. In the earlier form, "it likes me," this derivation is plainer.

Each nation, each locality, each family, each individual, "likes," in large measure, those things to which it has been accustomed. What else it might have liked, if it had had it, can never be known; but the slow penetration of new tastes and habits, the reluctant adoption of the potato, the tomato, maize, and other new vegetables by old countries, show that it is quite possible to change a liking.

In the narrow range of family capacity to supply and of family ability to prepare our food, and in our exaggerated intensity of personal preference, we have grown very rigid in our little field of choice. We insist on the superiority of our own methods, and despise the

methods of our neighbors, with a sublime ignorance of any higher standard of criticism than
our own uneducated tastes. When we become
accustomed from childhood to scientifically and
artistically prepared foods, we shall grow to
know what is good and to enjoy it, as we learn
to know good music by hearing it.

As we learn to appreciate a wider and higher
range of cooking, we shall also learn to care
for simplicity in this art. Neither is attainable
under our present system by the average person.
As cooking becomes dissociated from the home,
we shall gradually cease to attach emotions to
it; and we shall learn to judge it impersonally
upon a scientific and artistic basis. This will
not, of course, prevent some persons' having
peculiar tastes; but these will know that they
are peculiar, and so will their neighbors. It
will not prevent, either, the woman who has a
dilettante fondness for some branch of cookery,
wherewith she loves to delight herself and her
friends, from keeping a small cooking plant
within reach, as she might a sewing-machine or
a turning-lathe.

In regard to the eating of food we are still
more opposed by the "privacy of the home"
idea, and a marked — indeed, a pained — disincli-
nation to dissociate that function from family
life. To eat together does, of course, form

a temporary bond. To establish a medium
of communication between dissimilar persons,
some common ground must be found,— some
rite, some game, some entertainment,— something that they can *do* together. And, if the
persons desiring to associate have no other
common ground than this physical function,—
which is so common, indeed, that it includes
not only all humanity, but all the animal kingdom,— then by all means let them seek that.
On occasions of general social rejoicing to celebrate some event of universal importance, the
feast will always be a natural and satisfying institution.

To the primitive husband with fighting for
his industry, the primitive wife with domestic
service for hers, the primitive children with no
relation to their parents but the physical,— to
such a common table was the only common tie;
and the simplicity of their food furnished a
medium that hurt no one. But in the higher
individualization of modern life the process of
eating is by no means the only common interest
among members of a family, and by no means
the best. The sweetest, tenderest, holiest
memories of family life are not connected with
the table, though many jovial and pleasant ones
may be so associated. And on many an occasion of deep feeling, whether of joy or of pain,

the ruthless averaging of the whole group three times a day at table becomes an unbearable strain. If good food suited to a wide range of needs were always attainable, a family could go and feast together when it chose or simply eat together when it chose; and each individual could go alone when he chose. This is not to be forced or hurried; but, with a steady supply of food, easy of access to all, the stomach need no longer be compelled to serve as a family tie.

We have so far held that the lower animals ate alone in their brutality, and that man has made eating a social function, and so elevated it. The elevation is the difficult part to prove, when we look at humanity's gross habits, morbid tastes, and deadly diseases, its artifice, and its unutterable depravity of gluttony and intemperance. The animals may be lower than we in their simple habit of eating what is good for them when they are hungry, but it serves their purpose well.

One result of our making eating a social function is that, the more elaborately we socialize it, the more we require at our feasts the service of a number of strangers absolutely shut out from social intercourse,— functionaries who do not eat with us, who do not talk with us, who must not by the twinkling of an eyelash show any interest in this performance, save to minister to the grosser needs of the occasion on a strictly commercial basis. Such extraneous presence must and does keep the conversation at one level. In the family without a servant both mother and father are too hard worked to make the meal a social success; and, as soon as servants are introduced, a limit is set to the range of conversation. The effect of our social eating, either in families or in larger groups, is not wholly good. It is well open to question whether we cannot, in this particular, improve our system of living.

When the cooking of the world is open to full development by those whose natural talent and patient study lead them to learn how better and better to meet the needs of the body by delicate and delicious combinations of the elements of nutrition, we shall begin to understand what food means to us, and how to build up the human body in sweet health and full vigor. A world of pure, strong, beautiful men and women, knowing what they ought to eat and drink, and taking it when they need it, will be capable of much higher and subtler forms of association than this much-prized common table furnishes. The contented grossness of to-day, the persistent self-indulgence of otherwise intelligent adults, the fatness and leanness and feebleness, the whole train of food-made disorders, together

with all drug habits,— these morbid phenomena
are largely traceable to the abnormal attention
given to both eating and cooking, which must
accompany them as family functions. When
we detach them from this false position by un-
tangling the knot of our sexuo-economic relation, we shall give natural forces a chance to
work their own pure way in us, and make us
better.

Our domestic privacy is held to be further
threatened by the invasion of professional
cleaners. We should see that a kitchenless
home will require far less cleaning than is
now needed, and that the daily ordering of
one's own room could be easily accomplished
by the individual, when desired. Many would so
desire, keeping their own rooms, their personal
inner chambers, inviolate from other presence
than that of their nearest and dearest. Such
an ideal of privacy may seem ridiculous to those
who accept contentedly the gross publicity of
our present method. Of all popular paradoxes,
none is more nakedly absurd than to hear us
prate of privacy in a place where we cheerfully
admit to our table-talk and to our door service —
yes, and to the making of our beds and to the
handling of our clothing — a complete stranger,
a stranger not only by reason of new acquaintance and of the false view inevitable to new

eyes let in upon our secrets, but a stranger by birth, almost always an alien in race, and, more hopeless still, a stranger by breeding, one who can never truly understand.

This stranger all of us who can afford it summon to our homes,— one or more at once, and many in succession. If, like barbaric kings of old or bloody pirates of the main, we cut their tongues out that they might not tell, it would still remain an irreconcilable intrusion. But, as it is, with eyes to see, ears to hear, and tongues to speak, with no other interests to occupy their minds, and with the retaliatory fling that follows the enforced silence of those who must not "answer back,"— with this observing and repeating army lodged in the very bosom of the family, may we not smile a little bitterly at our fond ideal of "the privacy of the home"? The swift progress of professional sweepers, dusters, and scrubbers, through rooms where they were wanted, and when they were wanted, would be at least no more injurious to privacy than the present method. Indeed, the exclusion of the domestic servant, and the entrance of woman on a plane of interest at once more social and more personal, would bring into the world a new conception of the sacredness of privacy, a feeling for the rights of the individual as yet unknown.

Closely connected with the question of cleaning is that of household decoration and furnishing. The economically dependent woman, spending the accumulating energies of the race in her small cage, has thrown out a tangled mass of expression, as a large plant throws out roots in a small pot. She has crowded her limited habitat with unlimited things,— things useful and unuseful, ornamental and unornamental, comfortable and uncomfortable; and the labor of her life is to wait upon these things, and keep them clean.

The free woman, having room for full individual expression in her economic activities and in her social relation, will not be forced so to pour out her soul in tidies and photograph holders. The home will be her place of rest, not of uneasy activity; and she will learn to love simplicity at last. This will mean better sanitary conditions in the home, more beauty and less work. And the trend of the new conditions, enhancing the value of real privacy and developing the sense of beauty, will be toward a delicate loveliness in the interiors of our houses, which the owners can keep in order without undue exertion.

Besides these comparatively external conditions, there are psychic effects produced upon the family by the sexuo-economic relation not altogether favorable to our best growth. One

is the levelling effect of the group upon its
members, under pressure of this relation. Such
privacy as we do have in our homes is family
privacy, an aggregate privacy ; and this does not
insure — indeed, it prevents — individual privacy.
This is another of the lingering rudiments of
methods of living belonging to ages long since
outgrown, and maintained among us by the
careful preservation of primitive customs in the
unchanged position of women. In very early
times a crude and undifferentiated people could
flock in family groups in one small tent without
serious inconvenience or injury. The effects of
such grouping on modern people is known in
the tenement districts of large cities, where
families live in single rooms ; and these effects
are of a distinctly degrading nature.

The progressive individuation of human beings requires a personal home, one room at least
for each person. This need forces some recognition for itself in family life, and is met so far
as private purses in private houses can meet it ;
but for the vast majority of the population no
such provision is possible. To women, especially, a private room is the luxury of the rich
alone. Even where a partial provision for personal needs is made under pressure of social
development, the other pressure of undeveloped
family life is constantly against it. The home

is the one place on earth where no one of the component individuals can have any privacy. A family is a crude aggregate of persons of different ages, sizes, sexes, and temperaments, held together by sex-ties and economic necessity; and the affection which should exist between the members of a family is not increased in the least by the economic pressure, rather it is lessened. Such affection as is maintained by economic forces is not the kind which humanity most needs.

At present any tendency to withdraw and live one's own life on any plane of separate interest or industry is naturally resented, or at least regretted, by the other members of the family. This affects women more than men, because men live very little in the family and very much in the world. The man has his individual life, his personal expression and its rights, his office, studio, shop : the women and children live in the home — because they must. For a woman to wish to spend much time elsewhere is considered wrong, and the children have no choice. The historic tendency of women to "gad abroad," of children to run away, to be forever teasing for permission to go and play somewhere else ; the ceaseless, futile, well-meant efforts to "keep the boys at home," — these facts, together with the definite absence of the man of the home for so much of the time, constitute a curious commentary upon our patient belief that we live at home, and like it. Yet the home ties bind us with a gentle dragging hold that few can resist. Those who do resist, and who insist upon living their individual lives, `find that this costs them loneliness and privation ; and they lose so much in daily comfort and affection that others are deterred from following them.

There is no reason why this painful choice should be forced upon us, no reason why the home life of the human race should not be such as to allow — yes, to promote — the highest development of personality. We need the society of those dear to us, their love and their companionship. These will endure. But the common cook-shops of our industrially undeveloped homes, and all the allied evils, are not essential, and need not endure.

To our general thought the home just as it stands is held to be what is best for us. We imagine that it is at home that we learn the higher traits, the nobler emotions,— that the home teaches us how to live. The truth beneath this popular concept is this : the love of the mother for the child is at the base of all our higher love for one another. Indeed, even behind that lies the generous giving impulse of sex-love, the out·going force of sex-energy. The family relations ensuing do underlie our higher, wider social relations. The "home comforts" are essential to the preservation of individual life. And the bearing and forbearing of home life, with the dominant, ceaseless influence of conservative femininity, is a most useful check to the irregular flying impulses of masculine energy. While the world lasts, we shall need not only the individual home, but the family home, the common sheath for the budded leaflets of each new branch, held close to the parent stem before they finally diverge.

Granting all this, there remains the steadily increasing ill effect, not of home life *per se*, but of the kind of home life based on the sexuo-economic relation. A home in which the rightly dominant feminine force is held at a primitive plane of development, and denied free participation in the swift, wide, upward movement of the world, reacts upon those who hold it down by holding them down in turn. A home in which the inordinate love of receiving things, so long bred into one sex, and the fierce hunger for procuring things, so carefully trained into the other, continually act upon the child, keeps ever before his eyes the fact that life consists in getting dinner and in getting the money to pay for it, getting the food from the market, working for·

ever and ever to cook and serve it. These are the prominent facts of the home as we have made it. The kind of care in which our lives are spent, the things that wear and worry us, are things that should have been outgrown long, long ago if the human race had advanced evenly. Man has advanced, but woman has been kept behind. By inheritance she advances, by experience she is retarded, being always forced back to the economic grade of many thousand years ago.

If a modern man, with all his intellect and energy and resource, were forced to spend all his days hunting with a bow and arrow, fishing with a bone-pointed spear, waiting hungrily on his traps and snares in hope of prey, he could not bring to his children or to his wife the uplifting influences of the true manhood of our time. Even if he started with a college education, even if he had large books to read (when he had time to read them) and improving conversation, still the economic efforts of his life, the steady daily pressure of what he had to do for his living, would check the growth of higher powers. If all men had to be hunters from day to day, the world would be savage still. While all women have to be house servants from day to day, we are still a servile world.

A home life with a dependent **mother,** a

servant - wife, is not an ennobling influence. We all feel this at times. The man, spreading and growing with the world's great growth, comes home, and settles into the tiny talk and fret, or the alluring animal comfort of the place, with a distinct sense of coming down. It is pleasant, it is gratifying to every sense, it is kept warm and soft and pretty to suit the needs of the feebler and smaller creature who is forced to stay in it. It is even considered a virtue for the man to stay in it and to prize it, to value his slippers and his newspaper, his hearth fire and his supper table, his spring bed, and his clean clothes above any other interests.

The harm does not lie in loving home and in staying there as one can, but in the kind of a home and in the kind of womanhood that it fosters, in the grade of industrial development on which it rests. And here, without prophesying, it is easy to look along the line of present progress, and see whither our home life tends. From the cave and tent and hovel up to a graded, differentiated home, with as much room for the individual as the family can afford; from the surly dominance of the absolute patriarch, with his silent servile women and chattel children, to the comparative freedom, equality, and finely diversified lives of a wellbred family of to-day; from the bottom grade of

industry in the savage camp, where all things
are cooked together by the same person in the
same pot,—without neatness, without delicacy,
without specialization,—to the million widely
separated hands that serve the home to-day in a
thousand wide-spread industries,—the man and
the mill have achieved it all; the woman has
but gone shopping outside, and stayed at the
base of the pyramid within.

And, more important and suggestive yet,
mark this: whereas, in historic beginnings, nothing but the home of the family existed; slowly,
as we have grown, has developed the home of
the individual. The first wider movement of
social life meant a freer flux of population,—
trade, commerce, exchange, communication.
Along river courses and sea margins, from
canoe to steamship, along paths and roads as
they made them, from "shank's mare to the
iron horse," faster and freer, wider and oftener,
the individual human beings have flowed and
mingled in the life that is humanity. At first
the traveller's only help was hospitality,—the
right of the stranger; but his increasing functional use brought with it, of necessity, the organic structure which made it easy, the transi-
tory individual home. From the most primitive
caravansary up to the square miles of floor-
space in our grand hotels, the public house has

met the needs of social evolution as no private house could have done.

To man, so far the only fully human being of his age, the bachelor apartment of some sort has been a temporary home for that part of his life wherein he had escaped from one family and not yet entered another. To woman this possibility is opening to-day. More and more we see women presuming to live and have a home, even though they have not a family. The family home itself is more and more yielding to the influence of progress. Once it was stationary and permanent, occupied from generation to generation. Now we move, even in families,— move with reluctance and painful objection and with bitter sacrifice of household gods; but move we must under the increasing irritation of irreconcilable conditions. And so has sprung up and grown to vast proportions that startling portent of our times, the "family hotel."

Consider it. Here is the inn, once a mere makeshift stopping-place for weary travellers. Yet even so the weary traveller long since noted the difference between his individual freedom there and his home restrictions, and cheerfully remarked, "I take mine ease in mine inn." Here is this temporary stopping-place for single men become a permanent dwelling-place for families! Not from financial necessity. These

are inhabited by people who could well afford
to "keep house." But they do not want to
keep house. They are tired of keeping house.
It is so difficult to keep house, the servant problem is so trying. The health of their wives is
not equal to keeping house. These are the
things they say.

But under these vague perceptions and ex-
pressions is heaving and stirring a slow, upris-
ing social tide. The primitive home, based on
the economic dependence of woman, with its unorganized industries, its servile labors, its smothering drag on individual development, is becoming increasingly unsuitable to the men and
women of to-day. Of course, they hark back
to it, of necessity, so long as marriage and child-
bearing are supposed to require it, so long as
our fondest sentiments and our earliest memories so closely cling to it. But in its practical
results, as shown by the ever-rising draught
upon the man's purse and the woman's strength,
it is fast wearing out.

We have watched the approach of this condition, and have laid it to every cause but the
real one. We have blamed men for not staying
at home as they once did. We have blamed
women for not being as good housekeepers as
they once were. We have blamed the children
for their discontent, the servants for their in-

efficiency, the very brick and mortar for their poor construction. But we have never thought to blame the institution itself, and see whether it could not be improved upon.

On wide Western prairies, or anywhere in lonely farm houses, the women of to-day, confined absolutely to this strangling cradle of the race, go mad by scores and hundreds. Our asylums show a greater proportion of insane women among farmers' wives than in any other class. In the cities, where there is less "home life," people seem to stand it better. There are more distractions, the men say, and seek them. There is more excitement, amusement, variety, the women say, and seek them. What is really felt is the larger social interests and the pressure of forces newer than those of the home circle.

Many fear this movement, and vainly strive to check it. There is no cause for alarm. We are not going to lose our homes nor our families, nor any of the sweetness and happiness that go with them. But we are going to lose our kitchens, as we have lost our laundries and bakeries. The cook-stove will follow the loom and wheel, the wool-carder and shears. We shall have homes that are places to live in and love in, to rest in and play in, to be alone in and to be together in ; and they will not be confused and declassed by admixture with any industry whatever.

In homes like these the family life will have all its finer, truer spirit well maintained; and the cares and labors that now mar its beauty will have passed out into fields of higher fulfilment. The relation of wife to husband and mother to child is changing for the better with this outward alteration. All the personal relations of the family will be open to a far purer and fuller growth.

Nothing in the exquisite pathos of woman's long subjection goes deeper to the heart than the degradation of motherhood by the very conditions we supposed were essential to it. To see the mother's heart and mind longing to go with the child, to help it all the way, and yet to see it year by year pass farther from her, learn things she never was allowed to know, do things she never was allowed to do, go out into "the world" — their world, not hers — alone, and

"To bear, to nurse, to rear, to love, and then to lose!"

this not by the natural separation of growth and personal divergence, but by the unnatural separation of falsely divided classes, — rudimentary women and more highly developed men. It is the fissure that opens before the boy is ten years old, and it widens with each year.

A mother economically free, a world-servant instead of a house-servant; a mother knowing the world and living in it,— can be to her children far more than has ever been possible before. Motherhood in the world will make that world a different place for her child.

XIII.

In reconstructing in our minds the position
of woman under conditions of economic independence, it is most difficult to think of her as
a mother.

We are so unbrokenly accustomed to the old
methods of motherhood, so convinced that all
its processes are inter-relative and indispensable, and that to alter one of them is to en-
danger the whole relation, that we cannot conceive of any desirable change.

When definite plans for such change are
suggested, — ways in which babies might be
better cared for than at present, — we either
deny the advantages of the change proposed
or insist that these advantages can be reached
under our present system. Just as in cooking we seek to train the private cook and to
exalt and purify the private taste, so in baby-
culture we seek to train the individual mother,
and to call for better conditions in the private
home; in both cases ignoring the relation between our general system and its particular
phenomena. Though it may be shown, with
clearness, that in physical conditions the private house, as a place in which to raise children, may be improved upon, yet all the more
stoutly do we protest that the mental life, the

emotional life, of the home is the best possible environment for the young.

There was a time in human history when this was true. While progress derived its main impetus from the sex-passion, and the highest emotions were those that held us together in the family relation, such education and such surroundings as fostered and intensified these emotions were naturally the best. But in the stage into which we are now growing, when the family relation is only a part of life, and our highest duties lie between individuals in social relation, the child has new needs.

This does not mean, as the scared rush of the unreasoning mind to an immediate opposite would suggest, a disruption of the family circle or the destruction of the home. It does not mean the separation of mother and child, — that instant dread of the crude instinct of animal maternity. But it does mean a change of basis in the family relation by the removal of its previous economic foundation, and a change of method in our child-culture. We are no more bound to maintain forever our early methods in baby - raising than we are bound to maintain them in the education of older children, or in floriculture. All human life is in its very nature open to improvement,

and motherhood is not excepted. The relation between men and women, between husband and wife, between parent and child,
changes inevitably with social advance; but
we are loath to admit it. We think a change
here must be wrong, because we are so convinced that the present condition is right.

On examination, however, we find that the
existing relation between parents and children
in the home is by no means what we unquestioningly assume. We all hold certain ideals
of home life, of family life. When we see
around us, or read of, scores and hundreds of
cases of family unhappiness and open revolt,
we lay it to the individual misbehavior of the
parties concerned, and go on implicitly be-
lieving in the intrinsic perfection of the institution. When, on the other hand, we find
people living together in this relation, in
peace and love and courtesy, we do not conversely attribute this to individual superiority
and virtue; but we point to it as instancing
the innate beauty of the relation.

To the careful sociological observer what
really appears is this: when individual and
racial progress was best served by the close
associations of family life, people were very
largely developed in capacity for family affection. They were insensitive to the essential

limitations and incessant friction of the relation. They assented to the absolute authority
of the head of the family and to the minor
despotism of lower functionaries, manifesting
none of those sharply defined individual characteristics which are so inimical to the family
relation.

But we have reached a stage where individual and racial progress is best served by the
higher specialization of individuals and by
a far wider sense of love and duty. This
change renders the psychic condition of home
life increasingly disadvantageous. We constantly hear of the inferior manners of the
children of to-day, of the restlessness of the
young, of the flat treason of deserting parents.
It is visibly not so easy to live at home as it
used to be. Our children are not more perversely constituted than the children of earlier
ages, but the conditions in which they are
reared are not suited to develope the qualities
now needed in human beings.

This increasing friction between members
of families should not be viewed with condemnation from a moral point of view, but studied
with scientific interest. If our families are
so relatively uncomfortable under present conditions, are there not conditions wherein the
same families could be far more comfortable?

No: we are afraid not. We think it is right to have things as they are, wrong to wish to change them. We think that virtue lies largely in being uncomfortable, and that there is special virtue in the existing family relation.

Virtue is a relative term. Human virtues change from age to age with the change in conditions. Consider the great virtue of loyalty, — our highest name for duty. This is a quality that became valuable in human life the moment we began to do things which were not instantly and visibly profitable to ourselves. The permanent application of the individual to a task not directly attractive was an indispensable social quality, and therefore a virtue. Steadfastness, faithfulness, loyalty, duty, that conscious, voluntary attitude of the individual which holds him to a previously assumed relation, even to his extreme personal injury, — to death itself, — from this results the cohesion of the social body: it is a first principle of social existence.

To the personal conscience a social necessity must express itself in a recognized and accepted pressure, — a force to which we bow, a duty, a virtue. So the virtue of loyalty came into early and lasting esteem, whether in the form of loyalty to one's own spoken word or vow —" He that sweareth to his hurt, and doeth it "— to a friend or group of friends in temporary union for some common purpose, or to a larger and more permanent relation. The highest form is, of course, loyalty to the largest common interest; and here we can plainly trace the growth of this quality.

First, we see it in the vague, nebulous, coherence of the horde of savages, then in the tense devotion of families, — that absolute duty to the highest known social group. It was in this period that obedience to parents was writ so large in our scale of virtues. The family feud, the *vendetta* of the Corsicans, is an over-development of this force of family devotion. Next came loyalty to the chief, passing even that due the father. And with the king — that dramatic personification of a nation, "Lo! royal England comes!" — loyalty became a very passion. It took precedence of every virtue, with good reason; for it was not, as was supposed, the person of the king which was so revered: it was the embodied nation, the far-reaching, collective interests of every citizen, the common good, which called for the willing sacrifice of every individual. We still exhibit all these phases of loyalty, in differently diminishing degrees; but we show, also, a larger form of this great virtue peculiar to our age.

The lines of social relation to-day are mainly industrial. Our individual lives, our social peace and progress, depend more upon our economic relations than upon any other. For a long time society was organized only on a sex-basis, a religious basis, or a military basis, each of such organizations being comparatively transient; and its component individuals labored alone on an economic basis of helpless individualism.

Duty is a social sense, and developes only with social organization. As our civil organization has become national, we have developed the sense of duty to the State. As our industrial organization has grown to the world-encircling intricacies of to-day, as we have come to hold our place on earth by reason of our vast and elaborate economic relation with its throbbing and sensitive machinery of communication and universal interservice, the unerring response of the soul to social needs has given us a new kind of loyalty,— loyalty to our work. The engineer who sticks to his engine till he dies, that his trainload of passengers may live; the cashier who submits to torture rather than disclose the secret of the safe,— these are loyal exactly as was the servitor of feudal times, who followed his master to the death, or the subject who gave up all for his king. Professional honor, duty to one's employers, duty to the work itself, at any cost,—this is loyalty, faithfulness, the power to stay put in a relation necessary to the social good, though it may be directly against personal interest.

It is in the training of children for this stage of human life that the private home has ceased to be sufficient, or the isolated, primitive, dependent woman capable. Not that the mother does not have an intense and overpowering sense of loyalty and of duty; but it is duty to individuals, just as it was in the year one. What she is unable to follow, in her enforced industrial restriction, is the higher specialization of labor, and the honorable devotion of human lives to the development of their work. She is most slavishly bound to her daily duty, it is true; but it does not occur to her as a duty to raise the grade of her own labor for the sake of humanity, nor as a sin so to keep back the progress of the world by her contented immobility.

She cannot teach what she does not know. She cannot in any sincerity uphold as a duty what she does not practise. The child learns more of the virtues needed in modern life — of fairness, of justice, of comradeship, of collective interest and action — in a common

277

school than can be taught in the most perfect
family circle. We may preach to our children as we will of the great duty of loving
and serving one's neighbor; but what the baby
is born into, what the child grows up to see
and feel, is the concentration of one entire
life — his mother's — upon the personal ag-
grandizement of one family, and the human
service of another entire life — his father's
— so warped and strained by the necessity of
"supporting his family" that treason to society is the common price of comfort in the
home. For a man to do any base, false work
for which he is hired, work that injures producer and consumer alike; to prostitute what
power and talent he possesses to whatever
purchaser may use them, — this is justified
among men by what they call duty to the family, and is unblamed by the moral sense of
dependent women.

And this is the atmosphere in which the
wholly home-bred, mother-taught child grows
up. Why should not food and clothes and the
comforts of his own people stand first in his
young mind? Does he not see his mother,
the all - loved, all - perfect one, peacefully
spending her days in the arrangement of these
things which his father's ceaseless labor has
procured? Why should he not grow up to

care for his own, to the neglect and willing injury of all the rest, when his earliest, deepest impressions are formed under such exclusive devotion?

It is not the home as a place of family life and love that injures the child, but as the centre of a tangled heap of industries, low in their ungraded condition, and lower still because they are wholly personal. Work the object of which is merely to serve one's self is the lowest. Work the object of which is merely to serve one's family is the next lowest. Work the object of which is to serve more and more people, in widening range, till it approximates the divine spirit that cares for all the world, is social service in the fullest sense, and the highest form of service that we can reach.

It is this personality in home industry that keeps it hopelessly down. The short range between effort and attainment, the constant attention given to personal needs, is bad for the man, worse for the woman, and worst for the child. It belittles his impressions of life at the start. It accustoms him to magnify the personal duties and minify the social ones, and it greatly retards his adjustment to larger life. This servant-motherhood, with all its unavoidable limitation and ill results, is the concomitant of the economic dependence of woman upon man, the direct and inevitable effect of the sexuo-economic relation.

The child is affected by it during his most impressionable years, and feels the effect throughout life. The woman is permanently retarded by it; the man, less so, because of his normal social activities, wherein he is under more developing influence. But he is injured in great degree, and our whole civilization is checked and perverted.

We suffer also, our lives long, from an intense self-consciousness, from a sensitiveness beyond all need; we demand measureless personal attention and devotion, because we have been born and reared in a very hotbed of these qualities. A baby who spent certain hours of every day among other babies, being cared for because he was a baby, and not because he was "my baby," would grow to have a very different opinion of himself from that which is forced upon each new soul that comes among us by the ceaseless adoration of his own immediate family. What he needs to learn at once and for all, to learn softly and easily, but inexorably, is that he is one of many. We all dimly recognize this in our praise of large families, and in our saying that "an only child is apt to be selfish." So is an only family. The earlier and more easily a child can learn that human life means many people, and their behavior to one another, the happier and stronger and more useful his life will be.

This could be taught him with no difficulty whatever, under certain conditions, just as he is taught his present sensitiveness and egotism by the present conditions. It is not only temperature and diet and rest and exercise which affect the baby. "He does love to be noticed," we say. "He is never so happy as when he has a dozen worshippers around him." But what is the young soul learning all the while? What does he gather, as he sees and hears and slowly absorbs impressions? With the inflexible inferences of a clear, young brain, unsupplied with any counter-evidence until later in life, he learns that women are meant to wait on people, to get dinner, and sweep and pick up things; that men are made to bring home things, and are to be begged of according to circumstances; that babies are the object of concentrated admiration; that their hair, hands, feet, are specially attractive; that they are the heated focus of attention, to be passed from hand to hand, swung and danced and amused most violently, and also be laid aside and have nothing done to them, with no regard to their preference in either case.

And then, in the midst of all this tingling self-consciousness and desire for loving praise, he learns that he is "naughty"! The grief, the shame, the anger at injustice, the hopeless bewilderment, the morbid sensitiveness of conscience or the stolid dulling of it, the gradual retirement of the baffled brain from all these premature sensations to a contentment with mere personal gratification and a growing ingenuity in obtaining it,—all these experiences are the common lot of the child among us, our common lot when we were children. Of course, we don't remember. Of course, we loved our mother, and thought her perfect. Comparisons among mothers are difficult for a baby. Of course, we loved our homes, and never dreamed of any other way of being "brought up." And, of course, when we have children of our own, we bring them up in the same way. What other way is there? What is there to be said on the subject? Children always were brought up at home. Isn't that enough?

And yet, insidiously, slowly, irresistibly, while we flatter ourselves that things remain the same, they are changing under our very eyes from year to year, from day to day.

Education, hiding itself behind a wall of books, but consisting more and more fully in the grouping of children and in the training of faculties never mentioned in the curriculum, — education, which is our human motherhood, has crept nearer and nearer to its true place, its best work, — the care and training of the little child. Some women there are, and some men, whose highest service to humanity is the care of children. Such should not concentrate their powers upon their own children alone, — a most questionable advantage, — but should be so placed that their talent and skill, their knowledge and experience, would benefit the largest number of children. Many women there are, and many men, who, though able to bring forth fine children, are unable to educate them properly. Simply to bear children is a personal matter, — an animal function. Education is collective, human, a social function.

As we now arrange life, our children must take their chances while babies, and live or die, improve or deteriorate, according to the mother to whom they chance to be born. An inefficient mother does not prevent a child from having a good school education or a good college education; but the education of babyhood, the most important of all, is wholly

in her hands. It is futile to say that mothers
should be taught how to fulfil their duties.
You cannot teach every mother to be a good
school educator or a good college educator.
Why should you expect every mother to be a
good nursery educator? Whatever our expectations, she is not; and our mistrained
babies, such of them as survive the maternal
handling, grow to be such people as we see
about us.

The growth and change in home and family
life goes steadily on under and over and
through our prejudices and convictions; and
the education of the child has changed and
become a social function, while we still imagine the mother to be doing it all.

In its earliest and most rudimentary manifestations, education was but part of the individual maternal function of the female animal.
But no sooner did the human mind begin to
show capacity for giving and receiving its
impressions through language (thus attaining
the power of acquiring information through
sources other than its own experience) than
the individual mother ceased to be the sole
educator. The young savage receives not
only guidance from his anxious mother, but
from the chiefs and elders of his tribe. For
a long time the aged were considered the only

suitable teachers, because the major part of knowledge was still derived from personal experience; and, of course, the older the person, the greater his experience, other things being equal, and they were rather equal then. This primitive notion still holds among us. People still assume superior wisdom because of superior age, putting mere number of experiences against a more essential and better arranged variety, and quite forgetting that the needed wisdom of to-day is not the accumulation of facts, but the power to think about them to some purpose.

With our increased power to preserve and transmit individual experience through literature, and to disseminate such information through systematic education, we see younger and younger people, more rich in, say, chemical or electrical experience than " the oldest inhabitant " could have been in earlier times. Therefore, the teacher of to-day is not the graybeard and beldame, but the man and woman most newly filled with the gathered experience of the world. As this change from age to youth has taken place in the teacher, it has also shown itself in the taught. Grown men frequented the academic groves of Greece. Youths filled the universities of the Middle Ages. Boys and, later, girls were

285

given the increasing school advantages of progressive centuries.

To-day the beautiful development of the kindergarten has brought education to the nursery door. Even our purblind motherhood is beginning to open that door; and we have at last entered upon the study of babyhood, its needs and powers, and are seeing that education begins with life itself. It is no new and daring heresy to suggest that babies need better education than the individual mother now gives them. It is simply a little further extension of the steadily expanding system of human education which is coming upon us, as civilization grows. And it no more infringes upon the mother's rights, the mother's duties, the mother's pleasures, than does the college or the school.

We think no harm of motherhood because our darlings go out each day to spend long hours in school. The mother is not held neglectful, nor the child bereft. It is not called a "separation of mother and child." There would be no further harm or risk or loss in a babyhood passed among such changed surroundings and skilled service as should meet its needs more perfectly than it is possible for the mother to meet them alone at home.

Better surroundings and care for babies,

better education, do not mean, as some mothers may imagine, that the tiny monthling is to be taught to read, or even that it is to be exposed to cabalistical arrangements of color and form and sound which shall mysteriously force the young intelligence to flower. It would mean, mainly, a far quieter and more peaceful life than is possible for the heavily loved and violently cared for baby in the busy household; and the impressions which it did meet would be planned and maintained with an intelligent appreciation of its mental powers. The mother would not be excluded, but supplemented, as she is now, by the teacher and the school.

Try and imagine for yourself, if you like, a new kind of coming alive,— the mother breast and mother arms there, of course, fulfilling the service which no other, however tender, could supervene; but there would be other service also. The long, bright hours of the still widening days would find one in sunny, soft-colored rooms, or among the grass and flowers, or by the warm sand and waters. There would be about one more of one's self, others of the same size and age, in restful, helpful companionship. A year means an enormous difference in the ages of babies. Think what a passion little children have for playmates of exactly their own age, because in them alone is perfect equality; and then think that the home-kept baby never has such companionship, unless, indeed, there are twins!

In this larger grouping, in full companionship, the child would unconsciously absorb the knowledge that "we" were humanity, that "we" were creatures to be so fed, so watched, so laid to sleep, so kissed and cuddled and set free to roll and play. The mother-hours would be sweetest of all, perhaps. Here would be something wholly one's own, and the better appreciated for the contrast. But the long, steady days would bring their peaceful lessons of equality and common interest instead of the feverish personality of the isolated one-baby household, or the innumerable tyrannies and exactions, the forced submissions and exclusions, of the nursery full of brothers and sisters of widely differing ages and powers. Mothers accustomed to consider many babies besides their own would begin, on the one hand, to learn something of mere general babyness, and so understand that stage of life far better, and, on the other, to outgrow the pathetic idolatry of the fabled crow, — to recognize a difference in babies, and so to learn a new ideal in their great work of motherhood.

This alone is reason good for a wider maternity. As long as each mother dotes and gloats upon her own children, knowing no others, so long this animal passion overesti mates or underestimates real human qualities in the child. So long as this endures, we must grow up with the false, unbalanced opinion of ourselves forced upon us in our infancy. We may think too well of ourselves or we may think too ill of ourselves; but we think always too much of ourselves, because of this untrained and unmodified concentration of maternal feeling. Our whole attitude toward the child is too intensely personal. Through all our aching later life we labor to outgrow the false perspective taught by primitive motherhood.

A baby, brought up with other babies, would never have that labor or that pain. However much his mother might love him, and he might enjoy her love, he would still find that for most of the time he was treated precisely like other people of the same age. Such a change would not involve any greater loss to home and family life than does the school or kindergarten. It would not rob the baby of his mother nor the mother of her baby. And such a change would give the mother certain free hours as a human being, as a member of a civilized community, as an economic producer, as a growing, self-realizing individual. This freedom, growth, and power will make her a wiser, stronger, and nobler mother.

After all is said of loving gratitude to our unfailing mother-nurse, we must have a most exalted sense of our own personal importance so to canonize the service of ourselves. The mother as a social servant instead of a home servant will not lack in true mother duty. She will love her child as well, perhaps better, when she is not in hourly contact with it, when she goes from its life to her own life, and back from her own life to its life, with ever new delight and power. She can keep the deep, thrilling joy of motherhood far fresher in her heart, far more vivid and open in voice and eyes and tender hands, when the hours of individual work give her mind another channel for her own part of the day. From her work, loved and honored though it is, she will return to the home life, the child life, with an eager, ceaseless pleasure, cleansed of all the fret and friction and weariness that so mar it now.

The child, also, will feel this beneficent effect. It is a mistake to suppose that the baby, more than the older child, needs the direct care and presence of the mother. Careful experiment has shown that a new-born baby does not know its own mother, and that a new-made mother does not know her own baby. They have been changed without the faintest recognition on either side.

The services of a foster-mother, a nurse, a grandma, are often liked by a baby as well as, and perhaps better than, those of its own mother. The mere bodily care of a young infant is as well given by one wise, loving hand as another. It is that trained hand that the baby needs, not mere blood-relationship. While the mother keeps her beautiful prerogative of nursing, she need never fear that any other will be dearer to the little heart than she who is the blessed provider of his highest known good. A healthy, happy, rightly occupied motherhood should be able to keep up this function longer than is now customary,— to the child's great gain. Aside from this special relationship, however, the baby would grow easily into the sense of other and wider relationship.

In the freedom and peace of his baby bed-room and baby parlor, in his easy association with others of his own age, he would absorb a sense of right human relation with his mother's milk, as it were,— a sense of others' rights and of his own. Instead of finding life a place in which all the fun was in being carried round and "done to" by others, and a place also in which these others were a tyranny and a weariness unutterable; he would find life a place in which to spread out, unhindered, getting acquainted with his own unfolding powers of body and mind in an atmosphere of physical warmth and ease and of quiet peace of mind.

Direct, concentrated, unvarying personal love is too hot an atmosphere for a young soul. Variations of loneliness, anger, and injustice, are not changes to be desired. A steady, diffused love, lighted with wisdom, based always on justice, and varied with rapturous draughts of our own mother's depth of devotion, would make us into a new people in a few generations. The bent and reach of our whole lives are largely modified by the surroundings of infancy; and those surroundings are capable of betterment, though not to be attained by the individual mother in the individual home.

There are three reasons why the individual mother can never be fit to take all the care of her children. The first two are so commonly true as to have much weight, the last so absolutely and finally true as to be sufficient in itself alone.

First, not every woman is born with the special qualities and powers needed to take right care of children: she has not the talent for it. Second, not every woman can have the instruction and training needed to fit her for the right care of children: she has not the education for it. Third, while each woman takes all the care of her own children herself, no woman can ever have the requisite experience for it. That is the final bar. That is what keeps back our human motherhood. No mother knows more than her mother knew: no mother has ever learned her business; and our children pass under the well-meaning experiments of an endless succession of amateurs.

We try to get "an experienced nurse." We insist on "an experienced physician." But our idea of an experienced mother is simply one who has borne many children, as if parturition was an educative process!

To experience the pangs of child-birth, or the further pangs of a baby's funeral, adds nothing whatever to the mother's knowledge of the proper care, clothing, feeding, and teaching of the child. The educative department of maternity is not a personal function: it is in its very nature a social function; and we fail grievously in its fulfilment.

The economically independent mother, wi-

293

dened and freed, strengthened and developed, by her social service, will do better service as mother than it has been possible to her before. No one thing could do more to advance the interests of humanity than the wiser care and wider love of organized human motherhood around our babies. This nobler mother, bearing nobler children, and rearing them in nobler ways, would go far toward making possible the world which we want to see. And this change is coming upon us overpoweringly in spite of our foolish fears.

XIV.

THE changes in our conception and expression of home life, so rapidly and steadily going on about us, involve many far-reaching effects, all helpful to human advancement. Not the least of these is the improvement in our machinery of social intercourse.

This necessity of civilization was unknown in those primitive ages when family intercourse was sufficient for all, and when any further contact between individuals meant war. Trade and its travel, the specialization of labor and the distribution of its products, with their ensuing development, have produced a wider, freer, and more frequent movement and interchange among the innumerable individuals whose interaction makes society. Only recently, and as yet but partially, have women as individuals come to their share of this fluent social intercourse which is the essential condition of civilization. It is not merely a pleasure or an indulgence: it is the human necessity.

For women as individuals to meet men and other women as individuals, with no regard whatever to the family relation, is a growing demand of our time. As a social necessity, it is perforce being met in some fashion; but

its right development is greatly impeded by
the clinging folds of domestic and social customs derived from the sexuo-economic relation. The demand for a wider and freer
social intercourse between the sexes rests,
primarily, on the needs of their respective
natures, but is developed in modern life to
a far subtler and higher range of emotion than
existed in the primitive state, where they had
but one need and but one way of meeting it;
and this demand, too, calls for a better arrangement of our machinery of living.

Always in social evolution, as in other evolution, the external form suited to earlier
needs is but slowly outgrown; and the period
of transition, while the new functions are
fumbling through the old organs, and slowly
forcing mechanical expression for themselves,
is necessarily painful. So far in our development, acting on a deep-seated conviction that
the world consisted only of families and the
necessary business arrangements involved in
providing for those families, we have conscien-
tiously striven to build and plan for family
advantage, and either unconsciously or grudg-
ingly have been forced to make transient provision for individuals. Whatever did not
tend to promote family life, and did tend to
provide for the needs of individuals not at the

time in family relation, we have deprecated in principle, though reluctantly forced to admit it in practice.

To this day articles are written, seriously and humorously, protesting against the increasing luxury and comfort of bachelor apartments for men, as well as against the pecuniary independence of women, on the ground that these conditions militate against marriage and family life. Most men, even now, pass through a period of perhaps ten years, when they are individuals, business calling them away from their parental family, and business not allowing them to start new families of their own. Women, also, more and more each year, are entering upon a similar period of individual life. And there is a certain permanent percentage of individuals, " odd numbers " and " broken sets," who fall short of family life or who are left over from it; and these need to live.

The residence hotel, the boarding-house, club, lodging-house, and restaurant are our present provision for this large and constantly increasing class. It is not a travelling class. These are people who want to live somewhere for years at a time, but who are not married or otherwise provided with a family. Home life being in our minds inextricably connected

297

with married life, a home being held to imply a family, and a family implying a head, these detached persons are unable to achieve any home life, and are thereby subjected to the inconvenience, deprivation, and expense, the often inhygienic, and sometimes immoral influences, of our makeshift substitutes.

What the human race requires is permanent provision for the needs of individuals, disconnected from the sex-relation. Our assumption that only married people and their immediate relatives have any right to live in comfort and health is erroneous. Every human being needs a home,— bachelor, husband, or widower, girl, wife, or widow, young or old. They need it from the cradle to the grave, and without regard to sex-connections. We should so build and arrange for the shelter and comfort of humanity as not to interfere with marriage, and yet not to make that comfort dependent upon marriage. With the industries of home life managed professionally, with rooms and suites of rooms and houses obtainable by any person or persons desiring them, we could live singly without losing home comfort and general companionship, we could meet bereavement without being robbed of the common conveniences of living as well as of the heart's love, and we could marry in

298

ease and freedom without involving any change in the economic base of either party concerned.

Married people will always prefer a home together, and can have it; but groups of women or groups of men can also have a home together if they like, or contiguous rooms. And individuals even could have a house to themselves, without having, also, the business of a home upon their shoulders.

Take the kitchens out of the houses, and you leave rooms which are open to any form of arrangement and extension; and the occupancy of them does not mean "housekeeping." In such living, personal character and taste would flower as never before; the home of each individual would be at last a true personal expression; and the union of individuals in marriage would not compel the jumbling together of all the external machinery of their lives,—a process in which much of the delicacy and freshness of love, to say nothing of the power of mutual rest and refreshment, is constantly lost. The sense of lifelong freedom and self-respect and of the peace and permanence of one's own home will do much to purify and uplift the personal relations of life, and more to strengthen and extend the social relations. The individual will learn to feel himself an integral part of the social structure, in close, direct, permanent connection with the needs and uses of society.

This is especially needed for women, who are generally considered, and who consider themselves, mere fractions of families, and incapable of any wholesome life of their own. The knowledge that peace and comfort may be theirs for life, even if they do not marry,— and may be still theirs for life, even if they do,— will develope a serenity and strength in women most beneficial to them and to the world. It is a glaring proof of the insufficient and irritating character of our existing form of marriage that women must be forced to it by the need of food and clothes, and men by the need of cooks and housekeepers. We are absurdly afraid that, if men or women can meet these needs of life by other means, they will cheerfully renounce the marriage rela-tion. And yet we sing adoringly of the power of love!

In reality, we may hope that the most val-uable effect of this change in the basis of living will be the cleansing of love and mar-riage from this base admixture of pecuniary interest and creature comfort, and that men and women, eternally drawn together by the deepest force in nature, will be able at last to meet on a plane of pure and perfect love. We shame our own ideals, our deepest instincts, our highest knowledge, by this gross assumption that the noblest race on earth will not mate, or, at least, not mate monogamously, unless bought and bribed through the common animal necessities of food and shelter, and chained by law and custom.

The depth and purity and permanence of the marriage relation rest on the necessity for the prolonged care of children by both parents, — a law of racial development which we can never escape. When parents are less occupied in getting food and cooking it, in getting furniture and dusting it, they may find time to give new thought and new effort to the care of their children. The necessities of the child are far deeper than for bread and bed: those are his mere racial needs, held in common with all his kind. What he needs far more and receives far less is the companionship, the association, the personal touch, of his father and mother. When the common labors of life are removed from the home, we shall have the time, and perhaps the inclination, to make the personal acquaintance of our children. They will seem to us not so much creatures to be waited on as people to be understood. As the civil and military protection of society has long since superseded the tooth-and-claw defence of the fierce parent, without in the least endangering the truth and intensity of the family relation, so the economic provision of society will in time supersede the bringing home of prey by the parent, without evil effects to the love or prosperity of the family. These primitive needs and primitive methods of meeting them are unquestionably at the base of the family relation; but we have long passed them by, and the ties between parent and child are not weakened, but strengthened, by the change.

The more we grow away from these basic conditions, the more fully we realize the deeper and higher forms of relation which are the strength and the delight of human life. Full and permanent provision for individual life and comfort will not cut off the forces that draw men and women together or hold children to their parents; but it will purify and intensify these relations to a degree which we can somewhat foretell by observing the effect of such changes as are already accomplished in this direction. And, in freeing the individual, old and young, from enforced association on family lines, and allowing this emergence into free association on social lines, we shall healthfully assist the development of true social intercourse.

The present economic basis of family life holds our friendly and familiar intercourse in narrow grooves. Such visiting and mingling as is possible to us is between families rather than between individuals; and the growing specialization of individuals renders it increasingly unlikely that all the members of a given family shall please a given visitor or he please them. This, on our present basis, either checks the intercourse or painfully strains the family relation. The change of economic relation in families from a sex-basis to a social basis will make possible wide individual intercourse without this accompanying strain on the family ties.

This outgoing impulse among members of families, their growing desire for general and personal social intercourse, has been considered as a mere thirst for amusement, and deprecated by the moralist. He has so far maintained that the highest form of association was association with one's own family, and that a desire for a wider and more fluent relationship was distinctly unworthy. "He is a good family man," we say admiringly of him who asks only for his newspaper and slippers in the evening; and for the woman who dares admit that she wishes further society than that of her husband we have but one name. With

the children, too, our constant effort is to
"keep the boys at home," to "make home
attractive," so that our ancient ideal, the
patriarchal ideal, of a world of families and
nothing else, may be maintained.

But this is a world of persons as well as of
families. We are persons as soon as we are
born, though born into families. We are persons when we step out of families, and persons still, even when we step into new families of our own. As persons, we need more
and more, in each generation, to associate
with other persons. It is most interesting to
watch this need making itself felt, and getting
itself supplied, by fair means or foul, through
all these stupid centuries. In our besotted
exaggeration of the sex-relation, we have
crudely supposed that a wish for wider human
relationship was a wish for wider sex-relationship, and was therefore to be discouraged, as
in Spain it was held unwise to teach women
to write, lest they become better able to com-
municate with their lovers, and so shake the
foundations of society.

But, when our sex-relation is made pure
and orderly by the economic independence
of women, when sex-attraction is no longer a
consuming fever, forever convulsing the social
surface, under all its bars and chains, we shall

not be content to sit down forever with half a dozen blood relations for our whole social arena. We shall need each other more, not less, and shall recognize that social need of one another as the highest faculty of this the highest race on earth.

The force which draws friends together is a higher one than that which draws the sexes together,— higher in the sense of belonging to a later race-development. " Passing the love of women " is no unmeaning phrase. Children need one another: young people need one another. Middle-aged people need one another: old people need one another. We all need one another, much and often. Just as every human creature needs a place to be alone in, a sacred, private " home " of his own, so all human creatures need a place to be together in, from the two who can show each other their souls uninterruptedly, to the largest throng that can throb and stir in unison.

Humanity means being together, and our unutterably outgrown way of living keeps us apart. How many people, if they dare face the fact, have often hopelessly longed for some better way of seeing their friends, their own true friends, relatives by soul, if not by body!

305

Acting always under the heated misconceptions of our over-sexed minds, we have pictured mankind as a race of beasts whose only desire to be together was based on one great, overworked passion, and who were only kept from universal orgies of promiscuity by being confined in homes. This is not true. It is not true even now in our over-sexed condition. It will be still less true when we are released from the artificial pressure of the sexuo-economic relation and grow natural again.

Men, women, and children need freedom to mingle on a human basis; and that means to mingle in their daily lives and occupations, not to go laboriously to see each other, with no common purpose. We all know the pleasant acquaintance and deep friendship that springs up when people are thrown together naturally, at school, at college, on shipboard, in the cars, in a camping trip, in business. The social need of one another rests at bottom on a common, functional development; and the common, functional service is its natural opportunity.

The reason why friendship means more to men than to women, and why they associate so much more easily and freely, is that they are further developed in race-functions, and that they *work together*. In the natural association of common effort and common relaxation is the true opening for human companionship. Just to put a number of human beings in the same room, to relate their bodies as to cubic space, does not relate their souls. Our present methods of association, especially for women, are most unsatisfactory. They arise, and go to "call" on one another. They solemnly "return" these calls. They prepare much food, and invite many people to come and eat it; or some dance, music, or entertainment is made the temporary ground of union. But these people do not really meet one another. They pass whole lifetimes in going through the steps of these elaborate games, and never become acquainted. There is a constant thirst among us for fuller and truer social intercourse; but our social machinery provides no means for quenching it.

Men have satisfied this desire in large measure; but between women, or between men and women, it is yet far from accomplishment. Men meet one another freely in their work, while women work alone. But the difference is sharpest in their play. "Girls don't have any fun!" say boys, scornfully; and they don't have very much. What they do have must come, like their bread and butter, on lines of sex. Some man must give

them what amusement they have, as he must
give them everything else. Men have filled
the world with games and sports, from the
noble contests of the Olympic plain to the
brain and body training sports of to-day, good,
bad, and indifferent. Through all the ages
the men have played; and the women have
looked on, when they were asked. Even the
amusing occupation of seeing other people do
things was denied them, unless they were
invited by the real participants. The "queen
of the ball-room" is but a wall-flower, unless
she is asked to dance by the real king.

Even to-day, when athletics are fast opening
to women, when tennis and golf and all the
rest are possible to them, the two sexes are
far from even in chances to play. To want
a good time is not the same thing as to want
the society of the other sex, and to make a
girl's desire for a good time hang so largely on
her power of sex-attraction is another of the
grievous strains we put upon that faculty.
That people want to see each other is con-
strued by us to mean that "he" wants to see
"her," and "she" wants to see "him."
The fun and pleasure of the world are so interwound with the sex-dependence of women
upon men that women are forced to court
"attentions," when not really desirous of any-

thing but amusement; and, as we force the association of the sexes on this plane, so we restrict it on a more wholesome one.

Even our little children in their play are carefully trained to accentuate sex; and a line of conduct for boys, differing from that for girls, is constantly insisted upon long before either would think of a necessity for such difference. Girls and boys, as they associate, are so commented on and teased as to destroy all wholesome friendliness, and induce a premature sex-consciousness. Young men and women are allowed to associate more or less freely, but always on a strictly sex-basis, friendship between man and woman being a common laughing-stock. Every healthy boy and girl resents this, and tries to hold free, natural relation; but such social pressure is hard to resist. She may have as many "beaux" as she can compass, he may "pay attention" to as many girls as he pleases; but that is their only way to meet.

The general discontinuance of all friendly visiting, upon the engagement of either party, proves the nature of the bond. Having chosen the girl he is to marry, why care to call upon any others? having chosen the man she is to marry, why receive attention from any others? these "calls" and "attentions" being all in the nature of tentative preliminaries to possible matrimony. And, after marriage, the wife is never supposed to wish to see any other man than her husband, or the husband any other woman than his wife. In some countries, we vary this arrangement by increasing the social freedom of married people; but the custom is accompanied by a commensurate lack of freedom before marriage, which causes questionable results, both in married life and in social life. In the higher classes of society there is always more freedom of social intercourse between the sexes after marriage; but, speaking generally of America, there is very little natural and serious acquaintance between men and women after the period of pre-matrimonial visiting.

Even the friendship which may have existed between husband and wife before marriage is often destroyed by that relation and its economic complications. They have not time to talk about things as they used: they are too near together, and too deeply involved in the industrial and financial concern of their new business. This works steadily against the development of higher and purer relations between men and women, and tends to keep them forever to the one primitive bond of sex-union.

A young man goes to a city to live and work. He needs the society of women as well as of men. Formerly he had his mother, his sisters, and his sisters' friends, his school-mates. Now he must face our constrained social conditions. He may visit two kinds of women, — those whom we call "good," and those whom we call "bad." (This classification rests on but one moral quality, and that a sexual one.) He naturally prefers the good. The good are divided, again, into two kinds, — married and single. If he visit a married woman frequently, it is remarked upon: it becomes unpleasant, he does not do it. If he visit an unmarried woman frequently, it is also remarked upon; and he is considered to have "intentions." His best alternative is to visit a number of unmarried women, and distribute his attentions so cautiously that no one can claim them as personal.

Here he enters on the first phase of our sexuo-economic relation: he cannot even visit girls freely without paying for it. Simply to see the girl by calling on her in the family circle is hardly what either wants of the other. One does not meet half a dozen people of various ages and of both sexes as one meets a friend alone. To seek to see her alone is an "attention." To "take her out" costs money, and he cheerfully pays it. But he cannot do this too often, or he will become involved in what is naturally considered a " serious " affair; and every step of the acquaintance is watched and commented upon from a sexual point of view.

There is no natural, simple medium of social intercourse between men and women. The young man can but learn that his popularity depends largely on his pocket-book. The money that he might be saving for marriage is wasted on these miscellaneous preliminaries. As he sees what women like and how much it costs to please them, his hope of marriage recedes farther and farther. The period during which he must live as an individual grows longer; and he becomes accustomed to superficial acquaintance with many women, on the shallowest side of life, with no opportunity for genuine association and true friendship. What wonder that the other kind of woman, who also costs money, it is true, but who does not involve permanent obligation, has come to be so steady a factor in our social life? The sexuo-economic relation promotes vice in more ways than one.

The economic independence of woman will change all these conditions as naturally and inevitably as her dependence has introduced sex-instinct lifted off the world, born clean and strong, of noble-hearted, noble-minded, noble-bodied mothers, trained in the large wisdom of thè new motherhood, and living freely in daily association with the best womanhood, a new kind of man can and will grow on earth. What this will mean to the race in power and peace and happiness no eye can foresee. But this much we can see:— that our once useful sexuo-economic relation is being outgrown, that it now produces many evil phenomena, and that its displacement by the economic freedom of woman will of itself set free new forces, to develope in us, by their natural working, the very virtues for which we have striven and agonized so long.

This change is not a thing to prophesy and plead for. It is a change already instituted, and gaining ground among us these many years with marvellous rapidity. Neither men nor women wish the change. Neither men nor women have sought it. But the same great force of social evolution which brought us into the old relation — to our great sorrow and pain — is bringing us out, with equal difficulty and distress. The time has come when it is better for the world that women be economically independent, and therefore they are becoming so.

them. In her specialization in industry, she will develope more personality and less sexuality; and this will lower the pressure on this one relation in both women and men. And, in our social intercourse, the new char acter and new method of living will allow of broad and beautiful developments in human association. As the private home becomes a private home indeed, and no longer the woman's social and industrial horizon; as the workshops of the world — woman's sphere as well as man's — become homelike and beautiful under her influence; and as men and women move freely together in the exercise of common racial functions, — we shall have new channels for the flow of human life.

We shall not move from the isolated home to the sordid shop and back again, in a world torn and dissevered by the selfish production of one sex and the selfish consumption of the other; but we shall live in a world of men and women humanly related, as well as sexually related, working together, as they were meant to do, for the common good of all. The home will be no longer an economic entity, with its cumbrous industrial machinery huddled vulgarly behind it, but a peaceful and permanent expression of personal life as withdrawn from social contact; and that social contact will be provided for by the many common meeting-places necessitated by the organization of domestic industries.

The assembling-room is as deep a need of human life as the retiring-room, — not some ball-room or theatre, to which one must be invited of set purpose, but great common libraries and parlors, baths and gymnasia, work-rooms and play-rooms, to which both sexes have the same access for the same needs, and where they may mingle freely in common human expression. The kind of buildings essential to the carrying out of the organization of home industry will provide such places. There will be the separate rooms for individuals and the separate houses for families; but there will be, also, the common rooms for all. These must include a place for the children, planned and built for the happy occupancy of many children for many years, — a home such as no children have ever had. This, as well as rooms everywhere for young people and old people, in which they can be together as naturally as they can be alone, without effort, question, or remark.

Such an environment would allow of free association among us, on lines of common interest; and, in its natural, easy flow, we should develop far higher qualities than are

brought out by the uneasy struggles of present "society" to see each other wi wanting to. It would make an enormous ference to woman's power of choosing right man. Cut off from the purch power which is now his easiest way to pass his desires, freely seen and known in daily work and amusements, a woman c know and judge a man as she is wholly un to do now. Her personality developed 1 free and useful life, clear-headed and o eyed, — a woman still, but a personality well as a woman, — the girl trained to nomic independence, and associating fr with young men in their common work play, would learn a new estimate of what constitutes noble manhood.

The young man, no longer able to cover his shortcomings with a dress-coat, and obtain absolution for every offence by simple penance of paying for it, unable rea to do much that was wrong for lack of the opportunity and the old incentive, constan helped and inspired by the friendly preser of honest and earnest womanhood, would ha all the force of natural law to lift him instead of pulling him heavily downward, it does now.

With the pressure of our over-develop

It is worth while for us to consider the case fully and fairly, that we may see what it is that is happening to us, and welcome with open arms the happiest change in human condition that ever came into the world. To free an entire half of humanity from an artificial position; to release vast natural forces from a strained and clumsy combination, and set them free to work smoothly and easily as they were intended to work; to introduce conditions that will change humanity from within, making for better motherhood and fatherhood, better babyhood and childhood, better food, better homes, better society,— this is to work for human improvement along natural lines. It means enormous racial advance, and that with great swiftness; for this change does not wait to create new forces, but sets free those already potentially strong, so that humanity will fly up like a released spring. And it is already happening. All we need do is to understand and help.

XV.

As WE learn to see how close is the connection of that which we call the soul with our external conditions, how the moral sense and the behavior of man are modified by the environment, we must of course look for marked results in psychic development arising from so important a condition as our sexuo-economic relation.

The relation of the sexes, in whatever form, has always been observed to affect strongly the moral nature of mankind; and this is one reason why we have placed such disproportionate stress upon the special virtues of that relation. The word "moral" in common use means "chaste"; and, in the case of women, the word "virtue" itself simply implies the one virtue of chastity. Large, popular conceptions are never baseless. They are rooted in deep truths, felt rather than seen, and, however false and silly in external interpretation, may be trusted in their general trend. It is not that the virtue of chastity is so much more important to the race than the virtue of honesty, the virtue of courage, the virtues of cheerfulness, of courtesy, of kindness, but that upon the sex-relation in which we live depends so much of the further development and arrangement of our whole moral nature.

What we call the moral sense is an intellectual recognition of the relative importance of certain acts and their consequences. This appears vaguely and weakly among early savages, and was for long mainly applied to a few clearly defined and arbitrary rites and ceremonies, set rules in a game of priest-and-people. But the habit of associating a sense of worthiness with certain acts by which came praise and profit grew in the childish soul, and the range of moral deeds widened. It has been widening ever since, growing deeper and higher and far more subtle, developing with the other social qualities.

No human distinction is more absolutely and exclusively social than the moral sense. Ethics is a social science. There is no ethics for the individual. Taken by himself, man is but an animal; and his conduct bears relation only to the needs of the animal, — self-preservation and race-preservation. Every virtue, and the power to see and strive for it, is a social quality. The highest virtues are those wherein we best serve the most people, and their development in us keeps pace with the development of society. It is the social relation which calls for our virtues, and which maintains them.

A simple instance of this is in the prompt

lapse to barbarism of a man cut off from his kind, and forced to live in conditions of savagery. Even a brief and partial change in condition changes conduct at once, as is shown by the behavior of the most pious New Englanders when in mining camps. It is shown, also, by the different scale of virtue in the different classes and industries.

Every social relation has its ethics; and the general needs of society, as a whole, are the basis of ethics. In every age and race this may be studied, and a clear connection established always between the virtues and vices of a given people and their local conditions. The principal governing condition in the development of ethics is the economic environment. This may seem strange to one accustomed to consider moral laws as not of this world, and to see how often virtue costs its possessor dear. The relative behavior of a given number of people depends, first, upon the existence of those people. Such conduct as should tend to exterminate them would exterminate their ethics. Such conduct as should tend to preserve and increase them is the only conduct of which ethical value can be predicated. Ethics is, therefore, absolutely conditioned upon life and the maintenance thereof. From the lowest and narrow-

320

est view which calls an act right or wrong, according to its immediate effects upon one's present life, to the clear vision of ultimate results which calls a course of conduct right or wrong, according to its final effects upon one's eternal life, our ethics, small and great, is the science of human conduct measured by its results.

It is inevitable, then, that in all races we should find those acts whereby men live considered right, and should see a high degree of approval awarded to him who best performs them. In the hunting and fighting period the best hunter and fighter was the best man, praised and honored by his tribe. The virtues cultivated were such as enabled the possessor to hunt and kill most successfully, to maintain himself and be a credit and a help to his friends. Savage virtues are the simple reflection of savage conditions. To be patient and self-controlled was an economic necessity to the hunter: to bear pain and arduous exertion easily was a necessity to the fighter. Therefore, the savage, by precept and example, cultivated these virtues.

In the long agricultural and military periods we see the same thing. In the peasant the virtues of industry and patience were extolled: it takes industry and patience to raise corn.

In the soldier the virtues of courage and obedience were extolled, and in every one the
virtue of faith was the prime requisite of the
existing religion. It took a great deal of
faith to accept the religions of those times.
The importance of faith as a virtue declines
as religion grows more intelligible and appli-
cable to life. It requires no effort to believe
what you can understand and do. Slowly the
industrial era dawned and grew, from the
weak, sporadic efforts of the cringing pack-
man and craftsman, the common prey of the
dominant fighting class, to our colossal industrial organization, in which the soldier is
ruthlessly exploited to some financial interests.
With this change in economic conditions has
changed the scale of virtues.

Physical courage has sunk: obedience, patience, faith, and the rest do not stand as they
did. We praise and value to-day, as always,
the virtues whereby we live. Every animal
developes the virtues of his conditions: our
human distinction is that we add the power of
conscious perception and personal volition to
the action of natural force. Not only in our
own race, but in others, do we call "good"
and "bad" those qualities which profit us;
and the beasts that we train and use develope,
of necessity, the qualities that profit them,—

as, for instance, in our well-known friend, the dog.

The dog is an animal long since cut off from his natural means of support, and depending absolutely on man for food. As a free, wild dog, he was profited by a daring initiative, courage, ferocity. As a tame, slave dog, he is profited by abject submission, by a crawling will-lessness that grovels at a blow, and licks the foot that kicks it. We have quite made over the original dog; and his moral nature, his spirit, shows the change even more than his body. The force which has accomplished this is economic, — a change of base in the source of supplies and the processes of obtaining them.

Let us briefly examine the distinctive virtues of humanity, their order of introduction and development, and see how this one peculiar relation has affected them.

The main distinction of human virtue is in what we roughly describe as altruism, — "otherness." To love and serve one another, to care for one another, to feel for and with one another, — our racial adjective, "humane," implies these qualities. The very existence of humanity implies these qualities in some degree, and the development of humanity is commensurate with their development.

Our one great blunder in studying these things lies in our failure to appreciate the organic necessity of such moral qualities in human life. We have assumed that the practice of these social virtues involved a personal effort and sacrifice, and that there is an irreconcilable contest between the cosmic process of development and the ethical process, as Huxley puts it. Social evolution brings with it the essential qualities of social relation, and these are our much boasted virtues. The natural processes of human intercourse and interrelation develope the qualities without which such intercourse would be impossible; and this development is as orderly, as natural, as "cosmic," as the processes of organic activity within the individual body. It is as natural for an industrial society to live in peace as for a hunting society to live in war; and this peace is not the result of heroic and self-sacrificing effort on the part of the industrial society; it is the necessity of their condition.

The course of evolution in human ethics is marked by a gradual extension of our perception of common good and evil as distinct from our initial perception of individual good and evil. This becomes very keen in the more socialized natures among us, as in the far-seeing devotion of statesmanship, patriotism, and philanthropy. Each of these words shows in its construction that the quality described is social,—the statesman, one who thinks and works for the State; the patriot, one who loves and labors for his country; the philanthropist, one who loves mankind. All these qualities, in their extreme and in their first beginnings, are a mere recognition of the equal right of the next man, common "fair play" and courtesy; they are but the natural product of social conditions acting on the individual through primal laws of economic necessity. The individual, in the absolute economic isolation of the beast, is profited by pure egoism, and he developes it. The individual, in the increasing economic interdependence of social relation, is profited by altruism; and he developes it.

All our virtues can be so traced and accounted for. The great main stem of them all, what we call "love," is merely the first condition of social existence. It is cohesion, working among us as the constituent particles of society. Without some attraction to hold us together, we should not be able to hold together; and this attraction, as perceived by our consciousness, we call love. The virtue of obedience consists in the surrender of the individual will, so often necessary to the common good; and it stands highest in military organization, wherein great numbers of men must act together against their personal interests, even to the sacrifice of life, in the service of the community.

As we have grown into fuller social life, we have slowly and experimentally, painfully and expensively, discovered what kind of man was the best social factor. The type of a satisfactory member of society to-day is a man self-controlled, kind, gentle, strong, wise, brave, courteous, cheerful, true. In the Middle Ages, strong, brave, and true would have satisfied the demands of the time. We now require for our common good a larger range of qualities, a more elaborate moral organization. All this is a simple, evolutionary process of social life, and should have involved no more confusion, effort, and pain than any other natural process.

But the moral development of humanity is a most tempestuous and contradictory field of study. Some virtues we have developed in orderly fashion, hardly recognizing that they were virtues, because they came so easily into use. Accuracy and punctuality are qualities which were unknown to the savage, because they were not needed in his business. They have been developed in us, because they were required, and so have been gradually assumed under pressure of economic necessity. Obedience, even in its extreme form of self-sacrifice, has been produced in the soldier; and no quality is more altruistic, more un natural, or more difficult of adoption by the sturdy individual will. The common, law-abiding citizen does not consider himself a hero; yet he is manifesting a high degree of social virtue, often at great personal sacrifice.

But in other virtues we have not progressed so smoothly. In the ordinary economic relations of life, and in our sex-relations, we are distinguished by peculiar and injurious qualities. Our condition may be described as consisting of a tenacious survival of qualities which we ought, on every ground of social good, to have long since outgrown; and an incessant struggle between these rudimentary survivals and the normal growth. This it is which has so forcibly assailed our consciousness since its awakening, and which we call the contest between good and evil. We have felt within ourselves the pull of diverse tendencies, — the impulse to do what was immediately good for ourselves, but which our growing social sense knew was bad for the community, and therefore wrong; and the impulse to do what might be immediately bad for ourselves, but which the same social sense knew was good for the community, and therefore right. This we felt, and cast about in our minds for an explanation of the way we behaved: we knew it was peculiar. The human brain is an organ that must have an explanation, if it has to make one. We made one.

The belated impulses of the individual beast — good in him because he needed them, bad in us because we were becoming human and had other needs — we lumped together, and, with our facile, dramatic, personifying tendency, called them "the devil." And, as these evil promptings were usually along the lines of physical impulse, we considered our own bodies, and nature in general, as part and parcel of the wrong, — "the world, the flesh, and the devil." We felt, also, within us the mighty stirrings of new powers and strange tendencies, that led us out of ourselves and toward each other, new loves and hopes and wishes, new desires to give instead of to take, to serve instead of to fight; and, realizing, with true social instinct, that this impulse tended to help us most, was really good for us, we called it the will of God, the voice of God, the way to God. The tearing contest between these ill-adjusted impulses and

tendencies, with our growing power of self-
conscious decision and voluntary adoption of
one or another course of action,—this process
in psychic evolution has given us the greatest
world-drama ever conceived, the struggle between good and evil.

And, fumbling vaguely at the sources of
our pain so far as we could trace them, judg-
ing always by persons, and not by conditions,
—as a child strikes the chair he bumps his
head upon,—race after race has located the
cause of the trouble in woman.   Not that she
primarily invented all the evil, and brought it
upon us,—our vague devil was the remoter
cause,—but that woman let the trouble in.
Pandora did not make the mischief-box; but
she perversely opened it, even against the
wise man's advice.   Eve did not plant that
apple-tree; but she ate of it, and tempted the
superior man.   It seems a childish and clumsy
guess, but there is something in it.   Nothing
of the unspeakable blame and shame with
which man has blackened the face of his
mother through all these centuries, but a
sociological truth for all that.

Not woman, but the condition of woman,
has always been a doorway of evil.   The
sexuo-economic relation has debarred her from
the social activities in which, and in which

alone, are developed the social virtues. She
was not allowed to acquire the qualities
needed in our racial advance; and, in her
position of arrested development, she has
maintained the virtues and the vices of the
period of human evolution at which she was
imprisoned. At a period of isolated economic
activity, — mere animal individualism, — at a
period when social ties ceased with the ties of
blood, woman was cut off from personal activity in social economics, and confined to the
functional activities of her sex.

In keeping her on this primitive basis of
economic life, we have kept half humanity
tied to the starting-post, while the other half
ran. We have trained and bred one kind of
qualities into one-half the species, and another kind into the other half. And then we
wonder at the contradictions of human nature!
For instance, we have done all we could, in
addition to natural forces, to make men brave.
We have done all we could, in addition to
natural forces, to make women cowards. And,
since every human creature is born of two
parents, it is not surprising that we are a
little mixed.

We have trained in men the large qualities
of social usefulness which the pressure of
their economic conditions was also develop-

ing; and we have done this by means of conscious praise and blame, reward and punishment, and with the aid of law and custom. We have trained in women, by the same means, the small qualities of personal usefulness which the pressure of their economic conditions was also developing. We have made a creature who is not homogeneous, whose life is fed by two currents of inheritance as dissimilar and opposed as could be well imagined. We have bred a race of psychic hybrids, and the moral qualities of hybrids are well known.

Away back in that early beginning, by dividing the economic conditions of women and men, we have divided their psychic development, and built into the constitution of the race the irreconcilable elements of these diverse characters. The incongruous behavior of this cross-bred product is the riddle of human life. We ourselves, by maintaining this artificial diversity between the sexes, have constantly kept before us the enigma which we found so hard to solve, and have preserved in our own characters the confusion and contradiction which is our greatest difficulty in life.

The largest and most radical effect of restoring women to economic independence will be in its result in clarifying and harmonizing the human soul. With a homogeneous nature bred of two parents in the same degree of social development, we shall be able to feel simply, to see clearly, to agree with ourselves, to be one person and master of our own lives, instead of wrestling in such hopeless perplexity with what we have called "man's dual nature." Marry a civilized man to a primitive savage, and their child will naturally have a dual nature. Marry an Anglo-Saxon to an African or Oriental, and their child haš a dual nature. Marry any man of a highly developed nation, full of the specialized activities of his race and their accompanying moral qualities, to the carefully preserved, rudimentary female creature he has so religiously maintained by his side, and you have as result what we all know so well, — the human soul in its pitiful, well-meaning efforts, its cross-eyed, purblind errors, its baby fits of passion, and its beautiful and ceaseless upward impulse through all this wavering.

We are quite familiar with this result, but we have not so far accurately located the cause. We have had our glimmering perception that woman had something to do with it; and she has been treated accordingly, by many simple races, to her further injury, and to that of the whole people. What we need to see is that it is not woman as a sex who is responsible for this mis-mothered world, but the economic position of woman which makes her what she is. If men were so placed, it would have the same effect. Not the sex-relation, but the economic relation of the sexes, has so tangled the skein of human life.

Besides the essential evils of an unbalanced nature, many harmful qualities have been developed in human characters by these conditions. For countless centuries we have sought to develope, by selection and education, a timid submission in woman. When there did appear "a curst shrew," she was left unmarried; and her temper perished with her, or she was "tamed" by some Petruchio. The dependence of women on the personal favor of men has produced an exceeding cleverness in the adaptation of the dependent one to the source of her supplies. Under the necessity of pleasing, whether she wished or no, of interceding for a child's pardon or of suing for new pleasures for herself, "the vices of the slave" have been forever maintained in this housemaid of the world.

Another discord introduced by the condition of servitude is that between will and action. A servant places his time and strength at the disposal of another will. He must hold himself in readiness to do what he is told; and the mere physical law of conservation of energy, to say nothing of his own conscious judgment, forbids wasting nerve-force in planning and undertaking what he may not be able to accomplish. This produces a condition of inactivity, save under compulsion, and, on the other side, a perverse, capricious wilfulness in little things,— the reaction from a forced submission.

A more insidious, disintegrating force to offset the evolution of human character could hardly be imagined than this steady training of the habits of servitude into half the human race,— the mother of all of it. These results have been modified, of course, by the different education and environment of men, developing in them opposite qualities, and transmitting the contradictory traits to the children indiscriminately.

Heredity has no Salic law. The boy inherits from his mother, as well as from his father; the girl from her father, as well as from her mother. This has prevented the full evil of the results that might have ensued, but has also added to the personal difficulties of each of us, and retarded the general progress of the race.

Worse than the check set upon the physical activities of women has been the restriction of their power to think and judge for themselves. The extended use of the human will and its decisions is conditioned upon free, voluntary action. In her rudimentary position, woman was denied the physical freedom which underlies all knowledge, she was denied the mental freedom which is the path to further wisdom, she was denied the moral freedom of being mistress of her own action and of learning by the merciful law of consequences what was right and what was wrong; and she has remained, perforce, undeveloped in the larger judgment of ethics.

Her moral sense is large enough, morbidly large, because in this tutelage she is always being praised or blamed for her conduct. She lives in a forcing-bed of sensitiveness to moral distinctions, but the broad judgment that alone can guide and govern this sensitiveness she has not. Her contribution to moral progress has added to the anguish of the world the fierce sense of sin and shame, the desperate desire to do right, the fear of wrong; without giving it the essential help of a practical wisdom and a regulated will. Inheriting with each generation the accumulating forces of our social nature, set back in each generation by the conditions of the primitive human female, women have become vividly self-conscious centres of moral impulse, but poor guides as to the conduct which alone can make that impulse useful and build the habit of morality into the constitution of the race.

Recognizing her intense feeling on moral lines, and seeing in her the rigidly preserved virtues of faith, submission, and self-sacrifice, — qualities which in the Dark Ages were held to be the first of virtues, — we have agreed of late years to call woman the moral superior of man.   But the ceaseless growth of human life, social life, has developed in him new virtues, later, higher, more needful; and the moral nature of woman, as maintained in this rudimentary stage by her economic dependence, is a continual check to the progress of the human soul.   The main feature of her life — the restriction of her range of duty to the love and service of her own immediate family — acts upon us continually as a retarding influence, hindering the expansion of the spirit of social love and service on which our very lives depend.   It keeps the moral standard of the patriarchal era still before us, and blinds our eyes to the full duty of man.

An intense self-consciousness, born of the ceaseless contact of close personal relation;

an inordinate self-interest, bred by the constant personal attention and service of this relation; a feverish, torturing, moral sensitiveness, without the width and clarity of vision of a full-grown moral sense; a thwarted will, used to meek surrender, cunning evasion, or futile rebellion; a childish, wavering, short-range judgment, handicapped by emotion; a measureless devotion to one's own sex relatives, and a maternal passion swollen with the full strength of the great social heart, but denied social expression, — such psychic qualities as these, born in us all, are the inevitable result of the sexuo-economic relation.

It is not alone upon woman, and, through her, upon the race, that the ill-effects may be observed. Man, as master, has suffered from his position also. The lust for power and conquest, natural to the male of any species, has been fostered in him to an enormous degree by this cheap and easy lordship. His dominance is not that of one chosen as best fitted to rule or of one ruling by successful competition with "foemen worthy of his steel"; but it is a sovereignty based on the accident of sex, and holding over such helpless and inferior dependants as could not question or oppose. The easy superiority that needs no striving to maintain it; the tempta-

tion to cruelty always begotten by irresponsible power; the pride and self-will which
surely accompany it, — these qualities have
been bred into the souls of men by their side
of the relation. When man's place was maintained by brute force, it made him more brutal: when his place was maintained by purchase, by the power of economic necessity,
then he grew into the merciless use of such
power as distinguishes him to-day.

Another giant evil engendered by this relation is what we call selfishness. Social life
tends to reduce this feeling, which is but
a belated individualism; but the sexuo-economic relation fosters and developes it. To
have a whole human creature consecrated to
his direct personal service, to pleasing and
satisfying him in every way possible, — this
has kept man selfish beyond the degree incidental to our stage of social growth. Even in
our artificial society life men are more forbearing and considerate, more polite and kind,
than they are at home. Pride, cruelty, and
selfishness are the vices of the master; and
these have been kept strong in the bosom of
the family through the false position of
woman. And every human soul is born, an
impressionable child, into the close presence
of these conditions. Our men must live in

the ethics of a civilized, free, industrial, democratic age; but they are born and trained in the moral atmosphere of a primitive patriarchate. No wonder that we are all somewhat slow to rise to the full powers and privileges of democracy, to feel full social honor and social duty, while every soul of us is reared in this stronghold of ancient and outgrown emotions, — the economically related family.

So we may trace from the sexuo-economic relation of our species not only definite evils in psychic development, bred severally in men and women, and transmitted indifferently to their offspring, but the innate perversion of character resultant from the moral miscegenation of two so diverse souls, — the unfailing shadow and distortion which has darkened and twisted the spirit of man from its beginnings. We have been injured in body and in mind by the too dissimilar traits inherited from our widely separated parents, but nowhere is the injury more apparent than in its ill effects upon the moral nature of the race.

Yet here, as in the other evil results of the sexuo-economic relation, we can see the accompanying good that made the condition necessary in its time; and we can follow the beautiful results of our present changes with comforting assurance. A healthy, normal moral sense will be ours, freed from its exaggerations and contradictions; and, with that clear perception, we shall no longer conceive of the ethical process as something outside of and against nature, but as the most natural thing in the world.

Where now we strive and agonize after impossible virtues, we shall then grow naturally and easily into those very qualities; and we shall not even think of them as especially commendable. Where our progress hitherto has been warped and hindered by the retarding influence of surviving rudimentary forces, it will flow on smoothly and rapidly when both men and women stand equal in economic relation. When the mother of the race is free, we shall have a better world, by the easy right of birth and by the calm, slow, friendly forces of social evolution.

INDEX

Academic groves of Greece, 285.
Accident of sex, man's sovereignty due to, 337.
Accompaniment to social life, home life only an, 282.
Action of heredity, 70.
—— in servitude, discord of will and, 333.
Activity in obstetrics, masculine, 197.
Advance, motherhood and racial, 189.
Advantage of professional cleaners, 255.
—— of family alone planned for, 296.
Advantages of home cooking, 249.
Africa, Darkest, 180.
African, hybrid progeny of Anglo-Saxon and, 332.
Age, the Augustan, 161.
—— Elizabethan, 161.
—— Periclean, 161.
Aggregate privacy of the family, 258.
Agony of Armenia, 162.
Allen, Grant, quotation from, 172.
Altruism, the main distinction of human virtue, 323.
—— the socialized individual profited by, 325.
—— of obedience, 327.
Amateur, the mother always an, 293.
America, 162.
—— the Englishman in, 79.
—— the human soul in, 148.
American, the, in England, 79.
"Americanitis."
Amusement, woman's, gained through sex-attraction, 308.
Anglo-Saxon blood, 147.
—— hybrid progeny of, and African, 332.
—— hybrid progeny of, and Oriental, 332.
Anthony, Susan B., 167.
Apartments, bachelor vs. marriage, 297.
Apple-tree, Eve and the, 329.
Arabellas of the last century, 148.
Armenia, the agony of, 162.
Arrested development of woman, result of, 330.
Art and science of cooking, 230.
Association, present methods of, unsatisfactory for women, 307.
—— value of, of the sexes, 314.
Associations of home, 221.
Attitude of women to marriage, 86.
Attraction, love a necessary, 325.

Augustan age, 161.

Baby, the first impressions of a, 281.
Baby-culture, wrong training of mothers for, 270.
Baby-education, the meaning of better, 287.
Baby-educator, the mother a bad, 284.
Babyhood, the ideal, 288.
Babylon, the girls of, 97.
Bachelor apartments vs. marriage, 297.
Balance of power in living organisms, 59.
Barton, Clara, 165.
Basis, change of, in family relations, 271.
—— the economic, of present family life, 303.
—— mingling on a human, 306.
Bela, the temple of, 97.
Benefits, of our sexuo-economic relation, 136.
—— of home life, 260.
Betterment, surroundings of infancy capable of, 292.
Bible, instructions of, 28.
Birth of free France, 137.
—— of historic crises, 146.
Blackwell, Dr. Elizabeth, 167.
Boston, 80.
—— Tea Party, 146.
Brain action, two laws of, 76.
Bridge's Food for infants, 196.
Britons, surprise of, over Boston Tea Party, 146.
Brought up at home, children that are, 282.
Burden, economic, of children, 169.
Business partners, husband and wife not, 12.
Byron, quotation from "Childe Harold," 24.

Camp, conduct of New Englanders in a mining, 320.
Captives, stripping of the Persian, 73.
Care of children, to marriage, value of, 301.
Cause of our exaggerated sex-development, 58.
—— of insanity, loneliness often a, 267.
Causes of the decline of home life, 266.

34 1

343

Index

353